T0367399

alternative
INVESTMENT
strategies
and
risk
management

Improve Your Investment Portfolio's Risk-Reward Ratio

Raghurami Reddy Etukuru, MBA, CAIA, FRM, PRM

Alternative Investment Strategies and Risk Mangaement
Improve Your Investment Portfolio's Risk–Reward Ratio

iUniverse books may be ordered through booksellers or by contacting:

iUniverse LLC
1663 Liberty Drive
Bloomington, IN 47403
www.iuniverse.com
1-800-Authors (1-800-288-4677)

ISBN: 978-1-4620-5007-9 (sc)
ISBN: 978-1-4620-5009-3 (hc)
ISBN: 978-1-4620-5008-6 (e)

Printed in the United States of America

iUniverse rev. date: 08/28/2014

Table of Contents

1. Alternative Investments

Alternative investments do not constitute a separate group of asset classes. In fact, they are an extension to existing asset classes. The main drivers that distinguish alternative investments from traditional investments are the fewer or no investment constraints and the style and risk/return characteristics of the underlying investments. Most alternative investment managers use traditional asset classes, such as equity, debt, cash, and real assets, and apply both strategic and tactic allocation to these assets. Alternative investments are private in nature and are purchased through a financial intermediary. Examples of alternative investments are hedge funds, managed futures, real estate, commodities, and private equities. Traditionally high-net-worth individuals have shown interest in alternative investments and were willing to bear the disadvantages, such as illiquidity and non-transparency. Due to the attractive risk/reward characteristics and low correlations to traditional asset classes, alternative investments became more of a favorite of institutional investors as well. Alternative investments have grown in popularity as a result of their anticipated impact on overall portfolio performance. Institutional and individual investors have been increasing their exposure to alternative investments in an attempt to improve the risk/reward balance within their investment portfolios.

Investors who invest in alternative investments use the historical returns of the fund as one of the inputs to the manager selection criteria. However, the future performance of any investment or investment portfolio is not certain, and reliance on historical information does not ensure any particular outcome. The past performance of any investment, including alternative investments, such as managed futures funds, is not necessarily indicative of future results. It can only be used as one of the factors, not the sole factor. The main reasons for the attractiveness of alternative investments are higher returns with low volatility and low correlation with traditional assets and the ability to produce absolute returns.

1.1 Sources of Returns

While the sources of returns for alternative investments depend on the type of the investment and underlying assets, the following are major and macro level sources of returns common to most of the types of alternatives.

Strategic-Tactical Allocation: Strategic-tactical allocation is also called *core-satellite allocation*. Strategic or core allocation is designed to accomplish long-term goals, to determine the fund's market or beta exposure, and to establish a policy risk. The returns earned through strategic allocation are called *beta returns* and can be estimated by using the capital asset pricing model (CAPM). Once the strategic asset allocation is set, the fund managers typically seek additional returns with the asset classes through tactical asset allocation. Tactical, or satellite, allocation is designed to accomplish short-term goals and to take advantage of dynamic market conditions. Tactical asset allocation requires more dynamic trading and is said to be more opportunistic. The additional returns earned through tactical allocation are called *active returns* or *alpha returns*. The alpha returns are in excess of the returns that are estimated by CAPM.

Mathematically,

$$Rp = Rf + \beta(R_m - R_f) + \alpha$$

Where Rp = Manager's Portfolio Returns

Rf = Risk-Free Returns

R_m = Market return

α = Excess return that is earned by using tactical allocation.

$Rf + \beta(R_m - R_f)$ = the return estimated by CAPM theory

Market Inefficiencies: Efficient market hypothesis asserts that financial markets are information efficient and one cannot achieve returns in excess of average market returns. Efficient market hypothesis comes in three forms. The weak form EMH assumes that current stock prices fully reflect all historical information. The semi-strong EMH form assumes that stock prices fully reflect all historical information and all current publicly available information. Finally, the strong-form EMH states that prices reflect not just historical and current publicly available information, but private information, too. In reality, information inefficiencies exist in all markets, and alternative investment managers take advantage of these inefficiencies to earn excess returns.

Manager Skill: Alternative investment managers build complex strategies using their skill. The strategies employ highly complex quantitative strategies and exploit pricing inefficiencies. The manager's skill at gathering information is also one of the sources of returns.

Unconstrained Investments: Traditional investment firms, such as pension funds and mutual funds, have some constraints in investing in certain types of investments. For example, they are restricted to short sell the assets and to use the leverage. Alternative investments are unconstrained and can invest anywhere and in any type of investment and to any extent of leverage. Traditional investment products earn returns through market exposure and not intended to beat market returns. Therefore, these funds are called beta drivers. The most common beta drivers are passive index funds, active index funds, long only funds, and 130/30 funds. These products do not take active risk and are not intended to earn excess returns. 130/30 funds engage in 130 percent of long assets and 30 percent of short assets, with net long exposure of 100%.

Alternative investment managers earn excess returns or alpha, and therefore these products are typically called alpha drivers. The alpha drivers' spectrum starts where the beta spectrum ends. There are several types of alpha drivers. Long/Short strategies do not have any restrictions on the portion of long or short assets. They can even be market neutral, meaning equal long and short exposure, or can be net long exposure. The goal is to earn returns from both positive and negative events. Long/Short strategy is a basic technique of alpha generation. The absolute return technique aims to earn profits regardless of the direction of the market. Managers take market-neutral or net long or net short positions to best utilize available opportunities. These are unconstrained in style and strategy and are less correlated with broad market indices. The global macro strategy is an example of an absolute return investment. Market segmentation is another source of alpha. Market segmentation occurs because not all investors have the same expectation about their investments. Some investors prefer high-liquid assets, while some investors want to take advantage of illiquidity. Some institutional investors are prohibited from investing in certain types of assets. Alternative investment managers take advantage of market segmentation and earn excess returns. High-yield bonds and CDOs are examples of segmented markets. Diversification minimizes the risk but at the same time minimizes the performance. Concentrated portfolios have the potential for losses but also provide greater opportunity for excess returns especially when dedicated research is conducted. Active investment managers engage in private equities such as venture capitals and leveraged buyouts. Leveraged buyouts build concentrated portfolios to earn active returns. Nonlinear investments are away from linear market exposure and exhibit option-like payoff with exposure to negative outlier events. Examples of nonlinear investments include option strategies, convertible arbitrage, merger arbitrage, and event-driven strategies. Alternative beta is gaining exposure in markets other than traditional markets. Alternative beta markets include commodities and real estate. Alternative beta investments are still exposed to the market but are outside of the normal market. Therefore alternative beta investments are considered as extension to beta investments and are different from alpha investments.

1.2 Benefits of Alternatives

Diversification Potential: Alternative investment returns exhibit low correlations to traditional asset classes like stocks and bonds, and therefore adding alternative investments to a portfolio can reduce volatility without sacrificing part of return. Alternative investments can produce returns that are not related to the direction of the market. In other words, alternative investments provide the opportunity to profit from both rising and falling markets. The diversification potential is one of the main reasons why institutional investors, such as pension plans, endowments, or foundations, invest in alternative assets.

Hedge Against Inflation: Some alternative asset classes, such as commodities and real estate investments, provide a good inflation hedge. Commodities and real estate are negatively correlated with interest rates and therefore are positively correlated with inflation and negatively correlated with stock and bond markets. However, there are a few exceptions, where these asset classes show positive correlation with stocks and bonds. This topic is discussed under the commodities and real estate section.

Access to Unreachable Markets: Alternative investments provide access to opportunities that are not commonly available to everyone. For example, venture capital funds invest in new and upcoming companies for which there is no public trading available. Investing in venture capital funds provides an opportunity to gain exposure to start-up firms.

Enhanced Returns: Returns of alternative investments vary over time depending on market conditions and the economic cycle, but in general provide returns either in-line with the S&P 500 or above the S&P 500. While not all funds or all strategies beat the S&P 500, most alternative investments perform better than the S&P 500.

Low Volatility: Most alternative investments exhibit lower volatility than the S&P 500. Though the volatility of alternatives is higher than bonds, they perform better than the average bond index. On a risk-adjusted basis, alternative investments perform better than both bonds and stocks.

1.3 Types of Alternatives

Alternative investments typically involve investing in equity, debt, and derivatives associated with equity and debt. Some alternative investments involve investing in real assets, such as commodities and real estate. Various types of alternative investments are listed below.

1. Hedge funds
2. Commodities and managed futures
3. Private equity
4. Real estate

As mentioned earlier, alternative investments are purchased through a financial intermediary. The organization of the intermediary varies depending on the type of alternative investment. Each of these structures is discussed in the following topics.

1.4 Hedge Funds

Hedge funds are private partnerships that seek to optimize profits. Though hedge funds were originally established to hedge portfolios against downside risk by using short selling, in modern days hedge funds became opportunistic and seek to profit by using complex and advanced strategies. Hedge funds are only available for accredited investors who have a net worth of $1 million or a history of income greater than $200,000. Since hedge funds are offered only to sophisticated investors, they are typically unregulated. If a fund has less than one hundred accredited investors, then the fund does come under the regulatory oversight of the Securities and Exchange Commission. However, since institutional investors, such as pension funds and endowments, started investing in hedge funds and since they are restricted from investing in unregulated funds, most hedge funds are seeking to register with the SEC even if they have less than one hundred investors. In contrast to mutual funds, hedge funds are restricted from advertising and soliciting and must concentrate marketing efforts on wealthy individuals and institutions.

It is often assumed that hedge funds cause calamities in financial markets. In reality, hedge funds often provide liquidation to financial markets. For example, during the global recession period of 2007 to 2008, many financial instruments became ineligible for institutional investors and, as such, they became illiquid. Since hedge funds typically do not have constraints on market segmentation, these funds started investing in the illiquid market, thus unfreezing the market.

There is also an argument that George Soros's large bet in 1992 that the British pound sterling would devalue caused the decline of the pound, which earned Soros a profit of $1 billion. However, analysis of George Soros's bet found that while his bet made the situation worse, he was not the primary cause of the devaluation. Therefore, it can be inferred that while hedge funds may not be the root cause of the directional changes of the market, they can magnify the change to some extent.

The two primary goals of hedge funds are enhancing return at a given level of investor risk and achieving volatility lower than that of traditional asset classes.

Since income tax rules for investors will differ depending on the country where they live, a hedge fund manager will often establish the hedge fund as a master and feeder structure. The assets for the funds are invested through a master trust, and the first feeder is set up as US-based and a second one is set up offshore to accommodate foreign investors. It is often assumed that this structure is established for the purpose of avoiding the investor's home-country taxation, but this is a wrong assumption. The master and feeder structure is to avoid double taxation or unrelated business income taxation. The master trust is tax neutral, so there are no tax consequences at the master trust level. The master trust is usually set up in a location that does not have corporate income taxes. Some of the no-tax domiciles, such as Bermuda and the Cayman Islands, are discussed in this topic. The master trust does not pay any tax at the corporate level and allows tax liabilities to flow down to the tax code of each investor's home country. On the other hand, had the master trust been established in tax-liable country, then the hedge fund would have to pay tax at the corporate level, which ultimately impacts the investor's profit. And the investor is also liable to taxation in the country where he resides. Therefore, the master trust and onshore/offshore structure avoids double taxation.

In general, any fund that wants to be incorporated usually has to be approved by the local regulatory authority; and the fund manager, administrator, prime broker, custodian, and auditors are subject to regulatory authority approval. A change of service providers requires the prior consent of the regulatory authority. The authority conducts due diligence on proposed service providers and investment manager personnel, including, for instance, background checks in databases to find out whether there has been any legal action or NASD or SEC disciplinary sanctions against such individuals. Incorporation can take a longer time because of all the approval rules. However, some countries offer a fast-track process, which enables hedge funds to operate quickly. Some of the special domiciles are discussed below.

Cayman Islands: Being the world's lowest tax domicile, the Cayman Islands have been the leading jurisdiction for fund formation, with an estimated 80 percent of the world's hedge funds domiciled there. As of December 2008, Cayman had over 10,000 hedge funds registered with the local regulatory authority. The Cayman Islands offer managers many competitive advantages and allow a fast-track establishment process. Nonpublic funds can be registered in as little as three to five days with the Cayman Island Monetary Authority (CIMA), and the vehicle of choice for the fund can be registered within one day prior to filing, if necessary. There are no restrictions on investment policy, issue of equity interests, prime brokers, and custodians. The quality and expertise of the Cayman Islands local services, infrastructure, and legal system are well above par. Cayman is a tax-neutral jurisdiction, and therefore there are no capital gains, income, profits, withholding, or inheritance taxes attaching to investment funds established there. Currently the Cayman Islands does not require a fund to file regular reports with CIMA.

The Bahamas: Due to its political stability, well-developed infrastructure, and skilled workforce of accountants, lawyers, trustees, and investment managers, the Bahamas has become a preferred jurisdiction for the hedge fund industry.

British Virgin Islands: With more than 2800 funds registered or recognized under the Securities and Investment Business Act 2010 (SIBA), the British Virgin Islands became one of the leading jurisdictions for alternative investment funds. In the British Virgin Islands, closed-ended funds are not subject to specific regulation, although BVI-established managers and other BVI-established functionaries of closed-ended funds will in many circumstances require a license under SIBA.

Bermuda: In Bermuda there are no local taxes on income, profits, dividends, and capital gains. A corporation is liable only for payroll taxes. The Bermuda Monetary Authority (BMA) oversees the approval of the fund, fund manager, administrator, prime broker, custodian, and auditors. In addition, any change of service providers requires the prior consent of the BMA. The BMA conducts due diligence on service providers and investment manager personnel, and finds out whether there has been any legal action or NASD or SEC disciplinary sanctions against such individuals. A fund needs to file monthly reports with BMA. Compared to the Cayman Islands, the establishing time is longer in Bermuda.

1.5 Commodities

One of the available ways to get access to commodities is through managed futures. A managed futures account (MFA), which is a special type of alternative investment, typically takes both long and short positions in futures contracts and options on futures contracts in the global commodity, interest rate, equity, and currency markets. Managed futures enable investors to profit from fluctuations in futures prices through active management by an experienced trader. There are three ways to access managed futures: public commodity pools, private commodity pools, and individual managed accounts. Commodity pools are similar in structure to hedge funds and pool the money from several investors for the purpose of investing in futures markets. Indeed, commodity pools are considered as a subset of the hedge fund market. Commodity pools are managed by a general partner and must register with the Commodity Futures Trading Commission (CFTC) and the National Futures Association (NFA) as a commodity pool operator (CPO).

Public commodity pools are open to general public investors and must file a registration with the Securities and Exchange Commission (SEC) before offering shares in the pool to investors. Similar to mutual funds, public commodity pools require a low minimum investment and provide higher liquidity.

Private commodity pools' investment objective is the same as that of public commodity pools, but they are sold only to high-net-worth individuals and institutional investors in order to avoid the lengthy registration requirements of the SEC. Depending on the nature of the account, they also avoid the reporting requirements of CFTC. The advantages of private commodity pools are lower brokerage commissions and the flexibility to implement investment strategies. Both public and private commodity pool operators typically hire professional money managers, called commodity trading advisors (CTAs), to manage the funds in the pool.

Individual managed accounts can be created directly with commodity trading advisors and are available to wealthy and institutional investors only. The advantages of individual accounts are more specific investment objectives and full transparency.

Due to enormous growth in the managed futures industry, the Commodity Exchange Act (CEA) was amended in 1974 and created two entities called CFTC and NFA. CPOs and CTAs are required to register with the CFTC and NFA and must meet continuing education requirements. In some cases, the CPO can also be registered as the CTA. The CFTC's mission is to protect market users and the public from fraud, manipulation, and abusive practices related to the sale of commodity and financial futures and options, and to foster open, competitive, and financially sound futures and options markets. As per CEA standards, traders and brokers must report their activity on the exchange to CFTC; each exchange is required to disclose information regarding the previous day's trades, and a daily record of each customer's trade must be maintained. The NFA oversees the continuing education required of CPOs and CTAs.

Similar to hedge funds, CPOs and CTAs follow a typical 2/20 fee structure. They usually charge a 2%-percentmanagement fee and a 20-percent performance fee. The management fee ranges from 0 percent to 3 percent, and the performance fee ranges from 10 percent to 35 percent.

1.6 Private Equities

Private equity firms employ various investment strategies and purchase privately traded equity or debt that is not available through public exchanges. Typically private equity firms raise a pool of capital from investors and invest in private firms. Depending on the nature and type of investment strategy, private equity firms fall into one of four categories:

1. Venture capitals
2. Leveraged buyouts
3. Mezzanine financiers
4. Distressed debt

1.6.1 Venture Capitals

Start-up companies, which are typically established by new entrepreneurs, will not have a sufficient track record and tangible assets to attract investment capital from traditional sources, such as public markets and lending institutions. Start-up firms will exhibit negative returns for the first few years. As a result, start-up firms are considered to be high-risk and illiquid investments. Venture capitalists, who are willing to take significant risks, finance these companies in the hope of cashing in on a few highly profitable ventures. Depending on the type of capital investment vehicle, venture capitals can be divided into four types; and again, depending on the stage of financing, each vehicle can be subdivided into five types. The four types of investment vehicles are limited partnership, limited liability companies, corporate venture capital funds, and venture capital fund of funds.

The limited partnership structure contains one general partner and one or more limited partners. The general partner acts as the venture capitalist and contributes capital to the fund along with pooled money from the limited partners. The limited partnership is not taxed; instead, all income and capital gains flow through to the limited partners. Limited partners pay taxes individually according to their tax status. The general partner is responsible for day-to-day management. As the name indicates, limited partners do not take part in management. Limited partnerships are generally formed with an expected life of seven to ten years, with an option to extend for another one to five years. Since a limited partnership requires the general partner's own committed investment to the fund, it is assured that the fund will be managed diligently.

Limited liability companies, or LLCs, are similar to limited partnerships in that all items of net income, losses, and capital gains are passed through to the shareholders of the LLC; they also have a life of ten years, with the possible option to extend for another one to five years. The difference arises from the knowledge level of the investors. In a limited partnership, investors or limited partners are usually passive and relatively uninformed, whereas in an LLC, the venture capitalist typically deals with a smaller group of knowledgeable shareholders. The LLC format allows the sale of additional shares in the LLC to new shareholders. In addition, LLCs usually have more specific shareholder rights and privileges.

Corporate venture capital funds are not available to outside investors and are typically formed only with the parent company's capital. Large public companies establish these types of venture capitals in order to supplement their internal research and development budgets and to gain access to new technologies. Corporate venture capital funds also gain the ability to generate new products and acquire stake in future potential competitors. There are several potential disadvantages to corporate venture capital funds. For example, there may be a conflict of goals between parent and subsidiary, or mismatches in investment horizons of parent and subsidiary.

Venture capital funds of funds do not invest in start-up firms directly; instead, they invest in other venture capital funds. This is a relatively new phenomenon and is similar to a fund of hedge funds. Venture capital funds of funds offer various advantages to both venture capitalists and investors. The venture capitalist receives one large investment instead of call-based investments from investors. Investors get exposure to a diverse range of venture capital firms and also get access to closed-end funds that are otherwise not available directly.

Depending on the stage of financing, venture capitals can be further divided into five types: seed financing, early stage, mid-late stage, mezzanine stage, and balanced venture capital funds.

Seed-financing venture capitals invest in very first-generation or beta-testing-stage prototypes and are typically considered as high risk. Seed-financing venture capitals are usually smaller and financing ranges from $1 million to $5 million. Early-stage-financing venture capitals involve with the second generation of a prototype with potential end users. Early-stage venture capital financing is usually $2 million and more. Mid-to late-stage venture capital funds deal with companies who have potential for growth but lack working capital. These are considered as low risk, but the returns are also low. However, there is a more rapid return of capital invested. Financing may range from $5 million to $25 million. Mezzanine venture capital funds invest in last-stage start-up companies and take them to public or sell to a strategic buyer. Balanced venture capitals invest in both early- and late-stage firms.

1.6.2 Leveraged Buyouts

Leveraged buyout employs borrowed money to acquire whole or part of the company. However the entity being acquired is used as collateral. Leveraged buyout is a way to take a publicly traded company private. If the investors are the company's current management, then the buyout is called a *management buyout*. Leveraged buyouts increase the value of a corporation by unlocking hidden value, exploiting existing but underfunded opportunities.

Most LBO funds are established as limited partnerships that are similar to hedge funds and venture capitals funds. The general partner is the LBO firm and is responsible for investment discretion and day-to-day operations, due diligence, and investing the committed capital of the fund. Limited partners, on the other hand, have a very limited role and rely on the general partners. Some LBOs have advisory boards filled with the general partner and selected limited partners. The advisory board advises on conflicts of interest that may arise as a result of acquisition, dividend payouts, and so forth. The fee structure of an LBO firm contains several components, such as: the management fee, which ranges from

1 percent to 3 percent; an incentive or profit-sharing fee, which ranges from 20 percent to 30 percent; a privatization fee of about 1 percent, which is charged to the firm that is being taken private; a breakup fee, which is charged in the event the LBO does not go through; and finally a divestiture fee, which is charged when the LBO firm arranges the sale of a division.

1.6.3 Mezzanine Financers

Mezzanine financers offer a debt that is a hybrid of debt and equity and falls in between senior debt and equity in a company's capital structure. The most typical form of mezzanine financing is an intermediate-term bond with an equity kicker in the form of option, warrant, or conversion right. The bond may have payment in cash or payment-in-kind. Payment-in-kind refers to repaying the bond with additional debt. In some cases, mezzanine financing is in the form of preferred stock with a set dividend payment as well as conversion right into the common stock.

1.6.4 Distressed Debt

Distressed-debt investing involves purchasing the debt issued by companies that are in financial trouble. The troubled companies may have already defaulted on their debt, may be on the brink of default, or may be seeking bankruptcy protection. Distressed-debt investors are sometimes called *vultures*. The distressed-debt market is an inefficient market. This makes the distressed bonds more illiquid, and as a result, the bonds are available at a deep discount. This is the first of the reasons that attract vultures to distressed debt. The other reason is that the distressed-debt market is segmented, as the debt was issued by noninvestment grade or nonrated firms. Institutional investors are restricted from investing in this debt. Vultures buy these bonds hoping to cash in when the health of the company improves.

1.7 Real Estate Investments

There is debate on whether or not to consider real estate as an alternative investment, as this investment existed even before the stock and debt market evolved. However, investing in real estate completely deviated from the traditional style and now is available in various forms. And real estate provides different systematic risk exposure that is otherwise not achieved through traditional stock and bond securities. In contrast to stocks and bonds, real estate is a tangible asset. For all of these reasons, real estate can be considered as an alternative investment.

Access to real estate investments can be obtained through real estate investment trusts, property indices, and mortgage-backed securities. All of these vehicles have their own advantages and disadvantages for investors.

Real Estate Investment Trusts

While real estate investment trusts (REITs) along with Property indices and mortgage-backed securities are discussed in depth in chapter nine, "Real Estate Investing," this chapter provides the structure, advantages, and disadvantages of REITs. REITs must obey certain rules and regulations in order to obtain REIT status and their pass-through structure of income and capital gains distribution.

Corporate Structure

1. Must be established as a corporation, a trust, or an association.
2. Must be managed by one or more trustees or directors.
3. Its shares must be transferable.
4. It cannot be a financial institution or an insurance company.
5. Must be owned by one hundred or more persons.
6. Five or fewer persons cannot own more than 50 percent of the REIT shares.

Tax Structure

1. At least 75 percent of an REIT's assets must be invested in real estate assets, cash, cash equivalents, treasuries, or short-term investments.
2. The remaining 25 percent can be held in the securities of other issuers but must not exceed 5 percent of the issuer's total assets or 10 percent of the total outstanding voting shares of the issuer.
3. At least 75 percent of gross income must be derived from real estate.
4. At least 95 percent of taxable income must come from dividends and interest, security sales, and the sources that meet the 75 percent test.
5. At least 95 percent of REIT taxable income must be distributed to shareholders annually.

Advantages

- REITs do not pay corporate taxes; instead, they allow all items of income and capital gains to flow through to shareholders, who pay taxes according to their tax status. Tax-exempt investors, such as pension funds and endowments, benefit from this pass-through structure.
- REIT shareholders can trade their shares on public stock exchanges and can purchase through a margin account.
- Investors can use REITs as either strategic allocation or tactical allocation.
- REITS are managed by professionals, who possess skills like evaluating, acquiring, managing, financing, and developing real estate properties—skills that investors may not have.
- REITs produce steady income to shareholders in the form of dividends.
- Independent boards of directors provide oversight and protect shareholders' interests.

Disadvantages

- Since REITs are listed on public exchanges and provide high liquidity, they tend to be more volatile. They are significantly correlated to small-cap and mid-cap stocks, thus reducing the diversification benefit.
- While the pass-through structure benefits tax-exempt investors, it may be a disadvantage to individual investors who fall in higher tax brackets.

2. Due Diligence

Due diligence is the most important phase of investing in hedge funds for both funds of hedge funds and individual investors. In broad terms, due diligence can be classified into three phases—operational, performance, and risk management—and investors typically expect all phases of due diligence to be passed. The due diligence process varies from firm to firm, investor to investor, and strategy to strategy. There is no industry-standard questionnaire that is readily available. This is one of the main reasons why the due diligence process cannot be quantified and automated. The following lists several areas that investors need to cover when performing due diligence, but it is certainly not all-inclusive:

1. Firm structure
2. Staff background
3. Service providers
4. Strategy-related review
5. Performance review
6. Risk review
7. Infrastructure review
8. Reporting and Data Providers
9. Administrative review
10. Legal review
11. References
12. Operational review

2.1 Firm Structure

As explained in hedge fund structures, most hedge funds may set up a master-feeder structure, having the master setup at low-tax or no-tax domiciles such as the Cayman Islands or Bermuda. If the corporation is not established in a low- or no-tax domicile, then the investor may end up paying double taxation either directly or indirectly. The investor should also seek to know where the primary contact office is located. If the time zone of the primary location does not fit into the investor's working hours, the investor should find out if the firm has any satellite office located in a time zone convenient to the investor. The investor should also know if the chief executive officer, investment officers, and chief operating officer are three different persons or one person playing more than one role. The latter case may be a red flag to the investor. The investor should also know who the current owner is and if there were any ownership changes in the past three years. The investor should seek to know what the company's original business goals were, if they were achieved, what the current goals are, and how the firm intends to achieve these goals.

Investors should seek to know if the hedge fund firm employs the strategy that utilizes funds of other hedge fund managers as well. Since a fund of hedge funds is also an investor of other companies' funds, then the investor may think those companies will ensure the interests of their investors.

Investors should understand all the tax laws and regulations in the country where the master trust is established. The tax laws and regulations vary from country to country, even for the same type of instruments or strategies. For example, according to Germany's accounting rules, all losses should be reported regardless of the source of the loss, whereas the gains from futures, even if they were meant for hedging, are not allowed to show. This is the reason why MGRM, a fund that was created using oil futures contracts, was required to show losses but was not allowed to show the gains from customers' futures contracts, which could have offset the loss to some extent. As a result of reported losses, MGRM's credit rating was dropped lower, increasing its received credit risk. As a result, MGRM was required to post more collateral. This is one of the reasons, along with other reasons, why the fund ultimately had to be liquidated.

Investors also need to document the firm's internal structure in terms of strategy execution and operations. For example, firms that establish clear barriers among the front office, risk management office, and back office exhibit long-term success. There have been a few examples where funds failed due to lack of separation between the front office and the risk management office, between the front office and the back office, or between the front office and the back office.

In 1994, Barings Trust lost millions through trading activities. The trader, Leeson, increased the magnitude of positions and even deviated from the original strategy. Leeson was Barings's floor manager on the Singapore International Monetary Exchange trading floor; he was also in charge of settlement operations. Due to his role in the settlement office, he was able to book fraudulent trades. Due to the lack of separation between the back office and the trading desk, and due to lack of oversight from the risk management unit, his activities went undetected until a huge loss was realized.

2.2 Staff Background

Since hedge fund returns are highly correlated to the manager's skill and the expertise of other staff in the firm, gathering staff-related information has become an important phase of due diligence. When conducting the staff information phase of due diligence, the investor should consider the number of employees currently employed, employees by department, maximum and minimum number of employees the firm had in the past three years, employee turnover, prior experience, education, and the compensation structure.

A higher number of employees alone does not necessarily need to be considered as a good sign. The proportionate number of employees will indeed be a good sign. An investor needs to know the maximum number of employees in the firm, as well as the number in each department. It is also necessary to find out the maximum and minimum number of employees the firm had in the past three years in order to determine whether the firm is growing or shrinking.

While it is common for employees to leave employers and pursue other opportunities, certain observations about employee turnover may raise red flags for investors. For example, if the CFO leaves the firm, that would create "media effect"; and if more people leave within a short span of time, that would raise concerns about the performance of the firm. Investors would want to find out details from the firm to see if the mass departure is because of any upgrade of infrastructure, merger activities, or otherwise. For example, the firm may let go employees with a certain skill level once it merges with another firm. Therefore, employee turnover need not necessarily mean a negative effect. Investors should document the reasons for employee turnover and make suitable judgments about the fund.

Investors should seek to know what the key manager's prior experience is. For example, if the manager is coming from long-only funds and is employed in a long/short strategy, then the investor may think that he does not have a competitive advantage over a manager who came from a long/short fund. The investor should also seek to know the educational background of key personnel at the firm. Employees with better packages may not tend to leave, and their compensation also indicates their skill level. The investor should understand the compensation structure of key personnel at the firm. Though it may often be difficult to arrive at conclusions about the proactive/reactive nature of staff, it is very important to know about it. While some firms perceive proactive nature as an added cost and speculative, the proactive behavior reduces potential loss when it occurs.

2.3 Service Providers

Hedge funds often rely on various service providers, such as prime brokers, administrators, auditors, legal counsel, custodians, and technology providers. The role of these service providers may be significantly different from what they play at traditional institutions. Relying on service providers exposes the fund to external risks. Each of these service providers is discussed below, along with what investors need to gather from the hedge fund related to the service providers.

2.3.1 Prime Broker

Prime brokers provide various standard and premium services to hedge funds. Standard services include executing trades on behalf of the hedge funds, lending securities for short sale, and leverage or margin financing. Some larger dealer banks that act as a prime broker provide premium services, such as custody of securities, clearing, cash management, and reporting. Other premium services include leasing space to start-up hedge funds, start-up services, capital introduction, compliance, and risk management.

Since prime brokers provide margin, the hedge funds will pledge the securities in their brokerage account to serve as collateral. The prime broker, in turn, uses this collateral as collateral against their loans through a process called rehypothecation. In the event of the prime broker's bankruptcy, the protection of hedge funds/investors against rehypothecation depends on the country of the prime brokers. In the United States, there is a legal process to segregate, identify, and return the assets, whereas in the United Kingdom the assets remain frozen until the broker works through the bankruptcy process. That is the main reason why investors under the US division of Lehman Brothers had an advantage over the investors in the UK division during the collapse of Lehman Brothers in 2008.

When hedge funds are concerned about the solvency of the prime broker, they typically demand margin loans from the prime broker, but the prime broker may not be able to use those same securities as collateral against his loans with other lenders since the other lender may also have concerns about the prime broker's solvency. When clients or hedge funds start leaving a prime broker, then the prime broker will start facing a liquidity crisis, causing systemic risk. Therefore, hedge funds may need to consider diversifying against multiple prime brokers.

From the prime brokerage point of view, the investor should, at the minimum, consider the following questions as part of due diligence:

1. Who is the prime broker, and what are the services he or she is offering?
2. In which country is the prime broker located?
3. Are the prime brokers engaging in rehypothecation?
4. How does the law protect clients in the event of prime broker bankruptcy?
5. Is the hedge fund relying on just one prime broker or multiple prime brokers?

2.3.2 Administrator

Administrators offer various accounting, pricing, and reporting services; and since they operate on economy of scale, they reduce the hedge funds' actual administrator costs. At the same time, they bolster average hedge fund investor confidence. However, it is very important for the investor to understand the type of services they offer and the track record of administrators. Typical services include accounting, fee calculations, ledger maintenance, tax preparation, daily P&L calculation, NAV (net asset value) calculation, trade captures, report preparation, preparing financial statements, anti-money laundering reporting, and so on.

From the administrator point of view, the investor should, at the minimum, consider the following questions as part of due diligence:

1. How many administrators are employed?
2. Who are the administrators?
3. What is the track record of the administrator?
4. How long has the hedge fund been using the administrator?
5. How are the administrators compensated?
6. What are the standard strategies that the administrator serves for any hedge fund?

2.3.3 Auditors

Outside auditors provide services such as maintaining official books and records and preparing audited financial statements. Therefore, auditors are a primary source of information about the hedge fund's accounting statement. As part of due diligence, the investor should seek the latest and past audited financial statements, and if the investor should get clarifications of any unclear portion of the statements. Some hedge funds that are not registered with the Securities and Exchange Commission are not required to prepare audited financial statements. However, in order to improve their reach to investors, even unregistered hedge funds have started preparing audited statements, so investors should be cautious in allocating to a fund if audited statements are not available.

In 2003, Bing Liang researched on the accuracy of fund performance reported to hedge fund databases and found that the funds that audited hedge funds had smaller discrepancies in various databases than non-audited funds. He also found that defunct funds were less effectively audited than live funds.

Recent history shows that it is required to determine the legitimacy of auditing firms as well. A key lesson that was learned from Bernie Madoff's case was that due diligence must be performed not only at the fund level but also at the outside auditor level, as it was ultimately found that the accounting firm that served as the independent auditor for Madoff was not a legitimate operation.

2.3.4 Legal Counsel

Legal counsels offer services such as start-up documentation, registering a hedge fund with the monetary or regulatory authority, compliance consulting, ongoing legal services, dealing with civil or criminal filings, and so on. Since the law varies from domicile to domicile, master-feeder hedge funds typically have two legal counsels: one onshore and the other offshore. As part of due diligence, investors should seek from the legal counsel information as to whether there are any civil, criminal, or legal actions pending against the hedge fund.

2.3.5 Custodian

Hedge fund assets, including cash and funds, are typically held with the custodian, who essentially deals with dividend collection and margin payments. However, it is not mandatory for the hedge fund to hold assets with a custodian. In the event that custodian becomes insolvent, the hedge fund assets will be at risk. Therefore, the investor needs to find out the exact role of the custodian related to the hedge fund in which the investor wants to invest.

2.4 Strategy-Related Review

Strategic review is one of the most important phases of due diligence, and the review should be conducted from the context of the investor's portfolio as well as the fund portfolio. The key issues to be considered in the strategy review phase are strategy type, style, type of financial instruments used, target markets, target return, sources of idea generation, capacity, and a snapshot of portfolio and competitive advantage.

In order to determine whether or not the fund should be added to the portfolio, the investor needs to know the strategy behind the fund. Hedge funds employ various strategies, as discussed in later sections of this book. While most funds tell what the specific strategy behind a fund is, it is not necessary that all hedge funds give the strategy description narrowed down to the bottom. Instead, they give a broader picture. Due to the similarities, ambiguities, and substrategies, it sometimes becomes difficult for the investor to figure out the specific strategy that the fund employs. For example, a fund manager may quote that, "the Fund is seeking capital appreciation and holding period income through disciplined investing in mortgage-backed securities that may include securities classified as distressed-priced securities in RMBS, CMBS markets." From the quotation, it is easy to figure out that the fund involves investing in mortgage-related securities; however, the investor will not know if the fund employs an arbitrage or non-arbitrage strategy; whether it considers prime, alt-A, or subprime mortgages; or from which geographic area these securities originate.

Therefore, the investor should apply various techniques and document the findings to determine what the strategy is. The investor should also apply some mathematics in order to find out whether it is opportunistic to add the fund to his or her portfolio.

The investor can use either the bottom-up or the top-down approach in order to narrow down the fund's primary strategy. In the bottom-up approach, for example, if the manager says he uses convertible bonds in the funds, then the investor should ask if the fund employs only long positions or long/short positions. If the answer is long/short, then it is narrowed down to convertible arbitrage. Then the investor should ask what the frequency of re-hedging is; if the answer is "many times a day," then it can be narrowed down to a dynamic hedging strategy, which falls under gamma trading. In the top-down approach, on the other hand, if the fund manager says that he is employing a relative value strategy, then the investor should ask what types of instruments are used. If the answer is fixed-income, then the strategy is narrowed down to the fixed-income arbitrage strategy. Then the investor should know what the specific types of bonds are. If the answer is mortgage securities, then the investor should further see if the fund employs all mortgages or only subprime or only prime mortgages. Now the investor can narrow down the strategy to, for example, the subprime mortgage relative value strategy. Whether the investor uses bottom-up or top-down, it is necessary to document the hedge fund strategy type and the approach used within the strategy.

It is also necessary to know what type of financial instruments are used. For example, are the instruments just plain securities, or derivatives such as options and futures? It is necessary to know what portion of the fund employs options. The use of options will result in nonlinear payoff and magnifies the returns, but sometimes it may lead to short volatility risk if the options are short options.

Unless the managers claim that the strategy is global macro, it is necessary to find out what the target markets are, including whether the fund invests just in the United States or outside the United States, and whether outside of the United States includes any emerging markets. For the same type of instruments, the level of risk varies from country to country due to country-specific risks and regulations.

While hedge funds do not promise target returns, the investor should find out the historical return pattern and compare it to the portfolio hurdle rate and the standard benchmark. The hurdle rate is similar to opportunity cost, what the investor can earn on his own without paying a management and performance fee to the fund manager. For example, if the return of the fund is 5 percent and the average S&P return is 5 percent, then the investor could invest in a passive index and pay a lower fee instead of a 2/20 fee structure. The investor should also compare fund returns with the aggregated strategy index as well as with the hedge fund industry aggregated index.

The investor should find out what the source of idea generation is and whether the ideas work in all the markets and all the time. For example, the fund manager may employ fundamental analysis or pure automated quantitative techniques. The quantitative techniques may not work in certain periods, such as during contagion market periods, unless the model is updated and back tested more frequently. If the model is designed for a bull market and does not perform well in a bear market, then it is only as good as investing in passive indices, such as the S&P 500 index.

Capacity measures the maximum industry capital a strategy can employ without diluting market inefficiency. If the market for strategy is small, for example, a CTA who does only copper trading, the more investors compete for initial attractive returns, then the investor returns may get diluted. In addition, smaller capacity markets may be prone to market manipulation. For example, Yasuo Hamanak, a copper trader at Sumitomo, built a strategy by establishing long positions in futures contracts and simultaneously purchasing large quantities of physical copper. As the copper market is very small and most of the copper was acquired by Yasuo, the futures writers found very little copper in the market at the time of expiration and were forced to either pay a large premium for physical copper or unwind their positions by taking an offsetting long position. In 1995, the Commodity Futures Trading Commission (CFTC) began an investigation, and Sumitomo was held responsible for market manipulation.

On the other hand, the global macro strategy has the highest capacity due to its broader spectrum of investment countries and financial instruments. So the investor is required to do his own research about the capacity of strategy. In addition, the investor should know what the capacity of the manager is as well. Manager capacity can be determined from the level of concentration. If managers prefer a concentrated portfolio even after employing a higher capacity strategy, then the manager may not be able to deploy all the available capital.

This transparency is a trade-off issue to the hedge fund manager. Most investors would like to know what the positions in the portfolio are in order to assess the risk. And a manager can attract more investors if he can reveal the position information. At the same time, the manager thinks that revealing the portfolio snapshot will make his competitors replicate the strategy and dilute his skills. The investor should at least seek to know the level of concentration and the broader picture of the portfolio in order to determine whether the fund is more exposed to market risk or security-specific risk. If the portfolio is concentrated, then the investor can infer that the portfolio is exposed to more security-specific risk and the manager skill matters a lot in achieving higher returns. The investor should find out the manager's net exposure by finding out total long exposure and total short exposure. The investor should also find out the available free cash. Too much cash may raise concerns that the manager is lacking investment ideas.

The investor should find out what competitive advantage the manager possesses over the competitors. The level of risk and return varies from manager to manager, even if two managers employ the same strategy. Competitive advantages include quantitative research, risk management practices, technologies, expertise, and so on.

2.5 Performance Review

The goal of an investor is to earn higher returns for a given level of risk. The performance review phase of due diligence holds the same level of importance that operational and risk management phases hold. During this phase, the investor should investigate the following type of information: fund history, statistical measures of performance, drawdown, pricing models.

Measuring the level of autocorrelation in fund returns and peer group analysis are major components of performance review. Investors should get all the monthly statements from all the prime brokers and see if the returns are persistent over both the short term and the long term. Academic studies reveal that hedge fund returns are persistent over the short term, but over the long term they lack persistency. The academic studies also reveal that the funds that show positive performance continue to show positive performance, and funds with negative performance continue to show negative performance over time. The investor should compare the return history with other funds and other firms with the same strategy and see if there is disparity in returns, as well as knowing if the disparity is temporary or persisting for a long time. The investor should also observe the performance history of other funds that the manager manages, even if the investor is not interested in those funds. This will help the investor to determine the skill level of the manager.

The important characteristic that needs to be investigated during the performance phase is statistical measures. The goal of the hedge fund manager is not to beat the risk-free rate. The investor should compare the returns with standard passive benchmarks like the S&P 500 and Russell and should measure the correlation between the benchmark and the fund. The fund should exhibit low correlation with the benchmark, while earning significantly higher returns than the passive indices. As mentioned earlier, the manager's goal is not only to earn excess returns but also to reduce the volatility. Therefore, the returns should be measured in terms of excess returns per unit of risk. The Sharpe ratio measures the excess returns over the desired risk-free rate per unit of strategy volatility. However, it does not measure the excess returns over the benchmark. In addition, the Sharpe ratio uses the standard deviation of the portfolio, for which the returns may not be stable. The other statistical measure that gives the excess returns over the desired benchmark is the information ratio, which uses the relative risk or tracking error as the denominator. The tracking error is the standard deviation of excess returns over the benchmark. The higher the information ratio, the better the fund. Hedge fund investors should expect an information ratio of greater than one.

Drawdown is defined as the decline in net asset value of the fund for a given day. In traditional investments, the drawdown is quite observable, as the drawdown is correlated with market declines. However, since the hedge fund manager's goal is to protect the fund against market declines, the hedge funds should, in theory, not exhibit drawdown. Nonetheless, drawdown is observed in a hedge fund but at a low level compared to traditional investment drawdown. The investor should document the maximum drawdown the manager experienced and how long the drawdown continued. In annual and monthly return history, the returns may have smoothed and the drawdown may not be observable. Therefore, the investor should try to get daily returns, if possible, in order to better understand the nature of drawdown. The investor should document the reason for the drawdown, and whether the drawdown was because of loss of skill or because of market shocks. In either case, the fund manager should have tuned the skill set in order to recover the loss.

The investor should seek to know how much free cash the fund manager keeps aside. Since investors often demand redemption, if the fund manager does not have enough cash in reserve, he must sell some of the assets, which will result in transaction costs. The transaction costs are shared among all the investors. If the exhibited returns were after keeping moderate cash in reserve, then it is a positive sign for the investor. Too much excess cash can be interpreted that the fund manager is lacking investment ideas or the strategy is lacking capacity.

Since hedge fund strategies can employ illiquid assets that lack the interest of a public market, the pricing of an asset is challenging for the managers and investors. Assets for which there is no public trading are priced using internal models instead of marking them to market. Pricing the assets using a model is called *mark-to-model*. The investor should ask how the mark-to-model behaves in stressed markets. The investor should document both mark-to-market and mark-to-model methodologies and should observe significant illiquidity premiums.

Fund valuation or individual security valuation is a key determinant of the accuracy of fund performance. Investors need to document valuation mechanisms. They need to know if managers are using their own justifications or using standard market models or quotes from a market dealer. Funds may show a significant difference in NAV when mark-to-model is used versus mark-to-market. Investors should document what method they use to mark to the market. Does the manager review and approve the NAV calculated by the administrator before it is sent out to investors? Has the manager ever had to revise the NAV after it was final?

2.6 Risk Review

Risk review is the most important part of due diligence, and a significant part of the book has been dedicated to risk management. In addition, risk characteristics of various strategies have been discussed in later sections of this book.

There are several types of information that the investor needs to document related to the risk-review phase of due diligence and the post investment phase.

Hedge fund managers combine short positions in most strategies. While some managers use the short positions to suppress unwanted risks, some managers use them as opportunistic and bet against upward pricing movements of assets. Betting against downward movement is as risky as long positions, and sometimes may even worsen the situation. For example, if the fund is using short options, then the fund will enjoy the premium as profit, but unfavorable sudden pricing movements may cause serious damages to the fund. Therefore, the investor needs to document the manager's intention of using the short positions in the fund. In addition, the investor should seek what types of risk are being hedged. For example, if the fund is engaging in international markets and the fund strategy's intention is not to profit from the fluctuations of currency and interest rates, then the investor should know if the manager is hedging against interest-rate risk and currency risk.

Traditional funds typically employ long-term strategies and therefore do not involve frequent trading. In contrast to traditional funds, hedge funds rely on both strategy and dynamic trading of the positions. The dynamic nature of the trading may cause the manager's style to be deviated from the original style. The investor should seek to know if the dynamic trading is for the purpose of re-hedging or for some other purpose. There are several reasons why managers drift away from the original style. The manager may be trying to move from a poorly performing style to a perceived outperforming style, the manager may be seeing more incoming investors and the current style may not be sufficient to sustain the increased funds, or the fund manager may be trying to increase the level of risk as he could not beat the benchmark, or the fund manager may be trying to recoup some of the drawdown. Nonetheless, it is very important for the investor to detect any style drifts in the fund before or after investing.

The investor should document how the manager is measuring the risk. Risk can be measured using a simple standard deviation or a very complex expected shortfall and extreme value theory. The investor should also seek how the manager is measuring tail risk, because most strategies exhibit non-elliptical distributions. Not all risk measures fit for all portfolios. Standard deviation is simple but cannot be decomposed easily; it also violates the monotonicity condition of coherent measures. Value-at-risk meets the monotonicity condition but violates the sub additive condition for non-elliptical distributions and depends on the assumption of distribution. Expected shortfall may be stable and meet all of the coherent conditions, but it is not easy to interpret. The investor should document how the manager performs stress testing and how the risk estimates are being back tested.

Since hedge funds often involve over-the-counter transitions, they are exposed to counterparty risk. The investor should document how the manager is reducing the credit exposure and how the risk is being controlled.

The use of leverage is specifically set in the partnership agreement and is bound to have certain limits. Even with the limit, the hedge fund manager is free to use more leverage than the traditional manager uses. Some hedge funds may prefer not to have the leverage limits, while others set limits. The investor should document the limit of leverage, what was the maximum limit reached in the past three years, and what was the performance pattern during the use of high leverage. There are numerous examples where many funds failed due to high use of leverage.

Finally the investor needs to document about the risk culture at the hedge fund firm. Some hedge funds employ the same division for both generating the investment ideas and risk analysis. In that case, some conflicts may appear, and risk may not be measured independently and accurately. Hedge funds that employ two different persons as the heads of the investments division and the risk management division exhibit success in business.

During risk review, investors should at least document the following:

Risk Measures: Various quantitative techniques are available to measure the risk of the fund. Risk measures range from simple standard deviation and variance to mid-advanced value-at-risk and expected tail loss to advanced measures that employ extreme value theory. Investors should document what the various risk measures are.

Risk Management Systems: Investors should know if the firms are using in-house or third-party systems for risk management. Investors should know the level of sophistication of the risk systems.

Other risk-related due diligence should at least address the below questions:

- How is the hedging mechanism implemented?
- Is the fund using any options?
- How are the options used?
- Are they being used to leverage the capital or for a hedging purpose?
- What are the various derivatives used?
- Are swaps, forwards, and futures used?
- What is the loss tolerance for a position?
- Are the stop-loss rules used?
- What are the stop-loss levels?

2.7 Infrastructure Review

In evaluating the hedge fund firm's infrastructure, there are three key issues to concentrate on. They are business continuity and disaster planning, technologies or software products, and outside technology providers.

Business continuity and disaster planning deals with continuing business in the event that a disaster shuts down the systems and also deals with how to recover the data that was lost, if any. While every part of the system is critically important, the need is understood to have a highly reliable and backup plan in place for trading and regular operations. The investor should seek to know a few things from the hedge fund, including how systems are protected from disasters, whether there are duplicate systems established in multiple locations, if the firm has the expertise to quickly restore crashed systems, how the lost data, if any, can be recovered, and whether the backup systems were tested by simulating the recovery.

Many firms often use either overfitting or underfitting software products internally. While the overfitting products create much hype and publicity, they cost the company millions, and the cost ultimately flows down to the investors. Underfitting products may require additional manual work, which may cause the manager to lose any short-lived opportunities. The investor must also seek how the existing systems are adaptable to new and emerging technologies. The investor will need to find out if the firm is using readily available products or if they were customized, in order to gauge the sophistication level of the firm.

Many hedge funds also rely on outside technology providers. While IT outsourcing provides many advantages, it brings some disadvantages as well.

The advantages include cost savings, access to advanced technologies and skills, quality of services, allocating on-site resources to core activities while allocating off-site resources to tactic or rapid technologies, scalability of resources, and shorter time to market. The disadvantages include providers' financial difficulties, slower communication, and buyer consolidation of providers. There are numerous examples where emerging technology providers went bankrupt, with no available backup for the clients. Due to the operating location of providers, it is sometimes found to be difficult to communicate in time. When providers are acquired by other providers, then the new provider may renegotiate the terms and conditions.

The following questions typically help the investor in due diligence:

1. Was the duplicate or triplicate infrastructure established at a colocation?
2. Can the colocation be reached easily?
3. Were the colocation systems tested with simulated disasters?
4. Who are the outside technology providers, and where are they located?
5. What are the terms and conditions of their license agreements?
6. When the systems are upgraded, will they be filled with historical data or started with new data?
7. Is the firm using any out-of-the-box products, or were they customized?

2.8 Reporting and Data Providers

The reporting and database review phase of due diligence is applicable at the aggregation level rather than the fund level. In selecting a specific fund to add to an existing portfolio, the investor should compare the performance of the fund being investigated to the average hedge fund industry indices, either at a strategy level or at an aggregated industry level. The depth of explanation in any index is only as good as the underlying data. There are many hedge fund databases available that collect, analyze and prepare research reports and indices. Hedgefund.net is one of the hedge fund databases with the largest number of funds. While the database providers try to maintain as much accuracy as possible, they may sometimes be subject to various biases, which are described below. The biases overstate the returns and understate the risk and may sometimes make the funds more attractive than is justifiable.

Survivorship Bias: Survivorship bias occurs when the hedge fund database excludes funds that have gone out of business. The perception is that only poorly performing hedge funds will go out of business. If the nonperforming funds are excluded, then the database may contain a majority of positive performing funds. It is quite possible that funds exhibit high volatile returns before operations are ceased. Therefore, the survivorship bias will overstate the returns and understate the risk of the fund index. In an academic study conducted during 2006, Fung and Hsieh found that survivorship bias added 3 percent per year to the reported hedge fund returns. However, as the hedge fund industry matures the survivorship bias declines.

Self-Selection Bias: Since hedge funds are little regulated, they have the choice whether to report performance at any and all times. Some hedge funds that want to market their fund may suddenly decide to report to hedge fund data providers and they report only if they are performing well. On the other hand, the hedge fund may stop reporting if it is not performing well. This is called self-selection bias. This can be compared to a forum where exam candidates, for example, discuss about the exam. When the results are announced, candidates may post the result. It is quite possible that only candidates who pass the exam may come back to the forum and post as passed. Out of a hundred posts during the exam day, we may find 70 percent of "passed" posts, but that does not necessarily mean that 70 percent of the aspirants passed the exam. On the other hand, a successful candidate who was not a member of the forum until the day results were announced may register and post a message as "passed". The self-selection bias will lead to an upward bias in performance measurement.

Backfill or Instant History Bias: When positive-performing funds are added to the database, it backfills all the historical data as well. Since the hedge fund managers have the option when to report the performance, it is rational that they report only when the numbers look attractive. A study by Princeton professor Burton Malkiel that appeared in the *Financial Analysts Journal* found that backfill bias overstated hedge fund returns by 5 percent per year.

Liquidation Bias: Liquidation bias is somewhat similar to survivorship bias but occurs before the fund goes out of business. Unsuccessful hedge funds, before they liquidate operations, will be busy with preparing internal reports and other formalities. During this time, they may stop reporting their performance to hedge fund databases. While closing the fund may take months, the database will lose the tail part of the data stream. This may cause the index to overestimate the returns and underestimate the risk. The liquidation bias is also called *catastrophe bias.*

Quantifying bias issues is certainly not an easy task, and investors should apply subjective analysis when comparing a fund performance with a corresponding index. Investors should try to get custom data that includes any excluded funds and then make the necessary adjustments to calculate unsmoothed risk and returns.

In addition to the bias issue, another issue that investors should keep in mind after adding the fund to the portfolio is performance reports. There are three main issues related to reports:

1. Ensure that the fund is publishing the report periodically.
2. Even if the fund is publishing the report periodically, ensure that it doesn't contain lagged data. For example, some funds may publish the data the first day of every quarter, but may include data only until the last day two quarters prior.
3. Ensure that the report is easily interpretable and understandable.

2.9 Administrative Review

During the administrative-review phase of the due diligence, the investor needs to document two types of information: Form ADV and account representative. While the investor is expected to earn a premium for bearing certain risks the fraud risks do not typically compensate the investors. Therefore, the investor needs to detect any past or present fraudulent activities of the manager and document them.

2.9.1 Form ADV Inspection

In the Unites States, investment managers who manage more than $25 million, require a lockup period of less than two years, and have at least fourteen clients are required to file form ADV. International hedge funds having at least fourteen US-based investors are also required to file Form ADV. The forms are required to be filed either annually or whenever there is a material change. In addition to lots of other information, Form ADV contains fraudulent activities—which include regulatory violations and civil and criminal allegations—and non-fraudulent activities, which include conflicts of interest the manager may have with their investors, soft-dollar arrangements, custodian, broker/dealer, and so on. Investors should seek form ADV from the SEC and detect any suspicious activity.

2.9.2 Account Representative

Investors are assigned to account representatives on behalf of the hedge fund manager. The representative will handle issues regarding performance reporting, withdrawals, and on-site meetings. While most of the communication can be handled remotely, certain operational events can be detected more easily with on-site meetings. Firms that allow frequent site visits are less exposed to negative operational events. Investors should document how frequently the firms allow site visits, whom they can meet, and what type of information can be gathered during site visits.

2.10 Legal Review

Investors should perform legal review regarding the structure of the hedge fund firm and rules and regulations of the country of the firm incorporation. This was discussed under the firm structural review phase of due diligence. In addition, investors should also perform legal review related to the fund. The review should include fee structure, hurdle rate, high watermark, clawbacks, lockups, redemptions, minimum subscriptions, and advisory committees.

The most common fee structure for hedge funds is a 2 percent management fee and a 20 percent performance fee. The structure may vary from firm to firm and strategy to strategy. A fund of hedge funds may charge an additional layer. The performance fee is subject to the hurdle rate, high watermark, and clawback, and the investor needs to document these three characteristics. Hurdle rate is defined as the minimum rate that the investor can earn on his own by investing in passive indices and is used as the minimum expected rate of return from the fund. Some fee structures deduct the hurdle rate from the hedge fund return while calculating the performance fee. For example, assume that the investor invests $100 in the fund and the agreed hurdle rate is 10 percent and the performance fee is 20 percent. At the end of the year, the fund is valued as $200. Now the investor's annual profit is $100. However, the investor does not pay a fee for the hurdle rate, 10 percent of profit. He only pays a fee for $90, which is equal to $18. While hedge funds do not guarantee a rate of return, most fund managers allow investors to use the hurdle rate while calculating the management fee. The above example describes a hard hurdle rate. In a soft hurdle rate, the fund manager is eligible to claim the performance fee on the entire returns as long as the returns exceed the hurdle rate. The high watermark is defined as the previous highest NAV before the drawdown occurs. Let us assume that the investor invests $100 and the performance fee is 20 percent. For simplicity, assume that the hurdle rate is zero and the management fee is also zero. At the end of year one, the fund earns a profit of $100. The investor pays a $20 performance fee, and the fund value becomes $180 after the management fee. In the second year, the manager loses $50, and the fund value becomes $130. In year three, the manager earns $100, and the fund value becomes $230. Without the high watermark, the investor would need to pay a performance fee on $100 profit, but the high watermark allows the investor to pay a performance fee only on $50 profit, which is in excess of the previous highest value of $180. The last important characteristic of fee structure is clawback. Clawbacks are rare in the hedge fund industry and are common in venture capitals. Clawbacks allow investors to take back the previously paid performance fee if the fund does not produce the hurdle rate over the agreed-upon period.

There are two concepts related to liquidity of the fund. They are the lockup period and redemptions. The lockup period refers to the period of time beginning with the investment over which the investor cannot redeem any part of the investment. If allowed to redeem, the investor is subject to a redemption fee. After the initial lockup period, investors are allowed to redeem periodically, and redemptions are available normally monthly or quarterly. The redemptions are entitled to a notice period as well. The notice period specifies the deadline date for receipt of the redemption notice. An investor willing to take part or all of his money out of the fund sends a redemption notice. For example, assume that a fund allows quarterly redemption and requires a thirty-day notice. Then the fund manager must receive the notice thirty days before the first day of the next quarter in order to redeem for that date at that valuation.

The investor should document all the details pertaining to the lockup period, the redemption period, and redemption notice times. Lockups and disciplined redemptions allow the manager to achieve superior performance. During temporary shocks, the funds may perform badly as the convergence strategies diverge temporarily before converging back. If the fund survives during the shock, then the fund may be back on track. However, if a majority of investors react to the panic and seek redemption within a short period of time, then the manager will have to liquidate the fund at unfavorable prices, and the mass liquidation in turn will increase the downward pressure. On the other hand, if the fund agreement prevents investors' redemption of the fund at irregular times, then the manager will have an opportunity to either show the positive returns or reduce the losses. Lockup periods provide the manager enough time to implement the strategy. Frequent redemptions also cause unnecessary transition costs, which affect other investors as well. If the investor is willing to invest for longer times, then he should consider fund managers who have stringent rules regarding redemption. It is common belief and historical observation that the fund with no redemption restrictions, no lockups, and no management fee usually liquidates early. However, this may not be true always, and investors need to perform subjective research on these issues.

Another important characteristic of the fund that the investor needs to document during the legal review phase is subscription amount. As we already know, hedge funds are meant for high-net worth and sophisticated investors. They require a minimum subscription amount. Hedge funds may also impose restrictions on the maximum subscription amount. A maximum limit allows the managers to diversify away from a small group of concentrated investors and protects the fund from mass redemption. Investors should document subscription amount details. Most investors prefer funds that have maximum limits.

Like many private equity firms, hedge funds also employ advisory committees, which advise fund managers on various critical issues. Utilization of advisory committees by hedge funds is a positive signal for investors.

2.11 References

The last part of the due diligence is checking the references. Investors should inquire with service providers as well as with existing and old investors. Outside auditors possess better information regarding the firm's accounting system. Investors should acquire audited statements from outside auditors and seek the explanation if there is any unqualified information. Prime brokers contain more insight about the hedge fund manager's transactions. The investor should seek to know about the leverage used, number of margin calls, if the manager is responding in time for the margin calls, and the size of the calls. The investor should contact existing clients as well as old clients.

2.12 Operational Review

Hedge fund managers either hedge away the most unwanted risks or expect a premium for bearing those risks. However, the hedge fund firm itself can be a source of operational risks, and the NAV may not reflect this operational risk. Therefore, investors need to evaluate the hedge fund firm-specific risk while performing the due diligence of the funds. There is no clear definition of operational risk; different experts define it differently. As per Basel's definition, operational risk is "the risk of loss resulting from inadequate or failed internal processes, people and systems, or from external events." Operational risk measurement techniques have been discussed in depth under the risk management part of the book.

Measuring operational risk, both subjective and objective, is one of the most challenging tasks for any firm. It is even more challenging for investors who sit outside of the firm to measure a hedge fund's operational risk. Part of the information contained in Form ADV can be used to evaluate operational risk. Form ADV has been discussed under the administrative review section. Hedge fund firms that are exposed to operational risk are more prone to failure during any financial crisis. There are numerous examples where hedge funds failed mainly due to lack of operational control.

2.12.1 Hedge Fund Disasters

Various researches reveal that more than half of the funds fail due to operational issues rather than performance issues. Most of the hedge fund operational issues were related to model risk, fraud, and limited risk management. An incorrect model is not necessarily intentional. It could be due to failure in analyzing relationships among various factors or could be due to data issues with input. Due to its importance, model risk has been discussed separately under its own topic in this book.

Some of the common reasons for hedge fund failures are listed below:

- Incorrect valuations
- Lack of experienced managers
- Limited or no stress testing
- Lack of opportunities to drift away from current underperforming style
- Single and concentrated strategies
- Mix of trades on both regulated and unregulated exchanges

While various hedge fund failures have been discussed throughout the book, the following are some other highly visible failures.

2.12.2 Millennium Partners

Millennium earned a substantial amount of profit by committing fraud using the concept called "flying under the radar" transactions, designed to get around defenses set up by mutual funds to deter market timing by disguising or concealing Millennium's identity. Millennium Partners earned more than

$100 million from market timing transactions from 1999 to 2003. Millennium Partners created more than one hundred shell companies, which were then used to open one thousand accounts at thirty-nine different clearing brokers. This process is referred to as *cloning the accounts*. In addition, Millennium rented postal office boxes and used them as addresses on account applications to deceive mutual funds that tracked unwanted market timing activity by their clients' street addresses. When a mutual fund company identified Millennium as a market timer and blocked its activity, it opened a new account in the name of a new company and continued the activity. By using the bogus accounts, Millennium made more than 76,000 timing transactions that might otherwise have been detected by monitors at mutual funds.

2.12.3 Mother Rock

The blowup of Mother Rock was mainly due to its large bets against natural gas prices. It was a highly concentrated single strategy. While the magnitude was not enough to affect the systemic risk, the similar failure of Amaranth at the same time magnified the headline risk of Mother Rock.

Important factors that led to Mother Rock's failure were:

- Single strategy
- Large bets
- Excessive leverage
- Less-experienced traders
- Limited capacity of the natural gas sector
- Lack of transparency of natural gas positions owned by other hedge funds

2.12.4 Bayou Fund

In 1992, Samuel Israel III and Daniel Marino created a hedge fund with capital of $1.2 million. Bayou attracted clients with its unique fee structure of zero percent management fee and 20 percent fee on profit. It also attracted small investors by reducing the minimum capital requirement to $225,000. In addition, investors were provided the ability to withdraw their funds at any time rather than being subject to lockup provisions. Bayou claimed that Grant Thornton was its auditor. In reality, Daniel Marino, CFO of Bayou Fund, created a fictitious accounting firm called Richmond-Fairfield, with just three listed employees. When the fund started losing money, Richmond-Fairfield was fabricating financial records. The firm was misrepresenting the fund's performance by hiding the losses. Bayou also created its own broker-deal firm called Bayou Securities and claimed to have used it for the clearance. Bayou's marketing materials mentioned that its books were audited on a periodic and surprise basis by the NASD and the SEC. Bayou claimed that the regulators had the right to examine the books as the firm owned the brokerage unit. In reality, the trades were being handled by a third-party firm that acted as Bayou's prime broker. However, Bayou Securities started earning profit from trading commissions. Authorities found that the firm wired a large amount of money to its bank accounts. Several other red flags were raised, and the fund was finally liquidated in mid-2005. Both the principals pled guilty to investment advisory fraud, mail fraud, wire fraud, and conspiracy.

The following concerns would have helped investors to detect the fraud earlier:

1. Too good a fee structure
2. No lockups
3. The need of an in-house broker for a small firm
4. Inquiry about an audit firm
5. Firm's operating expenses

2.12.5 Askin Capital

Askin Capital purchased large quantities of high-risk mortgage-backed securities and then pooled them into CMOs and resold them to investors. Highly rated tranches were sold to institutional investors at a higher fee. Askin Capital claimed that the fund performed between 1 percent and 2 percent, while market valuation systems showed that the fund was losing between 20 percent to 28 percent from February 1994 through March 1994.When the SEC filed a suit against the company, David Askin, the principal at Askin Capital, stated that he had issued his own estimates on his CMO holdings rather than using standard market valuations or dealer quotes, despite allegedly mentioning in his marketing prospectuses that he would use market valuations.

The following due diligence would have helped investors to avoid Askin Capital:

1. Level of leverage
2. Demanding more transparency regarding valuation methods
3. Level of Askin's experience
4. Noticing the lack of hedging techniques
5. Evaluating risk management practice at Askin Capital

2.12.6 LF Global Investments

The LF Global Investments fund allegedly involved a traditional Ponzi scheme. Investors contributed more than $100m to the hedge fund between 1999 and 2004.Only one third of the amount was actually invested by managers, who lost half of the invested amount. By the time that the SEC embarked upon investigation in early 2005, the hedge fund held only $3m in investments and $8000 in cash. The firm reported fictional performance of 30 percent by developing a close relationship with Santa-Rosa-based advisory firm Zenith Capital LLC. Zenith sent at least 115 investors to LF Global investments, where the total number of investors was 240.Although LF principals invested their own money in the fund, they withdrew substantially more money than they had invested. The hedge fund allegedly became a personal bank account for the principals. The SEC investigation found that there was no independent audit of the hedge fund's performance. The founder enjoyed total control, and there was no supervision of his actions. The founder had also been involved with security violations in the past. There was a cross ownership and conflicts of interest between Zenith and LF. In February 2005, the SEC charged the principals of the hedge fund with defrauding investors.

3. Quantitative Fundamentals

3.1 Risk and Performance Metrics

3.1.1 Standard Deviation

Standard Deviation measures the degree of variation of returns around the mean return and is often used as a measure of investment risk. The higher the fluctuations in the returns, the higher the standard deviation will be.

The two variations of standard deviations are upside standard deviation and downside standard deviation.

Upside standard deviation uses the average return of only gains and then measures the variation of only the gain periods around this gain mean. This statistic measures the volatility of upside performance.

Downside standard deviation uses the average return of only losses and then measures the variation of only the loss periods around this loss mean. This statistic measures the volatility of downside performance.

3.1.2 Alpha

Alpha measures the excess return over the return predicted by the capital asset pricing model (CAPM).

According to CAPM, Portfolio Return

$$E[r_p] = r_f + \beta[E[r_m] - r_f]$$

Since the beta does not capture all the risk exposures, portfolio actual return may be higher than that predicted by the above formula. The higher returns are attributed to the manager's skill of exploiting market inefficiencies. Therefore,

$$E[r_p] = r_f + \beta[E[r_m] - r_f] + \alpha$$

As we learned earlier, alpha can be decomposed into multiple risk exposures and real alpha in order to distinguish true skill versus market factor exposures. Rewriting the above formula,

$$E[r_p] = r_f + \beta_1[E[r_{m1}] - r_f] + ... + \beta_n[E[r_{mn}] - r_f] + \alpha$$

3.1.3 Treynor Ratio

The Treynor ratio measures returns adjusted to systemic risk. It gives portfolio excess returns over risk-free rate per unit of systemic risk. The Treynor ratio is also called the *reward-to-volatility ratio* or *Treynor measure*. The higher the Treynor ratio, the better the performance of the portfolio.

$$Treynor\,Ratio = \frac{r_p - r_f}{\beta}$$

3.1.4 Sharpe Ratio

The Sharpe ratio is one of the most important measures in investment space and measures risk-adjusted returns of a portfolio. It gives excess returns over risk-free rate per unit of portfolio risk. If the Sharpe ratio needs to be calculated per security, the portfolio return and volatility shall be replaced with those of the security.

$$Sharpe\,Ratio = \frac{r_p - r_f}{\sigma_p}$$

The Sharpe ratio can be used as a hurdle rate to determine whether or not to add a fund to a portfolio. A Sharpe ratio comparison tells whether a fund can be added to a portfolio or not. The higher the Sharpe ratio, the better the performance of the fund. When comparing the Sharpe ratio of portfolios, the fund's Sharpe ratio must be higher than the portfolio's Sharpe ratio.

$$\frac{r_m - r_f}{\sigma_m} > \rho \frac{r_p - r_f}{\sigma_m}$$

Where $\dfrac{r_p - r_f}{\sigma_m}$ = manager's Sharpe ratio

$$\frac{r_p - r_f}{\sigma_p} = \text{portfolio's Sharpe ratio}$$

ρ = correlation between manager's return and portfolio's return

σ_m = standard deviation of manager's return

σ_p = standard deviation of portfolio's return

Similarly, when comparing two funds, the fund with the higher Sharpe ratio is a better candidate for the portfolio.

3.1.5 Sortino Ratio

Standard deviation is not a good measure of risk, especially when there are more observations above the mean or below the mean. That means standard deviation is not good for non-normal distributions, which are quite common in alternative investments.

The Sharpe ratio, which adjusts the performance to standard deviation, can often be misleading because standard deviation penalizes portfolios for positive upside returns as much as the undesirable downside returns.

An alternative to the Sharpe ratio is the measure that uses an alternative to standard deviation. The downside semivariance or downside semistandard deviation is a better alternative to standard deviation or total risk.

The Sortino ratio takes only the downside size and frequency of returns into account and measures the reward to negative volatility trade-off. The Sortino ratio can be expressed mathematically as follows:

$$SortinoRatio = \frac{r_p - r_f}{\sigma_{down}}$$

σ_{down} = downside semistandard deviation

3.1.6 Information Ratio

The information ratio is similar to the Sharpe ratio except that the numerator is excess return over the benchmark instead of the risk-free rate and the denominator is the standard deviation of alpha. The standard deviation of alpha is also called *tracking error* or *active risk*.

Therefore, the information ratio gives excess returns over benchmark per unit of tracking error:

Information Ratio IR = alpha / tracking error

The above information ratio is calculated at the end of the returns period in analysis. It may often be required to know the information ratio in advance, or ex-ante. An ex-ante information ratio can be calculated using the fundamental law of active management developed by Richard Grinold.

According to the fundamental law of active management, the information ratio comprises two components: breadth (BR), which refers to the number of independent forecasts of alpha that are made in a year; and the information coefficient (IC), which is calculated as the correlation between the manager's forecasts and the actual values of active investments.

Ex-ante Information Ratio = $\sqrt{BR} * IC$

The greater the ability to produce higher ex-ante information ratios, the greater the opportunity for excess returns. For example, a 130/30 fund has gross exposure of 160 with net exposure of 100. Therefore, the additional 60 percent of bets increases the breadth, which in turn increases the information ratio.

3.1.7 Skewness

Skew is a very important statistical measure in the analysis of return distribution, as it tells us how the returns deviate from the normal distribution. A normal distribution is a symmetrical distribution with equal frequency of loss and gains. Since alternative investments employ complex option-like strategies, the return distribution is not always symmetrical. The skewness refers to the extent to which a distribution is not symmetrical. The distribution may be either positively or negatively skewed, as shown in the figures below. In negatively skewed distribution, a larger amount of outliers lie in the left tail, indicating potential for heavy losses; and in positively skewed distribution, a larger amount of outliers lie in the right tail, indicating potential for higher returns. For normal distribution, the skewness is zero. The following three diagrams depict normal distribution, distribution with positive skew, and distribution with negative skew.

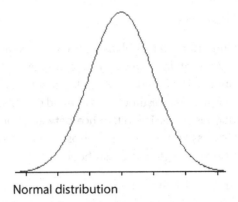

Normal distribution

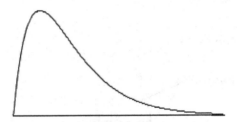

Distribution with a positive skew

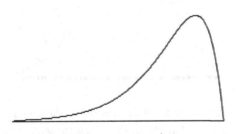

Distribution with a negative skew

Skewness represents the third momentum and is equal to the average of the cubed deviations from the mean divided by the sample standard deviation cubed.

$$\text{Skewness} = \frac{E\left[(x - \mu)^3\right]}{\sigma^3}$$

3.1.8 Kurtosis

Kurtosis is another important statistical measure for alternative investments; it measures the peakedness of distribution. The distribution that is more peaked than a normal distribution is referred to as leptokurtic, whereas the distribution that is less peaked than a normal distribution is referred to as platykurtic. Kurtosis for normal distribution is three. The difference between nonnormal kurtosis and three is called excess kurtosis. Excess kurtosis is negative for platykurtic distribution and positive for leptokurtic distribution.

Leptokurtic distribution will have more returns either around the mean or far from the mean, whereas platykurtic distribution will have fewer returns around and far from the mean.

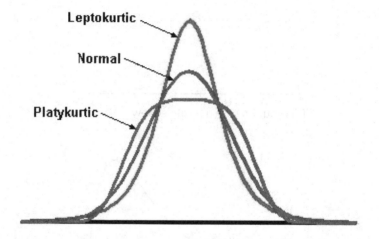

Efficient risk management puts more emphasis on skewness and kurtosis, as the risk estimated by traditional models either overestimates or underestimates the actual risk of alternative investments. As we will see in hedge fund strategies, most strategies exhibit negative skew and excess kurtosis, indicating a fat and prolonged left tail.

$$\text{Kurtosis} = \frac{E[(x - \mu)^4]}{\sigma^4}$$

3.1.9 Maximum Drawdown

Maximum drawdown (MDD) measures how sustained portfolio losses are over the specified period of time. It is the maximum loss from market peak to market low.

Maximum drawdown can be mathematically measured as follows:

MDD = ((Trough/Peak) -1) * 100

Trough = Lowest value of NAV during the specified time

Peak = Highest value of NAV

While the standard deviation takes both upside and downside values into account and may not accurately explain the downside risk, the maximum drawdown is more intuitive to the investors. However, maximum drawdown is sensitive to both time and valuation frequency. Since the MDD is not adjusted to time, the probability of NAV reaching more peak and trough values is high when used to measure returns over longer periods. Similarly, valuating the asset values more frequently may record either more peak or trough values. Investors should apply subjective judgments when using MDD.

3.1.10 D-Statistics

The D-statistic is another measure of downside risk, which gives the percentage of negative returns with respect to the absolute returns of all months.

$$\text{D-Statistic} = \frac{\sum |\text{Negative Returns}|}{\sum |\text{All Returns}|}$$

The lower the value of the D-statistic, the better the performance of the fund or portfolio.

3.1.11 Omega

While the D-statistic takes zero as demarcation, the omega can be calculated by using any value as a threshold.

It is the ratio of the sum of absolute returns above the reference point and the sum of absolute returns below the reference point. The threshold point is similar to the required rate of return and is positive.

$$\text{Mathematically, omega} = \frac{\text{sum of absolute returns above the threshold point}}{\text{sum of absolute returns below the threshold point}}$$

$$\Omega(L) = \frac{\sum \text{Returns}+}{\sum |\text{Returns}-|}$$

Where

L = threshold point

Returns+ = Returns above the threshold

Returns- = Returns below the threshold

The higher the values of the omega, the better the performance of the fund or portfolio. The omega can be used to monitor the style and performance of the fund manager. While standard deviation, skewness, and kurtosis take relative values above or below the mean, omega takes the actual value of returns. Therefore, omega represents actual distribution and provides the combined effects of standard deviation, skewness, and kurtosis. Omega is the most preferred measure for investors.

3.1.12 Greeks

Delta

Delta gives the rate of change of the option price with respect to the price of the underlying asset. For example, if delta is 0.4 for a call option, a one-dollar rise in stock price will result in a $0.40 rise in the call option price.

Mathematically,

$$\Delta = \frac{\partial V}{\partial S}$$

Where

V = Call option price

S = Stock Price

Delta is a first-order derivative and is a very useful measure in designing hedging strategies. For a call option on a nondividend-paying stock, delta is approximately 0.5 for the at-the-money option, 1 for a deep in-the-money option, and zero for a deep out-of-the-money option.

The Black-Scholes formula is mathematically expressed as:

$$V = S * N(d_1) - X * e^{-rt} * N(d_2)$$

Where

$$d_1 = \frac{ln(\frac{S}{X}) + (r + \frac{\sigma_2}{2})t}{\sigma\sqrt{t}}$$

$$d_2 = d_1 - \sigma\sqrt{t}$$

Taking the derivative of V with respect to S by keeping all other parameters constant,

Δ= N (d1).

From the put-call parity, the delta of a put option can be derived as follows:

Call + Ke⁻ʳᵗ = Put + Stock

C + Ke⁻ʳᵗ - P = S

Taking the derivative with respect to S,

Δ (call) - Δ (put) = 1

Δ (put) = Δ (call) -1

= N (d1) - 1

Therefore, for a put option on a nondividend-paying stock, delta is approximately -0.5 for the at-the-money option, -1 for a deep in-the money option, and zero for a deep out-of-the-money option.

Gamma

Gamma gives the rate of change of delta with respect to asset price. Therefore, it is a second-order derivative of an option with respect to underlying asset price.

$$\Gamma = \frac{\partial\Delta}{\partial S} = \frac{\partial^2 V}{\partial S^2}$$

Gamma gives the convexity of an option price relationship. Gamma is more pronounced for at-the-money options and is less for in-the-money and out-of-the money options. Gamma is also a function of time-to-maturity. For at-the-money options, gamma decreases as the time-to-maturity increases. For out-of-the-money options, near-to-expiration and far-from-expiration options will have less gamma, and medium-term options will have higher gamma. Gamma of in-the-money options also behaves like that of out-of-the-money options but is high at not-so-near but near expiration. Gamma is very useful in convertible arbitrage strategies and option strategies.

Theta

Theta gives the rate of change of the option price with respect to time-to-maturity. Theta is always negative, regardless of asset price and type of option. In other words, out-of-the-money, at-the-money, and in-the-money call and put options will all have negative theta. Therefore, option value increases with increased length of time, that is, far-from-maturity options will have a higher option price than those near to expiration. At-the-money options will have a higher absolute theta.

Vega

Vega gives the rate of change of the option value with respect to the volatility of the underlying asset. Vega is always positive and is higher for at-the-money options.

Rho

Rho gives the rate of change of the value of an option with respect to the interest rate. The option is more sensitive to rho at lower strike prices as the stock value goes down, the probability of the company value falling below the debt value increases, and the bond value in turn is more sensitive to the interest rate.

In the Black-Scholes formula, the term $N(d_2)$ gives the probability of a call option being exercised or the probability of debt being survived. The probability of a call option exercise means the stock being above the strike, which can also be interpreted as the company value being higher than the debt value.

The Black-Scholes formula gives the following equation for Rho:

$$Rho\ (call) = Kte^{-rt}N(d_2)$$

As we know from put-call parity, $C + Ke^{-rt} = P + S$

$$Dow\ C/\ Dow\ r - Kte^{-rt} = Dow\ P/\ Dow\ r$$

Rho (Put) = $Kte^{-rt}N(d2) - Kte^{-rt}$

$$=- Kte^{-rt}(1 - N(d_2))$$

$$=- Kte^{-rt}N(-d_2)$$

3.2 Probability Distributions and Applications

3.2.1 Binomial Distribution

The binomial distribution, a discrete probability distribution, describes the possible number of times that a particular event will occur in a sequence of observations. Let p be the probability of success and q the probability of failure. In each trial, the sum of probabilities of success and failure is equal to 1. In N number of trials, the total probability is $(p + q)^N$, which can be expanded as follows:

$$(p + q)^N = q^N + (N\ 1)\ q^{N-1}P + (N\ 2)\ q^{N-2}p^2 + \ldots\ldots + p^N$$

Where each term gives the probability of occurrence of X successes, X = 0, 1, 2, 3...N.

Generalizing each term gives the probability of occurrence of X successes and N-X failures.

$$P(X) = (N\ X)\ p^X\ q^{N-X}$$

In binomial distribution,

Mean = Np

Standard deviation = $\sqrt{Npq}$

The following scenario best describes the use of binomial distribution. Let the probability of stock value going up in any day be 1/7 and going down is 6/7, and the probability of each day is independent. The binomial tree of three consecutive days is shown below:

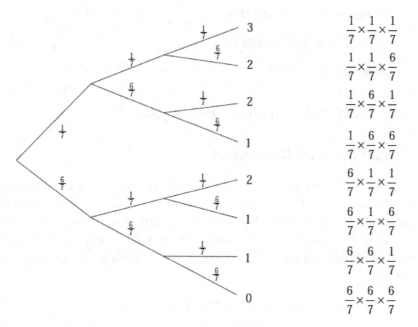

In three consecutive days, the probability of stock going up in two days is:

$$P(X=2) = \frac{1}{7} \times \frac{1}{7} \times \frac{6}{7} + \frac{1}{7} \times \frac{6}{7} \times \frac{1}{7} + \frac{6}{7} \times \frac{1}{7} \times \frac{1}{7}$$

$$= 0.0524$$

In the above example, one day is used as the time interval. As the time interval approaches zero or N approaches infinity, then the binomial distribution approaches the normal distribution. In other words, if continuously compound returns are used instead of daily returns, then the binomial distribution approaches the normal distribution.

3.2.2 Normal Distribution

Normal distribution, also known as the normal curve or Gaussian distribution, is a continuous distribution function and is defined by the equation

$$Y = \frac{1}{\sigma\sqrt{2\pi}}e^{-\frac{(x-\mu)^2}{2\sigma^2}}$$

Where μ = mean

σ = standard deviation

The total area bounded by the curve and the X-axis gives the cumulative probability and is equal to 1. The area under the curve between the two ordinates X=a and X=b, where a < b represents the probability that X lies between a and b.

The term $\dfrac{(x - \mu)}{\sigma}$ is referred to as the standardized unit and is denoted with z. In other words, z represents the distance between the mean and the sample per unit of standard deviation.

If we replace $\dfrac{(x - \mu)}{\sigma}$ with z in the normal distribution equation,

$$Y = \frac{1}{\sqrt{2\pi}} e^{-\frac{z^2}{2}}$$

In such a case, we say that z is normally distributed with mean 0 and variance 1, and the distribution is said to be a standard normal distribution.

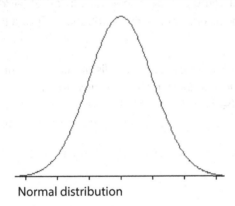

Normal distribution

The normal distribution is a two-tailed distribution with a bell shape. Its skew value is zero, kurtosis is 3, and mean=mode=median.

The value of z is used to measure the area of curve, which is the equivalent probability of an observation or confidence level. A z value of -1.645 gives the probability of 95 percent; in other words, 95 percent of the mass is distributed in the right side of -1.645. Since the normal distribution is symmetric, the same is true for the positive value of 1.645, that is, 95 percent of the mass is distributed to the left of 1.645. Hence, 90 percent of the mass is distributed between -1.645 and 1.645.

In terms of standard deviations:

- 68 percent of samples lie within 1 standard deviation, which indicates a 68percent confidence interval.
- 90 percent of samples lie within 1.645 standard deviations, which indicate a 90percent confidence interval.
- 95 percent of samples lie within1.96 standard deviations, which indicate a 95percent confidence interval.
- 99 percent of samples lie within 2.58 standard deviations, which indicate a 99percent confidence interval.

Risk-averse investors prefer returns of financial assets be normally distributed. In reality, very few asset classes exhibit normally distributed returns.

Most financial asset classes exhibit skewed and fat-tailed distribution. In a skewed distribution, less probable but large deviations appear in either tail; and in a fat-tailed distribution, mass is distributed in the tail and around the mean. Distributions with high excess kurtosis exhibit fat tails.

Smaller units of time series of returns may sometimes exhibit normal distribution, whereas the total series can be nonnormal. In other words, a nonnormal distribution can be a series of normal distributions. Such a behavior is called regime switching.

Binomial distribution approaches normal distribution as the number of samples N tends to large and if neither p nor q is too close to zero. "Neither p nor q is too close to zero" can be interpreted as the probability of occurring and probability of not occurring is less, which indicates less distribution in the tails.

Normal distribution and binomial distribution are related by the equation

$$z = \frac{x - Np}{\sqrt{Npq}}$$

As N increases, the skewness and kurtosis for the binomial distribution approach that of the normal distribution.

3.2.3 Lognormal Distribution

If a data set is known to follow a normal distribution, transforming the data by taking a logarithm of variables yields a data set that is lognormally distributed. Since the normal distribution allows variables to have negative values and negative values are not observed in asset prices, the lognormal distribution is used instead, in which the observed values take zero and above.

Let x be the continuously compounded asset return. Then the asset price at the end of the return period is calculated as pe^{x}. When x is normally distributed, the log value of e^{x} is said to be lognormally distributed.

As the standard deviation increases, the probability of an observation falling in the tail increases and shows skewness. Standard deviation σ determines the shape of the distribution.

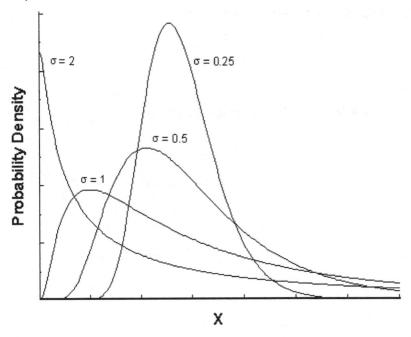

In the financial sector, the survival of certain investments is uncertain until a certain period has passed, and if the investment survives for that certain period, the probability of failure decreases dramatically. In other words, assets with a lognormal distribution have a higher chance of failing as they age for some period of time, but after survival to a specific age, the probability of failure decreases as time increases.

The lognormal distribution is left skewed with heavy tails. This can be observed from the above figure. Such a distribution is mostly observed in high-yield bonds.

3.2.4 Poisson Distribution

The Poisson distribution is a discrete probability distribution. It views the distribution as a function of the expected number of successes and was derived from the binomial distribution.

If the probability of occurrence of an event is p and the number of samples is N, then the mean occurrence of an event is Np and is denoted by lambda:

P = lambda/N

Replacing p with the above value in the binomial distribution,

$$P_{v/N}(n \mid N) = \frac{N!}{n!\,(N-n)!} \left(\frac{v}{N}\right)^n \left(1 - \frac{v}{N}\right)^{N-n},$$

As N becomes large, the distribution then approaches

$$P_v(n) \quad = \quad \lim_{N \to \infty} P_p(n \mid N)$$

$$= \quad \lim_{N \to \infty} \frac{N(N-1)\cdots(N-n+1)}{n!} \frac{v^n}{N^n} \left(1 - \frac{v}{N}\right)^N \left(1 - \frac{v}{N}\right)^{-n}$$

$$= \quad \lim_{N \to \infty} \frac{N(N-1)\cdots(N-n+1)}{N^n} \frac{v^n}{n!} \left(1 - \frac{v}{N}\right)^N \left(1 - \frac{v}{N}\right)^{-n}$$

$$= \quad 1 \cdot \frac{v^n}{n!} \cdot e^{-v} \cdot 1$$

$$= \quad \frac{v^n e^{-v}}{n!},$$

The Poisson distribution is very useful when the value of p is very small, that is, the events are very rare. Therefore, the Poisson distribution is called the law of small numbers.

When applying the Poisson distribution to analysis, the following conditions must be met:

1. The events must be countable whole numbers.
2. Each occurrence is independent of the other.

3. The average frequency of occurrence for the time period is known.
4. The number of counts must be measurable.

The Poisson distribution is very useful in operational risk measurement to estimate loss frequency distribution. Since there is a relationship between the Poisson distribution and the binomial distribution and again between the binomial distribution and the normal distribution, the Poisson distribution approaches a normal distribution with standardized variable $\dfrac{x - \lambda}{\sqrt{\lambda}}$.

3.2.5 Student's t Distribution

The z-statistic of normal distribution is good for analyzing various financial data series. However, one drawback with normal distribution is that it requires a very large number of observations, which is sometimes impractical. Instead of the z-statistic, the alternative t-statistic is used, which is derived from a small number of available samples. The t-statistic is very similar to the z-statistic, except that the standard deviation is replaced with the sample standard deviation.

The t-statistic is calculated by the following equation:

$$T = \frac{\overline{X} - \mu}{S/\sqrt{n}}$$

Where s is the sample standard deviation, which is calculated using the equation

$$S = \sqrt{\sum(X_i - \overline{X})^2/(n - 1)}$$

This distribution is called Student's t-distribution with n-1 degrees of freedom. The t-statistic varies based on the number of degrees of freedom. Therefore, it is a function of both confidence level and number of degrees of freedom. The t-distribution is centered at zero and symmetric, that is, the area to the left of 0 is half and the area to the right of 0 is half. The total area under the curve gives the cumulative probability, which is 1. The area in the tails of the t-distribution is larger than the area in the tails of the normal distribution. As sample size n increases, the distribution becomes approximately normal.

3.2.6 Chi-Square Distribution

The chi-square distribution is used to test the variance of a normally distributed population. The process is performed as follows. Suppose a random set of sample of size n is selected from a normal population, having a standard deviation equal to σ. Let s be the standard deviation of the sample set.

Then the chi-square statistic χ^2 is given by the equation $\chi^2 = \dfrac{(n-1)s^2}{\sigma^2}$

If the process is repeated for an infinite number of times, then the plot of χ^2 statistics gives the chi-square distribution.

The chi-square distribution has the following properties.

- The mean of the distribution is equal to the number of degrees of freedom.
- The variance is equal to twice the number of degrees of freedom.
- As the degrees of freedom increase, the chi-square curve distribution approaches a normal distribution.

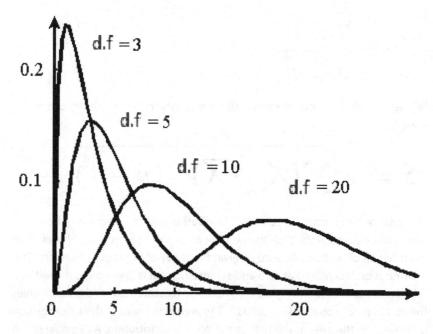

Chi-square distribution

3.2.7 Gamma Distribution

The gamma distribution is similar to the lognormal distribution and is very useful for high positive skewed variables. If the random variable Y is gamma-distributed with parameters α and β, then the probability of Y is

$$p(Y) = \frac{\beta^{\alpha}}{\Gamma(\alpha)} Y^{\alpha-1} e^{-\beta Y}$$

where the gamma function $\Gamma(x)$ is defined as

$$\Gamma(x) \equiv \int_0^{\infty} t^{x-1} e^{-t} dt$$

The parameter α is called the *shape parameter*, and the parameter β is called the inverse *scale parameter*. Both α and β must be positive. The standard deviation of the gamma distribution is proportional to 1/β. The mean of a gamma-distributed variable is α / β.

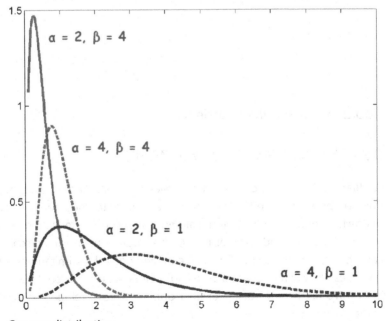

Gamma distribution

Gamma distribution belongs to a family of two-parameter probability distribution. When α =1, then the gamma distribution becomes exponential with respect to β.

3.2.8 Weibull Distribution

Weibull distribution is a two-parameter distribution and is defined as follows:

$$F_{\alpha,\beta}(x) = 1 - \exp\left[-\left(\frac{x}{\alpha}\right)^{\beta}\right] \quad \text{for} \quad x \geq 0 \quad \text{and} \quad F_{\alpha,\beta}(x) = 0 \quad \text{for } t < 0$$

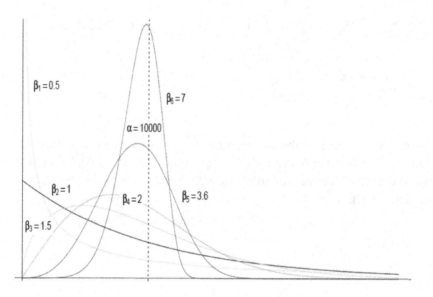

3.3 Popular Quantitative Models

3.3.1 The Black-Scholes-Merton Model

Fischer Black, Myron Scholes, and Robert Merton developed a model that became very popular in the 1970s and was used widely to price stock options and hedge the options. This book is not aimed at showing the derivation of the Black-Scholes-Merton model; rather, it takes the model equation and discusses how the model can be used in financial engineering and its limitations. The Black-Scholes-Merton model became the foundation for many models. Lots of models, even ones that are outside of stock options, were developed based on this model.

$$\text{Call Price } C = S * N(d_1) - X * e^{-rt} * N(d_2)$$

$$\text{Put Price } P = X * e^{-rt} * N(-d_2) - S * N(-d_1)$$

Where

$$d_1 = \frac{ln(\frac{S}{X}) + (r + \frac{\sigma_2}{2})t}{\sigma\sqrt{t}}$$

$$d_2 = d_1 - \sigma\sqrt{t}$$

r = Expected return on stock per year, equal to continuously compounded risk-free rate

σ = Volatility of the stock price per year

S = Price of the stock at the time of valuation of the option

K = Exercise price

T = Time period until expiration in years, normally measured as the number of trading days until expiration divided by the number of trading days in one year, that is, 250.

The function N(x) is the cumulative probability distribution function for a standardized normal distribution.

European options on dividend-paying stocks are valued by adjusting the stock price such that the present value of dividends will be deducted from the stock price. However, only dividends with ex-dividend dates during the life of the option should be included. The "dividend" should be the expected reduction in the stock price expected. According to the Black-Scholes formula, a non-dividend paying European call and put option are priced as follows:

$$\text{Call Price } C = S * e^{-qt} * N(d_1) - X * e^{-rt} * N(d_2)$$

$$\text{Put Price } P = X * e^{-rt} * N(-d_2) - S * e^{-qt} * N(-d_1)$$

$$d_1 = \frac{ln(\frac{S}{X}) + (r - q + + \frac{\sigma_2}{2})t}{\sigma\sqrt{t}}$$

$$d_2 = d_1 - \sigma\sqrt{t}$$

Where q = Continued dividend rate

Assumptions and Limitations of the BSM Model

- The BSM model assumes that there are no transaction costs. In reality, buying and selling options or hedging and rehedging of assets often are exposed to bid-ask spreads. This is even more pronounced for over-the-counter options.
- The BSM model assumes that volatility is a known and constant. In reality, the volatility is a function of both time and the underlying asset, and time series show that volatility is highly unstable.
- The BSM model assumes that the risk-free rate is known and constant. In reality, the risk-free rates change often, as the short-term interest rates are uncertain.
- The BSM model assumes that dividends are known and constant. This is not true in reality.
- The BSM model assumes that the underlying asset path is continuous. In reality, market prices are discontinuous, and from time to time they jump downward and upward. The sudden and large moves of prices are not contained in lognormal distribution, and the assumption that returns are normally distributed does not hold true.
- The BSM model assumes that price changes are exogenous. In reality, the buying and selling of large quantities of underlying assets moves the prices either in a fairly predictable fashion or an unpredictable fashion.
- The BSM model assumes that there is no autocorrelation in returns. In reality, in most cases, the returns are random and independent from what happened in the previous day or anytime in the past.
- The BSM model is applicable to only European options. That is, it assumes that options are exercised only at the time of expiration.

In reality, most stock options are American options and can be exercised at any time.

- The BSM model assumes that delta hedging eliminates the risk completely. In reality, there is always some residual risk.

3.3.2 Vasicek Model

The Vasicek model is one of the no-arbitrage and earliest stochastic interest rate models based on the evolution of an unspecified short-term interest rate. The Vasicek model gives an explicit formula for the zero coupon yield curve. It also gives explicit formulae for derivatives, such as bond options. It can also be used to create an interest rate tree. The model is based on mean reversion theory and assumes that the short rate follows the stochastic process, which is expressed as follows:

$$\text{Drift } dr = a(b - r)dt + \sigma * dz$$

Where dz is a standard Wiener process.

r is the current level of the interest rate.

b is the long-run normal interest rate.

a is a coefficient that adjusts the speed of the interest rate toward its long-run normal level.

σ is a volatility of interest rate and is assumed to be constant.

The mean reversion theory states that the factor approaches its long-run mean from its current level.

From the above model, it can be observed that if the interest rate is above the long-run mean, that is, r > b, then the drift (dr) become negative so that the rate will be pulled down in the direction of r.

Similarly, if the rate is less than the long-run mean, that is, r < b, then the drift (dr) become positive so that the rate will be pulled up in the direction of r.

This feature is particularly attractive because without it, interest rates could drift permanently upward or downward, which is not possible practically speaking. Mean reversion is reasonable for interest rates because it is economically unreasonable to think that interest rates can become infinite or become arbitrarily large.

In the Vasicek model, the mean reversion of interest makes the interest rate be normally distributed.

Based on the normal distribution, the Vasicek model gives an explicit formula for the (zero coupon) yield curve, as follows:

$$\text{Expected rate } E[R] = r * e^{-a(T-t)} + b * (1 - e^{-a(T-t)})$$

One drawback with normal distribution is that the variable can become negative. However, if the chosen value of coefficient a is greater than zero, the expected value will converge to b, which indicates mean reversion.

Weaknesses of the Vasicek Model

- While the model is based on no-arbitrage theory, real prices exhibit some sort of arbitrage. In other words, the Vasicek model generates prices that are inconsistent with the current term structure, and this could permit other dealers and counterparties to arbitrage against them.
- The Vasicek model is a one-factor model and cannot capture the more complex term structure shifts that occur.
- The Vasicek model assumes that all rates have the same volatility.
- Unless the coefficient is chosen properly, interest rates can go negative, which is not possible in any economy.

3.3.3 Cox, Ingersoll, and Ross Model

While the Vasicek model assumes that all rates have the same volatility, empirical evidence suggests that interest rate changes are more volatile when the level of interest rates is high. The Cox-Ingersoll-Ross (CIR) model has been developed to address such a limitation and is based on conditional volatility. The model also shows that interest rates will remain positive.

Thus, the CIR model has the same drift term as the Vasicek model, but with a modified volatility term:

$$\text{Drift } dr = a(b - r)dt + \sigma' * \sqrt{(rt)} * dz$$

When the short rate *rt* is high, the volatility of interest rate changes is high, and vice versa. The parameter σ' no longer represents the volatility of interest rate changes. It is just a parameter. The model provides solutions for bond prices and a complete characterization of the term structure that incorporates risk premiums and expectations for future interest rates. The CIR model process has the non-central chi-square distribution. The chi-square distribution makes the interest rate always be positive.

3.3.4 Heath, Jarrow, and Morton Model

All the models discussed so far use short-term interest rates to predict the expected future interest rate. Heath, Jarrow, and Morton modeled the whole forward rate curve, and this model is a major breakthrough in the pricing of fixed-income products.

The process for the short rate r in the Heath, Jarrow, and Morton (HJM) model is a non-Markov process. In a Markov process, it is only the present state of a variable that determines the possible future state. The general HJM model makes the motion of the spot rate non-Markov, that is, it utilizes the vector of past and present values of interest rates and bond prices at time t that are relevant for determining bond price volatilities at that time.

The non-Markov process is the real challenge of the implementation of the HJM model. It is required to generate Monte-Carlo simulation of the various paths. Using Monte-Carlo simulation can be a slow process and require powerful computers.

The one-factor HJM model is extremely popular due to its simplicity and mathematical tractability. The one-factor model essentially assumes that the term structure is affected by a single source of uncertainty. However, such a model can occasionally be insufficient in describing the complete evolution of term structure movements. Multifactor models can provide a more realistic description of the transition behavior of the term structure of interest rates. Multifactor HJM models are outside of the scope of this book.

The drawbacks of the HJM model are that the expressed instantaneous forward rates are not directly observed in the market. It is also difficult to calibrate the model to prices of actively traded instruments. These drawbacks are addressed by the Brace, Gatarek, and Musiela model, which is discussed below.

3.3.5 Brace, Gatarek, and Musiela Model

The Brace, Gatarek, and Musiela model, a discrete version of the HJM model, is also called the *Libor market model* (LMM). This model models the actively traded, observable quantities in the fixed-income sector. This model is favored by many traders as it can price any contract whose cash flows can be decomposed into functions of the observed forward rates. The model uses the discrete compounding definition of an interest rate rather than continuous compounding. The model uses the most convenient approach of valuing interest rates derivatives by working in a world that is always forward-risk neutral with respect to a bond maturing at the next reset date. This phenomenon is referred to as *rolling forward risk-neutral world*. The LMM can be extended to incorporate several independent factors.

The LMM can be used to value nonstandard caps, such as ratchet caps, sticky caps, and flexi caps. In a ratchet cap, the cap rate equals the previous reset date plus a spread. In a sticky cap, it equals the previous capped rate plus a spread. In a flexi cap, there is a limit on the total number of caplets that can be exercised.

Either the HJM or Libor market model can be used to simulate the behavior of interest rates month by month throughout the life of a Mortgage Backed Security.

3.4 Exotic Options

While exotic options are complex in nature and can be priced using variants of the Black-Scholes model and other complex models, the scope of this book is limited to explaining the features of various exotic options. Exotic options are used as part of a hedging strategy or as standalone instruments for arbitrage purposes.

3.4.1 Compound Options

A compound option is an option on an option, that is, the exercise payoff involves the value of another option. A compound option thus has two expiration dates and two strike prices. There are typically four types of compound options. A compound option is a two-dimensional, second-order derivative.

In a European style call on a call option, on the first expiration date T_1, the holder has the right to buy a new call using the strike price X_1. The new call has expiration date T_2 and strike price X_2.

In a European style call on a put option, on the first expiration date T_1, the holder has the right to buy a new put using the strike price X_1. The new put has expiration date T_2 and strike price X_2.

In a European style put on a put option, on the first expiration date T_1, the holder has the right to sell a new put using the strike price X_1. The new put has expiration date T_2 and strike price X_2.

In a European style put on a call option, on the first expiration date T_1, the holder has the right to sell a new call using the strike price X_1. The new call has expiration date T_2 and strike price X_2.

3.4.2 Chooser Options

A chooser option gives the holder of the option the right to choose whether the option is a call or a put at a specific time during the life of the option. Chooser options are similar to compound options except that the holder has an additional option of choosing the type of second option. The value of the second option at the time of expiration determines whether the option is a call or a put. A chooser option is a two-dimensional, second-order derivative.

3.4.3 Barrier Options

Barrier options have payoffs that depend on the strike and the barrier. Barrier options work well in a market where the future is not clear, that is, it is not certain if the future is going to be bullish or bearish.

A barrier option comes in two types, with two forms in each type. In essence, there are four types of barrier options. An up barrier is above the current stock level; if it is ever crossed, it will be from below. A down barrier is below the current stock level; if it is ever crossed, it will be from above. An in-barrier (knock-in) pays off only if the stock finishes in the money and if the barrier is crossed sometime before expiration. An out-barrier (knock-out) option pays off only if the stock finishes in the money and the barrier is never crossed before expiration.

Based on the combination of the above, the four types of barrier options are: down-and-out call (put), down-and-in call (put), up-and-out call (put), and up-and-in call (put) options.

Down-and-out call (put)—A call (put) option that expires if the market price of the underlying drops below a predetermined expiration price.

Down-and-in call (put)—A call (put) that becomes a standard call (put) option if the market price of the underlying drops below a predetermined expiration price.

Up-and-out call (put)—A call (put) option that expires if the market price of the underlying hits above a predetermined expiration price.

Up-and-in call (put)—A call (put) that becomes a standard call (put) option if the market price of the underlying hits above a predetermined expiration price.

Out options are inversely related to volatility. Increased volatility increases the probability of the underlying hitting the barrier, which in turn makes the options expire. Barrier options are two-dimensional, first-order derivatives.

3.4.4 Parisian Options

Parisian options are a special type of barrier options for which the barrier (in or out) feature is only triggered after the underlying asset price has spent a certain prescribed time beyond the barrier. Parisian options protect sellers and investors from market manipulation. Depending on the contract, the small fraction of time outside the barrier can be reset or saved and added to future times.

Parisian options are strongly path-dependent, three-dimensional (asset price, time, time spent outside the barrier), first-order derivatives.

3.4.5 Lookback Options

The payoffs of lookback options depend on the maximum or minimum underlying asset price attained during the option's life. Therefore, lookback options are strongly path-dependent options. Lookbacks provide investors a flexibility (if in the money) to buy at the ex-post low and sell at the ex-post high.

A standard or floating-strike lookback call gives the option holder the right to buy at the lowest price recorded during the option's life. Similarly a standard or floating-strike lookback put gives the right to sell at the highest price.

A call on maximum or fixed-strike lookback call pays off the difference between the realized maximum price and some predetermined strike or zero, whichever is greater. A put on minimum or fixed-strike lookback put pays off the difference between the predetermined strike and the realized minimum price or zero, whichever is greater.

Lookback options are three-dimensional—asset price, time, and maximum/minimum. They are first-order derivatives.

Lookback options are quite common in the fixed-income sector, as interest rates fluctuate up and down during a specified time.

3.4.6 Ladder Options

Ladder options are special types of lookback options for which the highest asset price is set to the floor in the series for call options and the lowest is set to the ceiling in the series for put options.

For example, in a series of multiples 5, 10,….45,50,55.., the asset price 53 is reset to 50 for call options and to 55 for put options. This will reduce the payoff to the investor. Ladder options are cheaper than the regular lookback options.

3.4.7 Shout Options

In shout options, the special feature, the payoff upon shouting, is another derivative, with contractual specifications different from the original derivative. The embedded shout feature in a call option allows its holder to lock in the profit via shouting while retaining the right to benefit from any future upside move in the payoff. The holder should shout only when the underlying asset is above strike. The number of shouting rights throughout the life of the contract may be more than one depending on the contract. The shouting instants may be limited to some predetermined times.

3.4.8 Binary Options

In regular European options, a call option pays off the difference between the asset price and strike if the asset price is above the strike. Similarly a put option pays off the difference between the strike price and asset price if the asset price is below the strike. Binary options are similar to European options, but the payoff amount is based on a special clause. The payoff amount is either a constant amount or the value of the asset itself.

If the payoff amount is a fixed quantity, then the option is called a cash-or-nothing option. For example, in a binary cash-or-nothing call option, if the predetermined amount is q and the asset price closes above the strike at the time of expiration, then the call writer pays off q amount on the expiration day. In a binary cash-or-nothing put option, the writer pays off the amount q if the asset price closes below strike at the time of expiration.

If the payoff amount is determined as the asset price, then the option is called asset-or-nothing. For example, in a binary asset-or-nothing call option, since the predetermined amount is the value of the asset at the time of expiration, if the asset price closes above the strike at the time of expiration, then the call writer pays off an amount equal to the asset price on the expiration day. In a binary asset-or-nothing put option, the writer pays off the amount equal to the asset price if the asset price closes below strike at the time of expiration.

3.4.9 Asian Options

Asian options link the payoff to the average price of an asset over a period of time. Due to the averaging concept, Asian options exhibit lower volatility and are less prone to market manipulation. The average is determined by taking the entire set of prices en route to expiration. The entire set can be discrete or continuous. A discrete set includes only the closing prices of each day, while a continuous set includes prices of every transaction or the closing prices of very short intervals. Again, the average can be arithmetic or geometric.

Depending on how the average price is used in option payoff, there are two types of Asian options:

1. Average Price Option—In this option, the average price is used in place of the asset closing price. Therefore, the average price Asian call option pays off max $(0, S_{ave} - K)$, where K is a strike price. Similarly, the average price Asian put option pays off max $(0, K - S_{ave})$.
2. Average Strike Option—In this option, the average price is used in place of the strike price. That is, the strike price is variable and is not determined at the time of initiation. Therefore the average strike Asian call option pays off max $(0, S_T - S_{ave})$, where S_T is a closing price of the asset. Similarly, the average strike Asian put option pays off max $(0, S_{ave} - S_T)$.

Advantages of Asian Options

- Lower volatility
- Less prone to market manipulation
- Easy to manage hedge ratio due to stability observed in average
- Less exposed to sudden jumps and crashes

3.4.10 Basket Options

In a basket option, the underlying asset is a basket of securities, currencies, or commodities, and the strike price is based on the weighted value of the basket's constituents. Basket options are a popular way to hedge portfolio risk. The cost of a basket option is significantly less than buying an option on the individual constituents of the portfolio. The buyer has the flexibility to choose the maturity of the option, the foreign currency amounts for the basket, and the aforementioned strike price. Basket options are also called *rainbow options*.

3.4.11 Forward-Start Options

Forward-start options are options whose strike price will be determined at some later date. A forward-start option is paid for in the present, but the strike price is not fully determined until an intermediate date before expiration. An application of forward-start options is employee stock options. An employee is typically promised that he will receive stock options at periodic dates in the future conditional upon his continued employment, and the strikes of these options will be set to be at-the-money on the periodical grant dates.

3.4.12 Bermuda Options

Just like Bermuda is situated in between America and Europe, the option's exercise style is also in between European and American style. The option can be exercised before maturity, but it can only be exercised at given times. Bermuda options are cheaper than American options but more expensive than European options. Investors prefer them when there is a lot of uncertainty about the dividends.

4. Risk Measurement and Management

4.1 Market Risk

4.1.1 Market Risk Management System

Market risk refers to the risk resulting from movements in market prices, in particular, changes in interest rates, foreign exchange rates, equity prices, and so on. Market risk is often propagated by other forms of financial risk, such as credit and liquidity risks. For example, a downgrading of the credit rating of an issuer could lead to a drop in the market value of securities issued by that issuer. Likewise, a major sale of a relatively illiquid security by another holder of the same security could depress the price of the security. On the other hand, the perceived market risk can impact liquidity and credit risk. Depending on the type of asset or security, exposure to other factors may also arise. The firm that is aiming to manage market risk should capture all risk factors that it is exposed to, and it must manage these risks soundly.

A sound and comprehensive risk management process should be designed to identify not only market risk, but other risks, such as liquidity, credit, operations, legal, and reputation. The risk management system should be commensurate with the scope, size, and complexity of an institution's trading and other financial activities and the market risks assumed. It should also enable the various market risk exposures to be accurately and adequately identified, measured, monitored, and controlled. All significant risks should be measured and aggregated on an institution-wide basis. An institution's risk management system should be able to quantify risk exposures and monitor changes in market risk factors and other market conditions on a daily basis. An institution whose risk levels fluctuate significantly within a trading day should monitor its risk profile on an intraday basis. The risk management system should, wherever feasible, be able to assess the probability of future losses. It should also enable an institution to identify risks promptly and take quick remedial action in response to adverse changes in market factors.

Limits for market risks that are consistent with the maximum exposures authorized by the board and senior management should be set. An independent risk management function should be established, with the responsibility of defining risk management policies, setting procedures for market risk identification, measurement and assessment, and monitoring the institution's compliance with established policies and market risk limits. It should also ensure that market risk exposures are reported in a timely manner to the board and senior management. Risk management staff should be separate from and independent of position-taking staff.

An institution should ensure that its treasury and financial derivative valuation processes are robust and independent of its trading function. Models and supporting statistical analysis used in valuations and stress tests should be appropriate, consistently applied, and have reasonable assumptions. These should be validated before deployment. Staff involved in the validation process should be adequately qualified and independent of the trading and model development functions. Models and analysis should be periodically reviewed to ascertain the completeness of position data, the accuracy of volatility, valuation, and risk factor calculations, as well as the reasonableness of the correlation and stress test assumptions. More frequent reviews may be necessary if there are changes in models or in the assumptions resulting from developments in market conditions.

The board and senior management should establish effective processes to manage market liquidity risk arising from treasury and financial derivative trading activities. Where feasible, the management of market liquidity risk should be an integral part of the institution's daily operations. The board and senior management should be aware of the size and depth of the markets the institution is active in and establish the appropriate risk-taking guidelines. These guidelines should take into account the institution's ability to access alternative markets or credit lines to continue trading under a broad range of scenarios. They should also consider the risks associated with early termination of treasury and financial derivative contracts.

4.1.2 Value-at-Risk

Value-at-risk measures the potential loss in value of a risky asset or portfolio over a defined period for a given confidence interval. Thus, if the VAR on a portfolio is calculated as $10 million at a one-week, 95 percent confidence level, then there is a 95 percent confidence that the loss of the portfolio will not exceed $10 million over any given week. In other words, there is a 5 percent chance that there will be a loss of at least $10 million over any given week. There are three basic approaches that are used to compute value-at-risk, though there are numerous variations within each approach. The measure can be computed analytically by making assumptions about return distributions for market risks. It can also be estimated by running hypothetical portfolios through historical data or from Monte-Carlo simulations.

4.1.2.1 Parametric Approach

The parametric approach is also known as the linear approach. The approach is parametric in that it assumes that the probability distribution is normal and then requires calculation of the variance-covariance parameters. The approach is linear in that changes in instrument values are assumed to be linear with respect to changes in risk factors. For example, for bonds, the sensitivity is described by duration, and for options it is described by the Greeks. The assumption that the asset returns are normally distributed provides a straightforward formula to calculate the value-at-risk. These approaches are called parametric approaches because they require parameters, such as mean, standard deviation, and correlation. Historical data is used to measure mean, standard deviations, correlations, and risk factors like beta, delta, duration, and so on. Measuring VAR with normal distribution uses one tail (only the loss part of the tail), so the significance level used in the formula is one-tailed.

In a simplistic form, VAR with normal distribution, or normal VAR, is calculated as follows:

$$VAR_\alpha = (\sigma * z_\alpha + \mu) * \text{Asset Value}$$

Where σ = Standard deviation of asset per holding period in percentage

μ = Mean returns for the holding period in percentage

α = One-tailed significance, or $1 - \alpha$ =confidence level.

Z is a negative value, as the VAR is interested only in the left tail.

If population mean and standard deviation are not available, then the researchers use sample mean and standard deviation.

VAR with lognormal distribution, or lognormal VAR, is calculated as follows:

$$VAR_\alpha = (1 - e^{\sigma z - \mu}) * \text{Asset Value}$$

When the asset exhibits a linear relationship with the risk factor, then the VAR is adjusted to the risk factor. The delta-normal method, a type of parametric approach, is used to calculate VAR for the options that exhibit a linear relationship. The delta-normal approach requires one additional parameter, which is the delta. Δ is defined as the rate of change of the option price with respect to the underlying asset price.

$$VAR_\alpha = \Delta * \sigma * z_\alpha * \text{Asset Value}$$

For instruments that exhibit risk factors like beta, duration, the Δ should be replaced accordingly with that risk factor.

The delta-normal method described above is appropriate when there is only one asset in a portfolio or the assets are not correlated. That means the simple delta-normal method ignores the diversification benefit. The variance-covariance method, on the other hand, utilizes both the variance and covariance, considering the correlation between assets. Note that some researchers also call the variance-covariance method the delta-normal method. Whatever the name we give it, the difference between the two approaches (diversified and undiversified) should be noted.

Measuring VAR using the variance-covariance method involves the following steps:

1. Obtain the risk factors.
2. Get the transpose of the risk factors matrix.
3. Obtain the variance-covariance matrix.
4. Multiply the transpose of the risk factors matrix with the variance-covariance matrix.
5. Multiply the resultant matrix of the above with the risk factors matrix.
6. Take the square root of the above value.
7. Multiply the above square root with the z-value of corresponding significance.

Using Δ as an example risk factor, the above steps can be expressed mathematically as follows:

$$VAR_\alpha = z_\alpha * \sqrt{(\Delta^T \Omega \Delta)} * \text{Portfolio Value}$$

Where Δ = Risk factor matrix

Ω = Variance-covariance matrix

Advantages of the Parametric Approach

- It is typically many times faster to calculate parametric VAR compared with Monte-Carlo or historical simulation.
- Simple to implement.

Disadvantages of the Parametric Approach

- It gives a poor description of nonlinear risks.
- If conditional returns are not normally distributed, the computed VAR will understate the true VAR. In other words, if there are far more outliers in the actual return distribution than would be expected given the normality assumption, the actual value-at-risk will be much higher than the computed value-at-risk. In reality, the risk-factor distributions have a high kurtosis, with more extreme events than would be predicted by the normal distribution.
- Even if the standardized return distribution assumption holds up, the VAR can still be wrong if the variances and covariance that are used to estimate it are incorrect. To the extent that these numbers are estimated using historical data, there is a standard error associated with each of the estimates. In other words, the variance-covariance matrix that is input to the VAR measure is a collection of estimates, some of which have very large error terms.
- A related problem occurs when the variances and covariance across assets change over time. This nonstationary behavior in values is not uncommon because the fundamentals driving these numbers do change over time. For example, the correlation between the US dollar and the Japanese yen may change if oil prices increase by 15 percent. This, in turn, can lead to a breakdown in the computed VAR.

4.1.2.2 Historical Simulation Approaches

Historical simulation approaches are called *nonparametric approaches*. The parametric approaches assume that the returns are distributed normally or lognormally. In reality, most assets do not follow normal distribution. Historical simulation makes an assumption that near-future returns will likely follow the pattern of most-recent returns. In the traditional historical simulation approach, researchers rank the historical returns in the order of returns and then separate bottom X percent of samples. The variable X is the significance level at which VAR is being calculated. For example if there are 100 samples in the data then bottom 5 values are separated from the list after ranking in descending order and the top value in the separated list i.e., the cutoff point is used to calculate the VAR.

One basic assumption that traditional historical simulation makes is that the future returns pattern will likely follow the historical return pattern, and therefore it places equal weight in all returns. There are various methods that adjust the series of historical returns. Three such methods are described below.

Age-Weighted Historical Simulation

The age-weighted simulation weighs the recent observations more and distant observations less. Let us assume that w1 is the weight given to a one-day-old observation. Each subsequent past observation is decayed using the decay paramete λ.

So the weight of a two-days-old observation is $\lambda w1$, the weight of a three-days-observation is $\lambda^2 w1$, and so on.

The weight of an i-days-old observation is $\lambda^{i-1} w1$.

Since all the weights must sum to 1,

$$\lambda w1 + \lambda^2 w1 + \ldots + \lambda^{i-1} w1 = 1$$

$$w1(\lambda + \lambda^2 + \ldots + \lambda^{i-1}) = 1$$

$$w1 = \frac{1-\lambda}{1-\lambda^n}$$

$$w(i) = \lambda^{i-1} \frac{1-\lambda}{1-\lambda^n}$$

The main goal of the decay parameter is to reduce the impact of ghost effects that may not reoccur.

Volatility-Weighted Historical Simulation

The volatility-weighted historical simulation approach weighs the observation by volatility rather than the age. Let us assume $R_{t,i}$ is the actual return for asset i on day t, $\sigma_{t,i}$ is the volatility forecast for asset i on day t, and $\sigma_{T,i}$ is the current forecast of volatility for asset i; then, the volatility-adjusted return is given by

$$R_{t,i}^{*} = \frac{\sigma_{T,i}}{\sigma_{t,i}} R_{t,i}$$

Thus, the volatility-adjusted return, $R_{t,i}^{*}$, is replaced by a larger value if the current forecasted volatility exceeds the previous forecasted volatility, and similarly by a smaller value if the current forecasted volatility is below the previous forecasted volatility. The volatility-weighted historical simulation approach allows the current forecasted VAR to be more sensitive to current market conditions.

Filtered Historical Simulation

Empirical evidence suggests that negative shocks increase market volatility more than positive shocks of the same magnitude, a phenomenon that has been called *asymmetric volatility*. Therefore, the traditional historical simulation method may not be efficient during asymmetric volatility periods. The filtered historical simulation method refines the basic historical simulation by using standardized residuals from a time-varying volatility model. Because the standardized residuals are likely to be independent and identically distributed, they are ideally suited for bootstrapping. Second, filtered historical simulation uses Hull and White's volatility updating so that increases in volatility during the risk measurement period affect the risk measures themselves. Thus, the method contains both the advantages of the basic historical simulation method and sophisticated volatility models like GARCH.

Advantages of Historical Simulation Approaches:

- They are intuitive and often computationally simple.

- Since they do not depend on an assumption of distribution, they can accommodate fat tails, skewness, and any other nonnormal features that can underestimate the actual VAR.
- They avoid complex variance-covariance matrices.
- They use data that is often readily available either from in-house or from vendors.
- Historical simulation approaches can be modified to allow a weighting scheme either by age or volatility.
- There is no need to calculate the correlations.
- There is no need to assume they are joint-normal with stable correlation.
- Empirical evidence suggests that historical simulation works quite well.

Disadvantages of Historical Simulation Approaches:

- Quiet periods may underestimate VAR and expected shortfall.
- Volatile periods may overestimate VAR and expected shortfall.
- It is difficult to detect structural/regime shifts in the data.
- They ignore plausible extreme events if they did not occur in the past.
- New financial instruments and markets may not have sufficient data.

4.1.2.3 Monte-Carlo Simulation

The VAR measurement methodologies described until now possess various disadvantages. The Delta-normal method does not work well for complex instruments, such as exotic options. Historical simulation methods do not work well if there is not sufficient data available. To overcome these issues, researchers use the Monte-Carlo simulation approach. This process is both parametric and a full valuation model, and it is tailor-made.

This process involves five basic steps in calculating VAR:

1. Specify the stochastic process and parameters. For example, Brownian motion.
2. Simulate a large number of outcomes based on assumptions.
3. Calculate the value of the asset for each outcome.

4. Run many iterations of steps 2 and 3. The more the iterations, the higher the accuracy. The number of iterations ranges from five thousand to a few hundred thousand.

5. Rank the asset values. The VAR at alpha % of significance level corresponds to the cutoff value at alpha % of the calculated values.

Monte-Carlo simulation techniques are the most flexible and powerful, since they are able to take into account all nonlinearity of the portfolio value with respect to its underlying risk factor and to incorporate all desirable distributional properties, such as fat tails and time-varying volatilities. Also, Monte-Carlo simulations can be extended to apply over longer holding periods. However, these techniques are also by far the most expensive computationally.

Advantages of Monte-Carlo Simulation:

•   Descriptive for both linear and nonlinear risks
•   Can include time decay factor
•   Flexible and extensible to other risk factors
•   Produces perfect distribution using an unlimited number of scenarios

Disadvantages of Monte-Carlo Simulation

•   Slow process
•   Intellectual and technical expertise is required.
•   Subject to model risk of the stochastic process chosen
•   Subject to sampling error at lower number of simulations

4.1.6 Principal Component Analysis

The variance-covariance method for estimating value-at-risk is very useful, but it has some limitations. When there are n number of assets in a portfolio, then there will be n number of variance terms, n(n-1)/2 number of covariance terms, and n*n number of total elements in a matrix. Analyzing that many parameters will become a difficult and time-consuming process. However, the common risk factors may be limited and are very highly correlated. The dimension reduction technique and analysis is called principal component analysis, or simply PCA. To understand principal component analysis, let us take a practical example of a portfolio of bonds. For simplicity, ignore the credit risk, and map the cash flows to spot market rates at the interval of one month using the volatility, present value, and duration invariants. Hence, the portfolio will contain long positions (cash-flow receivables) and short positions (the amount paid to purchase bonds). Based on these positions and risk factors, it would become easy to calculate the value-at-risk.

The major disadvantage of principal components is that interpretation can be more difficult since we are no longer working with the original variables and the principal components are heavily affected by the scaling of the variables.

Advantages of Principal Component Analysis

- Dimension reduction
- Easy to analyze second-order derivative changes, such as gamma and convexity
- Easy to perform stress test
- Lower noise and model risk

4.1.7 Limitations and Alternatives of VAR

Coherent Risk Measures

In order to measure and understand the risk involved in any event, it is necessary to find out if the risk quantification method is meeting coherent risk measures. The list of coherent risk measures is provided below:

1. **Translation Invariance:** The risk of a portfolio is dependent on the individual assets. If a deterministic quantity of l is added to a portfolio with a quantified loss of rho(R), then the resulting loss will be rho (R) – l; and similarly if the same quantity is subtracted, then the resulting loss will be rho (R) + l.
2. **Subadditivity:** Subadditivity reflects the idea that the total risk of a portfolio can be reduced by diversification and makes decentralization of risk management possible. Thus, the total risk of a portfolio is at most equal to the sum of the risks of the individual assets. Rho(R1+R2) <= rho (R1) + rho (R2).
3. **Positive Homogeneity:** The risk of a portfolio will increase with its size. For a constant value of X, the risk of a portfolio with XR events, rho (XR) = X*rho (R).
4. **Monotonicity:** A portfolio with higher potential returns will likely have less risk. For R1 >= R2, rho (R1) <= rho (R2).

VAR does not meet all of the coherent measures as explained below.

1. VAR VAR meets at most only three of the coherent risk measures, that is, VAR is translation invariant, positive homogeneous, and monotone. VAR is not generally subadditive. VAR is subadditive only if the portfolio returns are linear and the risk-return distribution follows a normal or elliptical distribution. Most portfolios in alternative investments contain options or events that cause the distribution to be skewed. Therefore, VAR is not subadditive in this case.

   Alternative: Expected shortfall or expected tail loss or conditional tail is used, all of which meet the subadditive measure. Expected tail loss has been discussed in the section "Quantifying Tail Risk."

2. VAR assumes a normal distribution of returns. Calculation of the confidence level assumes a normal distribution. But most alternative investment returns are not normal and contain fat tails. Some extreme events, such as the short volatility risk of short options, can lead to fat tails.

   Alternative: The extreme value theory is used to measure VAR for nonnormal distributions; this is discussed below under "Quantifying Tail Risk."

3. The VAR measure gives a maximum loss level at a given confidence level. It does not tell what the loss will be beyond the given confidence level.

   Alternative: Expected shortfall.

4. VAR assumes the portfolio position is constant over time. However, trading positions change frequently, and the VAR will need to be revalued. Revaluing VAR is complex and time-consuming.

   Alternatives: As an alternative to revaluation of VAR, marginal VAR, incremental VAR, and component VAR can be used in order to determine the possible change of VAR due to a change in positions. These VARs are discussed below under "VAR in Active Portfolios."

5. VAR methodologies assume the database with historical information is large enough. Due to the nature of products and continuous evolution of new products, there may not be enough historical information.

Alternative: If historical information on a particular financial instrument is not available, then the instruments are mapped to known instruments. This process is called the mapping method.

6. VAR models do not work efficiently in contagion markets, where correlations are broken. And VAR models are also not good if strategic risks are significant.

4.1.8 VAR in Active Portfolios

VAR will change each time the positions are changed in a portfolio. Portfolio managers would like to know which position should be altered in order to achieve the desired level of VAR or what will be the change in VAR if a particular position is added or subtracted. There are three tools available to address these issues: marginal VAR, incremental VAR, and component VAR.

Marginal VAR

Marginal VAR gives the per unit change in a portfolio VAR with respect to an additional investment in a portfolio. That is, the marginal VAR is the partial derivative of the portfolio VAR with respect to the position.

The marginal VAR of asset i in a portfolio P is given by the following equation:

$$MVaR_i = \frac{VaR_p}{P}\beta_i$$

Where β_i is the risk factor of asset i

VaR_p is the value-at-risk of the portfolio

If the portfolio manager wants to reduce the portfolio value by X amount, then the manager should rank all marginal VARs and pick the asset with the highest marginal VAR. Similarly if the portfolio manager wants to increase the portfolio value by X amount but not add new instruments, then the manager should pick the asset with the lowest marginal VAR.

Incremental VAR

While marginal VAR gives the impact of changing an existing position on the portfolio VAR, incremental VAR gives the change in VAR from the addition or deletion of an entire position in a portfolio. Thus, the incremental VAR is the difference between the portfolio VAR after adding/deleting the position and the VAR before adding/deleting the position. For accurate measurement of incremental VAR, it is necessary to reevaluate the portfolio fully. Since the full revaluation VAR is a complex process and time-consuming, for small changes to a portfolio, the incremental VAR may be calculated approximately by using the variance-covariance matrix.

The portfolio manager will need to consider the tradeoff between accuracy and faster computation. Since most arbitrage opportunities exist for a very short span of time and since the number of calculations in full revaluation increases with the square of the risk factors, the shortcut method provides a good approximation for a large portfolio, where a proposed trade is likely to be small relative to the entire portfolio.

Component VAR

The component VAR of an asset i is the amount of risk that asset contributes to the portfolio of assets N. Because of the diversification effect, it is generally less than the individual VAR of that asset.

Mathematically, component VAR is the marginal VAR multiplied by the dollar weight in position i:

Component VAR= MVAR * wi * P

From the equation of marginal VAR, it is known that MVAR*P is equivalent to the portfolio VAR * beta of the asset.

Therefore, CVAR = Portfolio VAR * Beta of i * wi.

Component VAR can be used to breakdown the risk contributions of the portfolio by a desired criterion, such as by a type of currency, by a class of asset, by geography of an asset, or even by business unit.

4.1.9 Quantifying Tail Risk

4.1.9.1 Expected Tail Loss

As described earlier, the VAR process has some disadvantages, such as VAR assumes a normal distribution, market conditions are not always normal, and

VAR does not meet the subadditive property. Expected tail loss addresses these drawbacks.

The assumption of a normal distribution underestimates extreme losses and fails to capture skewness and kurtosis. For example, a portfolio manager who writes options receives the option premium. If asset prices move as expected and options expire worthless, then the manager will keep the premium, profiting from the strategy. However, in unfavorable price movements, the losses will be extreme. This is called *short volatility risk,* and it is one of the sources of fat tails in a return distribution. Since traditional VAR measurement does not consider kurtosis and skewness, the actual VAR is underestimated. Expected tail loss (ETL) is simply the average of losses larger than VAR. This VAR acts as a benchmark for ETL. ETL is not a substitute for VAR; it only supplements VAR.

In summary, the following are attractive properties of expected tail loss:

- Expected tail loss reveals the loss hidden in tails.
- Expected tail loss gives the losses beyond the VAR.
- Expected tail loss is subadditive.
- Expected tail loss is risk-averse.
- Expected tail loss is very useful for scenario-based portfolio optimization.

Even after having numerous advantages, ETL is not yet a popular risk measure for the financial industry, whereas it is widely being used in the insurance industry. Due to the nature of alternative investments, it is very much required to adopt the expected tail loss in measuring risk.

If the value-at-risk used in ETL is measured relative to the benchmark, then such an ETL is called the *expected shortfall* (ESL). In other words, expected shortfall is the same as expected tail loss except that it measures the average of relative VARs beyond the confidence level. Both ETL and ESL are called conditional VARs.

4.1.9.2 Extreme Value Theory

Expected tail loss and expected shortfall overcome some of the disadvantages of traditional VAR, but they are still based on a central-limit theorem with certain assumptions about the changes to the shape of the normal distribution by considering skewness and kurtosis. In reality, extreme events may cause a complete deviation of normal distribution. Extreme values of distribution are important for proper risk management, as they are associated with extreme events, such as large market declines, market crashes, the failure of major financial institutions, the outbreak of political crises, or natural disasters. The major challenge of analyzing and modeling extreme events is that only a few extreme events occurred in the past and there are ranges of extreme events that have yet to occur. One solution to this problem is to use stress tests and scenario analysis. These can simulate the changes in the value of the portfolio under hypothesized extreme market conditions. While these are certainly very useful, they are inevitably limited, as it is not possible to explore all possible scenarios. Extreme value theory (EVT), a special branch of statistics, attempts to make the best possible use of little information about the extremes of the distribution and draw meaningful conclusions. EVT applies only to the tails and is inaccurate for the center of the distribution. The two parameters that play important roles in extreme value theory are scale (beta) and shape (epsilon). According to the Fisher-Tippett theorem, as the sample size gets larger, the distribution of tail converges to the generalized extreme value (GEV) distribution.

The shape parameters determine the speed at which the tail disappears. Depending on the shape of epsilon, the GEV takes three forms of distribution:

- A shape parameter of greater than zero indicates heavy tails, and the distribution is called a Frechet distribution.
- A shape parameter of zero indicates light tails, and the distribution is called a Gumbel distribution.
- A shape parameter of less than zero indicates very thin tails, and the distribution is called a Weibull distribution.

The peaks-over-threshold (POT) approach, a special application of EVT, is used to analyze the tail distribution over a high threshold. Instead of analyzing the entire data in tails, the POT limits the analysis to maximum and minimum ranges by setting a threshold.

Value-at-risk calculated from EVT will be higher than historical-simulation VAR and normal VAR, especially at high confidence levels, proving the assumption of normality or lack of sufficient past events can lead to underestimation of risks.

The extreme value theory has several advantages over traditional parametric and nonparametric VAR approaches. In the parametric approach, due to the assumption of normality, most observations lie close to the center of distribution, whereas tail observations are more important for VAR calculation. Nonparametric or historical simulation approaches estimate VAR by using a histogram of returns. However, the histogram may not contain the events that have yet to occur.

4.1.9.3 VAR with Cornish-Fisher Formula

Return distributions of certain asset classes exhibit close-to-normal distribution. Such a distribution is not completely away from normal but deviates slightly with skewness. The Cornish-Fisher expansion is a formula for approximating the value-at-risk for such a distribution.

The Cornish-Fisher formula provides an adjusted z-score based on the value of skewness.

$$\text{The adjusted } z = z + \frac{1}{6} * (z^2 - 1) * skewness$$

Since VAR is only interested in the left tail, the z-score is negative. Therefore, it is necessary to use the negative value of the z-score in the above formula.

The negative sign of the z-score and skewness magnifies the adjusted z-score, which in turn increases the VAR. Thus, the normal VAR, which is underestimated for skewed tail distribution, can be adjusted using the Cornish-Fisher formula.

The adjusted VAR = adjusted z-score * standard deviation.

4.1.9.4 VAR for Leptokurtic Distribution

Depending on the level of confidence, the VAR will be either underestimated or overestimated for leptokurtic distribution, as there is a higher probability of mass distribution in fat tails. For a lower confidence level (e.g., 95%), the normal assumption can overestimate VAR if the actual distribution is leptokurtic. On the other hand, for a higher confidence level (e.g., 99.5%), the normal assumption underestimates the actual VAR if the distribution is leptokurtic. The underestimation or overestimation depends on the value of excess kurtosis or fatness of the tails.

One approximate distribution for fat tail distribution is Student's distribution.

Let V be the degrees of freedom.

Hence, VAR with Student's distribution = $\mu + t_\alpha * \sqrt{(\frac{-\nu - 2}{\nu})} * \sigma$

As the number of samples increases, the VAR with Student's distribution approaches that of the normal distribution.

4.1.10 Back Testing VAR

Value-at-risk is an ex-ante measurement, meaning it is calculated before the loss occurs. In other words, VAR is a forecasted measure. So it is required to systematically compare the estimated value with real loss over a defined period and fine-tune the model to reduce the discrepancies. Basel sets certain rules to back test the VAR and imposes penalties depending on the number of exceptions.

One of the challenges in back testing the VAR is the dynamic nature of a portfolio. If the actual loss does not match with the estimated VAR, one cannot assume the mismatch arises from the changed positions or from the model. For this reason, the real VAR must be calculated on a hypothetical portfolio as well. A hypothetical portfolio is the one that is used to calculate ex-ante VAR. If the hypothetical VAR matches with the forecasted VAR and actual loss does not match, then it can be inferred that the loss is due to trading behavior. On the other hand, if the hypothetical VAR does not match with the forecasted VAR, then the methodology should be reexamined.

Basel Rules for Back Testing VAR

Under the internal models approach, Basel sets the market risk charge as one of the following two, whichever is higher:

1. The previous day's VAR.
2. The average VAR over the last sixty business days adjusted by a multiplication factor. The multiplication factor is equal to 3 + a penalty factor.

Basel sets three zones to adjust the penalty factor:

- Green Zone: With zero to four exceptions, then the penalty factor is 0.
- Yellow Zone: With five to nine exceptions, the penalty factor is provided in the table below.

Exceptions	Increase in Multiplier
5	0.40
6	0.50
7	0.65
8	0.75
9	0.85

- Red Zone: For ten exceptions or above, the penalty factor is 1.

Within the yellow zone, the supervisor may impose the penalties as follows:

- Basic Integrity of the model. The deviation occurred because the positions were reported incorrectly or because of an error in the source code. In this case, the penalty is applicable.
- Model accuracy could be improved. The deviation occurred because the model was not sophisticated. In this case, the penalty is applicable.
- Intraday trading. Positions changed during the day. Penalty may be considered.
- Bad luck: Markets were particularly volatile or correlations changed. Penalty will be excluded.

4.1.11 Annualization of VAR

Normal value-at-risk at an α of significance is defined as

$$VAR_\alpha = (\sigma * z_\alpha + \mu) * \text{Asset Value}$$

If the VAR is calculated on a daily basis and returns are assumed to be normally distributed, then the mean will be assumed to be zero.

Therefore,

$$VAR_\alpha = \sigma * z_\alpha * \text{Asset Value}$$

In this case, the annual VAR can be calculated as $\text{Daily VaR} * \sqrt{(250)}$

Where the number 250 represents the number of trading days in a year.

However, the above approximation does not hold true in the following cases:

1. When the returns are autocorrelated.
2. When the mean is not zero.

When the mean is not zero, then the annual mean is calculated by multiplying the daily VAR by 250, whereas the standard deviation is calculated by multiplying with the square root of 250.

Therefore, the VAR approximation using the square root of the time period rule will be over biased and overestimate the actual value-at-risk. This is because the higher positive mean and negative Z value should reduce the actual VAR by a higher value.

The actual value-at-risk, $VAR_\alpha = (\sigma * z_\alpha + \mu) * \text{Asset Value}$

Though a one-year (or 250 days) horizon was used above as an example, the same error is applicable for any time horizon. Therefore, it would be more accurate to calculate the direct annual VAR instead of using the square root of time rule.

However, for some securities that are newly issued, the data may not be available for longer periods. In that case, risk managers should use subjective decisions when using the short-term VAR to measure long-term VAR. The significance error increases with the time horizon chosen. The square root of time rule may be approximate for three months, but will overpenalize the fund for long time periods.

4.2 Liquidity Risk

Traditional asset pricing models such as CAPM assume that all assets are infinitely divisible as to the amount that may be held or transacted and can be transacted at no cost. Traditional value-at-risk models assume that portfolio positions are fixed over the horizon. The above models do not consider the fact that a portfolio cannot be liquidated without a significant impact on market prices. Liquidity risk is the degree to which a portfolio manager cannot trade a position without excess cost. Liquidity risk takes two forms: funding-liquidity risk and market-liquidity risk. **Funding-liquidity risk** arises from either the demand for payment from investors or margin calls from the lender, which may lead to involuntary liquidation of the portfolio at unfavorable prices. **Market-liquidity risk** arises when a trade cannot be executed at prevailing market prices due to the size of the position relative to normal market lots. Over-the-counter (OTC) derivatives and emerging markets usually have relatively high liquidity risk.

4.2.1 Market-Liquidity Risk

Taking liquidity risk into account improves the accuracy of value-at-risk. The VAR that incorporates liquidity risk is called *liquidity-adjusted VAR (LVAR)*.

LVAR is the sum of VAR and liquidity cost:

LVAR = VAR + LC

Where LC = Liquidity cost

Liquidity cost is the additional cost at which the manager will be able to liquidate the assets in a desired time. Liquidity cost depends on a variety of factors, such as type of instrument, market scope, business cycle, and geography. While the measurement of liquidity cost requires both subjective and quantitative tools, there are typically three standard approaches: the constant spread approach, the exogenous spread approach, and the endogenous price approach. The three methods look at different aspects of liquidity, and the researcher should select the appropriate method based on the nature of liquidity, sophistication, and ease of implementation.

Constant Spread Approach

This is the simplest approach, which assumes that the bid-ask spread is constant. The liquidity cost (LC) is equal to the product of half the spread and the size of the position to be liquidated. Half the spread has been used here as the liquidity risk incorporates selling the asset, which is a one-way trip as against a round-trip.

LC = 0.5*Spread*P

Where:

$$Spread = \frac{\text{ask price} - \text{bid price}}{\frac{\text{ask price} + \text{bid price}}{2}}$$

P = Value of the position

Therefore

LVAR = VAR + LC

= VAR + 0.5*Spread*P

When asset returns are assumed to be normally distributed, asset prices will be lognormally distributed.

So VAR using lognormal distribution can be calculated as follows:

$$VAR = \left[1 - e^{r - \sigma z}\right]$$

Where:

z = Confidence parameter

r = Mean return

σ = Standard deviation of returns

The higher the confidence level and the spread, the higher the liquidity-adjusted VAR.

Exogenous Spread Approach

The exogenous spread approach assumes that the bid-ask spread is not constant but the trades of a single trader do not impact the spread. This approach assumes that spread is stochastic, which follows normal distribution.

LVAR = VAR + LC

$$LVAR = [1 - e^{r - \sigma z}] + [r_s + z'\sigma_s]P$$

Where r_s and σ_s are the mean and the standard deviation of the bid-ask spread and Z' is the two-tailed confidence parameter.

Endogenous Price Approach

The endogenous price approach assumes that there exists a downward pressure on prices in response to trading. The downward pressure can simply be included in LVAR using elasticity and the size of the trade relative to the entire market.

$$LVAR = VAR[1 - E\frac{\Delta N}{N}]$$

Where:

E = Elasticity, which is always a negative

$\frac{\Delta N}{N}$ = Size of the trade relative to the entire market

4.2.2 Funding-Liquidity Risk

Funding-liquidity risk arises either from "liabilities or assets" or both when there are mismatches in timing of payments from one side to the other. Funding-liquidity risk is also called *liquidity-at-risk* or *cash flow-at -risk*.

Alternative investments engage either in leveraged portfolios or use futures to hedge the portfolio positions. In either case, there will be a margin call from prime brokers when the marked-to-market value of collateral falls. If the fund manager does not have enough funds to meet the margin demands, then some of the positions will be forced to liquidate at unfavorable prices. Fund managers reduce downside risk by hedging the market position using futures, thus reducing VAR. However, due to possible margin calls, there is the possibility of cash outflow, which increases cash flow-at-risk or liquidity-at-risk (LAR). Therefore, even though the hedged positions have small VAR, they will be subject to larger LAR. On the other hand, European options, which do not demand margin calls, have zero LAR but potentially large VAR prior to maturity. The asset side of funding-liquidity risk arises where there is a demand from investors for redemptions. Since most hedge funds invest in illiquid assets, such as distressed debt or structured products, hedge fund managers should impose a longer lockup period and longer notice periods.

A mismatch in timing of payments also causes liquidity risk. One such example is that most commercial banks fund long-term loans using short deposits. Mismatch occurs when there is a demand for withdrawal from depositors or when customers use an unused portion of their line of credit, thus forcing the bank into liquidity risk. Another example is when the coupon payment dates in a Collateralized Debt Obligations Special Purpose Vehicle do not match with the interest receiving date.

4.2.3 LTCM and Liquidity Issue

Long-Term Capital Management (LTCM) was a hedge fund founded in 1994 by former employees of Solomon Brothers. LTCM was a multistrategy fund that involved relative value and equity volatility with positions in fixed income, equity, and derivatives. It engaged in both balance sheet leverage and soft leverage using derivatives. The relative value strategy was built on the assumption that although the yield differences between risky and risk-free fixed-income securities varied over time, the risk premium or credit spread would tend to revert to average historical levels. Similarly, the equity volatility strategy was built on the assumption that implied volatility on options would tend to revert to long-term average levels. LTCM shorted the volatility when the volatility implied by equity options was abnormally high. The fund performed very well until 1998. In 1998, the unexpected default of Russia on its debt caused the Russian interest rates to soar and devaluation of the ruble. This economic shock caused an increase in yields and a flight to quality government bonds of developed countries. As a result, credit spreads increased opposite to the assumption of decreased credit spread. In addition, Brazil also devalued its currency, thereby further increasing interest rates and credit spreads. The overall panic also caused an increase in volatility, which generated losses in equity volatility strategies.

The severe impact in marked-to-market values of positions resulted in margin calls and cash-flow problems. Although relative value strategies sometimes diverge temporarily and converge ultimately, LTCM could not wait until convergence was returned back, as it had to force the liquidation of some of its positions in order to meet funding requirements for margin calls. As an added disadvantage, many other hedge funds, which mimicked the LTCM strategy, flooded the forced liquidation of positions into market. The unfavorable price movements ultimately caused the US government to bailout LTCM and close the fund.

Even though LTCM implemented various risk management strategies, such as implementing longer redemption periods for investors and conducting stress tests in historical returns, it failed to adjust VAR measures with stress scenarios of the possibility that a larger portion of the fund might be liquidated and other fund managers might be holding similar positions that might also require liquidation at the same time in the event of extreme market movements.

4.2.4 Managing Liquidity Risk

One can ask whether liquidity risk is a standalone risk or falls under market risk, credit risk, or operational risk. What are the major sources of liquidity risk? What are the corresponding risk factors to measure and hedge the liquidity risk? In fact, there is no single source of liquidity risk, and there is no risk factor that can be mapped to liquidity risk. Liquidity risk is not a standalone risk. Liquidity risk is a complex risk and can arise from unexpected tail risks, operational failures, internal imbalances, counterparty failures, market crises, systemic risks, or from the combined effects of all those shocks. Internal imbalances arise when market conditions alter the value of assets and collateral, or when external factors disrupt the funding sources. The economic cycle is also one of the sources of liquidity risk. In a rising economy, more banks lend money. When the economy starts falling, the value of collateral will also fall, and banks will demand more margins or ask to sell some of the assets. In order to meet margin requirements, clients will sell the assets. However, there may not be interested buyers to buy the assets that the client wants to sell. Instead, buyers will ask for the assets that they are interested in. This situation will make even liquid assets illiquid. Liquidity risk cannot be hedged with a single process or model. The risk management culture must be tuned to aim to routinize unexpected events. The liquidity risk management process should have governing rules and should deeply root within the corporate culture as an immune system. Assessing liquidity risk should involve both quantitative and qualitative approaches. Hedging liquidity risk is very expensive and cannot be priced accurately due to its complexity. It may not be advantageous to remove illiquid positions completely from a portfolio; instead, proper liquidity risk management should be in place in order to sustain the portfolio from unfavorable and extreme market movements.

In February 2008, the Basel Committee on Banking Supervision published "Liquidity Risk Management and Supervisory Challenges. "The difficulties outlined in that paper highlighted that many banks had failed to take account of a number of basic principles of liquidity risk management when liquidity was plentiful. Some liquidity risk management principles outlined by that paper are provided below.

Cash flow projections: Firms should have a robust liquidity risk management framework providing prospective, dynamic cash flow forecasts that include assumptions on the likely behavioral responses of key counterparties to changes in conditions. Firms should make realistic assumptions about future liquidity needs for both the short and long term that reflect the complexities of their underlying businesses, products, and markets. In estimating the cash flows arising from liabilities, a firm should assess the stability of its funding sources to ensure its sources will not dry up quickly under stress.

Maturity gap analysis: The firm should attempt to manage the timing of incoming flows in relation to known outgoing sources in order to obtain an appropriate maturity distribution for its sources and uses of funds.

Monitoring the quality of products: The firm should analyze the quality of assets that could be used as collateral, in order to assess their potential for providing secured funding in stressed conditions.

Monitoring margin forecasts: A firm should incorporate cash flows related to the repricing, exercise, or maturity of financial derivatives contracts in its liquidity risk analysis, including the potential for counterparties to demand additional collateral in an event such as a decline in the product credit rating or a decline in the price of the underlying asset. Timely confirmation of OTC derivatives transactions is fundamental to such analyses, because unconfirmed trades call into question the accuracy of a firm's measures of potential exposure.

Monitoring wrong-way risk: "Wrong-way risk" refers to the phenomenon that counterparty credit quality deteriorates at the same time when firms need to claim against their credit quality deterioration. A firm should consider the liquidity needs it would encounter if it has "wrong-way" risk with a counterparty that provides guarantees on its assets. For example, a firm that holds assets whose creditworthiness is dependent on the guarantees of a third party or has raised funds against such assets could face significant demands on its funding liquidity if the third party's credit standing deteriorates. In such cases, the firm could be required to write down the value of assets backed by the third party or repurchase, or post additional margin against, such assets.

Imposing limits: A firm should set limits to control its liquidity risk exposure and vulnerabilities and should regularly review such limits and corresponding risk escalation procedures. Limits should be relevant to the business in terms of its location, complexity of strategy, nature of products, currencies, and markets served. Limits should be used for managing day-to-day liquidity within and across lines of business and legal entities under normal conditions.

Liquidity Cushion: A firm should maintain a cushion of unencumbered, high-quality liquid assets to be held as insurance against a range of liquidity stress scenarios, including those that involve the loss or impairment of unsecured and typically available secured funding sources. A critical element of a firm's resilience to liquidity stress is the continuous availability of an adequate cushion of unencumbered, high-quality liquid assets that can be sold or pledged to obtain funds in a range of stress scenarios. This requires explicitly relating the size of the cushion of unencumbered, high-quality liquid assets held as insurance against liquidity stress to the estimates of liquidity needs under stress. Estimates of liquidity needs during periods of stress should incorporate both contractual and noncontractual cash flows, including the possibility of funds being withdrawn, and they should assume the inability to obtain unsecured funding as well as the loss or impairment of access to funds secured by assets other than the safest, most liquid assets. The size of the liquidity cushion should be aligned with the established risk tolerance. Key considerations include assumptions of the duration and severity of stress and the liquidation or borrowing value of assets in stress situations.

Early warning indicator system: A firm should design a set of indicators to identify the emergence of increased risk or vulnerabilities in its liquidity risk position or potential funding needs. Such early warning indicators should identify any negative trend and cause an assessment and potential response by management in order to mitigate the firm's exposure to the emerging risk. Early warning indicators can be qualitative or quantitative in nature and may include but are not limited to:

- rapid asset growth, especially when funded with potentially volatile liabilities
- growing concentrations in assets or liabilities
- increases in currency mismatches
- a decrease of weighted average maturity of liabilities
- repeated incidents of positions approaching or breaching internal or regulatory limits
- negative trends or heightened risk associated with a particular product line, such as rising delinquencies
- significant deterioration in the firm's earnings, asset quality, and overall financial condition
- negative publicity
- a credit rating downgrade
- stock price declines or rising debt costs
- widening debt or credit-default-swap spreads
- rising wholesale or retail funding costs
- counterparties that begin requesting additional collateral for credit exposures when the value of assets deteriorate.
- correspondent firm's that eliminate or decrease their credit lines
- difficulty accessing longer-term funding
- difficulty placing short-term liabilities

Funding source diversification: A firm should diversify available funding sources in the short term, medium term, and long term. Diversification targets should be part of the medium- to long-term funding plans and should be aligned with the budgeting and business planning process. Funding plans should take into account correlations between sources of funds and market conditions. The desired diversification should also include limits counterparty-secured versus unsecured market funding, instrument type, securitization vehicle, currency, and geographic market. As a general liquidity management practice, firms should limit concentration in any one particular funding source. For institutions active in multiple currencies, access to diverse sources of liquidity in each currency is required, since institutions are not always able to swap liquidity easily from one currency to another. Senior management should be aware of the composition, characteristics, and diversification of the firm's assets and funding sources. Senior management should regularly review the funding strategy in light of any changes in the internal or external environments.

Stress Test: A firm should conduct stress tests on a regular basis for a variety of institution-specific and market-wide stress scenarios to identify sources of potential liquidity strain and to ensure that current exposures remain in accordance with a firm's established liquidity risk tolerance. A firm's should use stress test outcomes to adjust its liquidity risk management strategies, policies, and positions and to develop effective contingency plans. While a firm typically manages liquidity under "normal" circumstances, it should also be prepared to manage liquidity under stressed conditions. A firm should perform stress tests or scenario analyses on a regular basis in order to identify and quantify its exposures to possible future liquidity stresses, analyzing possible impacts on the institution's cash flows, liquidity position, profitability, and solvency. The results of these stress tests should form the basis for taking remedial or mitigating actions to limit the exposures, build up liquidity buffers, and adjust its liquidity profile to fit its risk tolerance. The results of stress tests should also play a key role in shaping the firm's contingency planning and in determining the strategy and tactics to deal with events of liquidity stress. As a result, stress testing and contingency planning are closely intertwined.

Contingency funding plan: Senior management should incorporate the results of scenarios in assessing and planning for related potential funding shortfalls in the institution's contingency funding plan. A firm should assess the likelihood of loss of access to the foreign exchange markets, as well as the likely convertibility of the currencies in which the firm carries out its activities. A firm should negotiate a liquidity backstop facility for a specific currency, or develop a broader contingency strategy if the firm runs significant liquidity risk positions in that currency. A firm should be prepared to deal with unexpected disruptions to its intraday liquidity flows. Stress testing and contingency funding plans should reflect intraday considerations. A firm also should understand the level and timing of liquidity needs that may arise as a result of the failure-to-settle procedures of payment and settlement systems in which it is a direct participant. Robust operational risk management and business continuity arrangements are also critical to the effectiveness of a firm's intraday liquidity management.

4.2.5 Alternative Investments and Illiquidity

Most alternative assets have much lower liquidity than stocks or bonds, and lower liquidity is one of the reasons why alternative investment investors expect a higher return on investment as a premium for illiquidity. When investors decide to invest in illiquid investments, such as venture capital, real estate, and hedge funds, they need to ensure that the range of allocations that may occur over time is acceptable. Since alternative investments are long-term investments, investors must also have a long enough time horizon to ensure that they are able to benefit from the expected higher returns of the illiquid investments. Attempting to withdraw the investments, either partially or fully, will impact the performance of the fund, which in turn impacts the profits of other investors as well. Since a run on redemption hurts the performance of the fund and eventually the profit of other investors, the fund manager should impose restrictions on redemptions. However, overimposing the restrictions will not attract the investor, as there are always certain investors who want to redeem earlier than committed. As a tradeoff between redemption restrictions and performance compromise, the fund manager should adopt additional liquidity management principles. Some liquidity management principles are discussed below.

Enforcing lockup periods: A lockup period is an interval during which the investor is not allowed to withdraw funds from a particular fund. After the specified lockup period, investors are free to withdraw funds as defined in the disclosure document of each hedge fund. Almost all hedge funds have a lockup period ranging from as little as three months to longer than two years. Generally the more established the fund, the longer the lockup period. Lockup periods are established to give enough opportunity to the fund manager to draw the strategy and deploy the money. While managers prefer to establish lockup periods, investors often view them as an inconvenience. Managed futures, on the other hand, does not have lockup periods. There are a few that have lockups ranging anywhere from three months to a year, but this is not a stringent requirement in the futures fund industry.

Enforcing longer redemption notice periods: Longer redemption notice periods provide the fund manager time to assess the pros and cons of selling assets and decide which assets to sell that will have the least impact on the fund.

Enforcing redemption gates: Redemption gates protect the fund manager from the flooding of de-investments by investors. When few investors demand the withdraws then the manager may have to sell portion of the assets and since most funds invest at aggregated level rather than individual level it may often require to sell the investments of other investors as well. This will negatively impact the other investors. Withdrawing the funds may result in negative tax consequences. Redemptions gates allows manager to restrict the amount of withdrawals to a ceiling of between certain percentage of quarterly assets..

Side pockets: Side pockets hold special investments. A special investment is typically an illiquid asset or any asset that the fund manager determines is difficult to establish a market value for or should be held until the conclusion of a special event. However, managers do not label every asset in the fund as special. Each investor participating in illiquid investments will redeem a pro rata portion of their illiquid investments. Side pockets enable managers to invest and manage the funds efficiently because side pockets provide protection from unforeseen redemption pressures. Side pocketing allows fund managers to participate in private and less liquid investments in a way that is intended to be beneficial as well as fair and equitable to all investors. Side pockets are quite common in private equity funds.

Capital reserves: Reasonable cash reserves allow fund managers to fulfill redemption requests that they are obligated to meet as per the law.

Payment in kind: Payment in kind is more common in private equity investments. This provision allows fund managers to substitute cash redemptions with additional shares in the fund.

4.3 Interest Rate Risk

While interest rate risk is present in almost all financial instruments, some instruments, such as fixed-income securities, are heavily exposed to interest rate risk. Interest rate risk is a special type of market risk, as it is the risk that the investor realizes when he wishes to sell before maturity in the secondary market. However, interest rate risk also impacts business risk due to the exposure of the internal rate of return to the interest rate risk. Therefore, interest rate risk has been addressed in a separate section rather than being addressing under market risk. As far as the fixed-income market is concerned, the price of fixed-income securities usually changes inversely of interest rates, with some exceptions, such as securities with put options and interest-only mortgage-backed securities. This section covers simple techniques to measure interest rate sensitivity, such as duration, convexity, PVBP, or DV01, and advanced techniques, such as key rate shift and bucket shifts. The section also covers interest rate risk hedging techniques, such as interest rate swaps, swaptions, caps, and floors. Finally interest rate forecasting models are discussed.

4.3.1 Duration

Bond prices change when interest rates change. The new value of a bond can be calculated by revaluing the present values of coupons and par value using the new or forecasted interest rate as the discount rate. However, this process is time-consuming. Duration is a simple and less intensive measure that gives the percentage change in a bond's price for a 1 percent change in its yield to maturity (YTM).

In fact, duration is nothing but the weighted average of the present value of the bond's payments, and can be viewed as the average, or effective, maturity of a bond. The duration is measured in years, and it is more useful to interpret duration as a means of comparing the interest rate risks of different securities. Securities with the same duration have the same interest rate risk exposure. The longer the duration, the longer the average maturity, and, therefore, the greater the sensitivity to interest rate changes.

The duration can be calculated in a simple formula, as follows:

$$\text{Duration} = \frac{P_- - P_+}{2 P_0 \Delta_y}$$

Where P_0 = Bond price

P_- = Bond price when interest rate is incremented

P_+ = Bond price when interest rate is decremented

Δ_y = Change in interest rate in decimal form

The duration for a bond portfolio is equal to the weighted average of the duration for each type of bond in the portfolio.

$$\text{Portfolio Duration} = w_1 D_1 + w_2 D_2 + + w_i D_i$$

w_i = Market value of bond i / market value of portfolio

D_i = Duration of bond i

K = Number of bonds in portfolio

Macaulay Duration

Frederick Macaulay developed the concept of duration, equating it to the average time to maturity or the time required to receive half of the present value of the bond's cash flows. The relationship between modified duration and Macaulay duration can be expressed as follows:

$$D_m = \frac{D_{Mac}}{1 + \frac{y}{k}}$$

Where D_m = Modified duration

D_{Mac} = Macaulay duration

As the number of payments per year increases, y/k will become smaller, and the value of modified duration will approach Macaulay duration. In other words, for continues interest rate, k is equal to infinity and y/k will be zero, in which case modified duration and Macaulay duration will become equal.

Price Value of a Basis Point

PVBP or dollar value of an 01(DV01) gives the change in value of the bond for one basis point change in interest rate. Since duration gives the percentage change in bond value for a 1 percent change in interest rate, the change in value for one basis point (100th of 1%) is calculated as follows:

PVBP = Duration / 100

4.3.2 Convexity

Duration works well only for small changes in the yield. As shown in the figure below, the rate of change of bond price with respect to yield also changes as the yield moves further away. Thus, the duration underestimates the resulting bond prices. Convexity measures the rate of change of duration with respect to yield, and so it is a second derivative. The negative slope indicates the inverse relationship between interest rate and bond price.

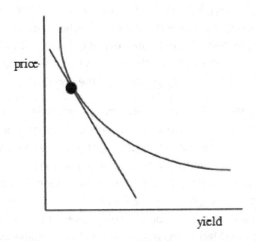

Convexity can also be calculated using the following approximate formula:

$$\text{Convexity} = \frac{P_+ + P_- - 2P_0}{2P_0(\Delta_y)^2}$$

Where P_0 = Bond price

P_- = Bond price when interest rate is incremented

P_+ = Bond price when interest rate is decremented

Δ_y = Change in interest rate in decimal form

The change in bond prices with respect to interest rates can be calculated as follows:

Change in Bond Price $\dfrac{\Delta_p}{P}$ = Duration + Convexity Adjustment

$$\frac{\Delta_p}{P} = -D_m\Delta_y + \frac{(\Delta_y)^2}{2}Convexity$$

Δ_y = Yield change

Δ_p = Bond price change

Convexity is usually a positive term, regardless of whether the interest rate is rising or falling; hence, it is positive convexity. From the above, it can be observed that the convexity increases the change in price when interest rates decline, that is, when delta y is negative, the convexity acts as an add-on. Similarly when interest increases, that is, when delta y is positive, the convexity reduces the price decline. In either case, convexity helps the investor.

However, some securities with embedded options or interest-only mortgage securities exhibit negative convexity. In this case, bond prices will increase with falling interest rates but will reach a ceiling at a certain point of yield. For example, for callable bonds, the price-yield curve follows the same positive convexity below the call price as an option-free bond, but as the yield falls and the bond price rises to near the call price, the positive convexity becomes negative convexity, where the bond price is limited at the top by the call price. Similarly the embedded prepayment option in mortgage loans causes the mortgage securities to exhibit negative convexity. The other instrument that exhibits negative convexity is IO mortgage securities or asset-backed securities. The falling interest rates make the borrowers prepay the loans, thus depleting the outstanding balance on which the interest is calculated to pay the IO investors.

4.3.3 Impact of Coupon Rate, Yield, and Maturity on Duration and Convexity

The duration also depends on the coupon rate of the bond. For a given yield, the lower the coupon, the higher the duration. For example, US treasuries usually have lower coupon rates and current yields than corporate bonds of similar maturities. Therefore, US treasuries should have higher durations than corporate bonds. Similarly for a given yield, bonds with lower coupons will have higher convexity. For a given yield d and duration, the lower coupon bonds will have lower convexity.

Duration is linearly related to maturity, that is, long-term bonds will have higher maturity. The convexity increases with the square of maturity.

4.3.4 Limitations of Duration

There are few limitations to duration. The first of them has been discussed earlier, which can be addressed by using convexity. The second limitation is the reinvestment risk. Since the duration is equal to the weighted average of the present value of the bond's payments, it assumes that the coupon payments are reinvested at the same yield. However, the yield may change from time to time, and the investor may end up reinvesting the coupon payments at lower rates. Reinvestment risk applies not only to coupon cash flows but also to principal repayment. The third limitation is that all the interest rates change in parallel, that is, duration assumes that the yield curve is shifted in parallel. But in reality, only a certain portion of the yield curve may change, while the other portion stays the same. This issue can be addressed using the key rate shift and bucket shift approaches, as discussed below.

4.3.5 Key Rate Shift Approach

In contrast to duration, which assumes that all the rates change in parallel, the key rate shift approach allows analysts to calculate price sensitivities by changing the rate at a particular area of the yield curve. This technique is useful to hedge the instruments against certain areas of yield curves. The key rate techniques assume that a change in interest rate of a particular term affects that term and terms on each side of it. The five-year interest rate affects five-year bonds and also three-year and seven-year bonds proportionately.

In order to implement efficient hedging strategies, managers typically choose a higher number of key rates. However, additional key rates will also require higher transaction costs and more monitoring time.

4.3.6 Bucket Shift Approach

In contrast to the key rate shift approach, the bucket shift approach incorporates much potential change within the region of the yield curve. This approach stands in between the key rate shift and the duration approaches, that is, the bucket shift assumes parallel shift only within the range. For example, when the manager anticipates that interest rates of terms three to five years will change, then the price sensitivity is calculated by assuming a parallel shift between three and five years while keeping all other interest rates constant.

4.3.7 Hedging Interest Rate Risk

Managers employ various strategies and instruments to hedge interest rate risk. The hedging products range from simple to complex. Some of the commonly used interest rate products are discussed below.

4.3.7.1 Forward Rate Agreements

A forward rate agreement (FRA) is an agreement between two parties that one party will pay a certain interest rate on a certain principal amount during a specified future time. FRAs are traded over the counter and are not traded on an exchange. Forward rate agreements are very flexible in nature and can be structured to mature on any date. They are an off-balance sheet instrument. They do not require a notional amount to be exchanged; instead, only the interest differentials are exchanged.

FRAs are not options; therefore, both the parties are required to share both losses and gains, depending on interest rate movements. The efficiency of hedging depends on the manager's skill in forecasting the interest rates. A FRA works in the following manner:

A manager is anticipating that interest rates will rise in two months and decides to hedge the interest rate risk by buying a three-month FRA two months from now. It is called a 2 X 5 FRA. Let us assume that the broker quotes 7.50 percent. The broker may be dealing with other counterparties on the other side, but the manager does not need to be aware of those details. The value date is two months from the spot date. The first fixing is two business days prior to the value date. Maturity will be three months from the value date.

Two months later, the interest rate rises to 8 percent, as the manager forecasted. Without the hedging, the manager would have paid 8 percent for the funding, but since he entered into a forward rate agreement, the broker would pay the differential of 0.5 percent on the agreed amount.

Mathematically, the value the manager receives =

$$P(R_y - R_{forward})(T2 - T1)e^{-R2*T2}$$

Where P = Principal

R_y = Agreed annualized interest rate for the period T2 – T1

T1 and T2 are one year and two years respectively

$R_{forward}$ = Forward interest rate between T1 and T2, for example LIBOR rate for the period T2-T1

R2 = Discount rate used to calculate the present value of the payment on T2 date

On the other hand, assume that the interest rate declined to 7.0 percent. In this case, the manager would need to pay the 0.5 percent differential to the broker.

Mathematically, the value the manager pays =

$$P(R_{forward} - R_y)(T2 - T1) * e^{-R2*T2}$$

4.3.7.2 Interest Rate Futures

Unlike the forward rate agreement, interest rate futures trade on standard exchanges, such as CME and CBOT. In futures, bonds are exchanged, rather than interest rate differentials. If the manager anticipates that the interest rate will decline, then he will buy the futures. If interest rates decline as anticipated, then the manager would take delivery of the futures and sell in the market at the higher prices. Similarly if the manager is anticipating interest-rate hikes, then he would sell the futures. If interest rates move in an unfavorable direction in either case, then the manager would have to bear the loss.

In order to prevent market manipulation, the exchanges set a rule that any government bond with more than fifteen years to maturity on the first day of the delivery month is deliverable on that contract. Since the deliverable bonds have different market prices, the CBOT has created a conversion factor.

Cash paid by a long position = Quoted Future Price * Conversion Factor + Accrued Interest

Cost to deliver the bond to buyer = Quoted bond price + AI

Profit/Loss to future buyer = Cost to deliver the bond to buyer - Cash paid by long position

= Quoted bond price - Quoted Future Price * Conversion Factor

Conversion factors are calculated as the present value of the bond minus accrued interest divided by face value.

If interest rates decline as anticipated, then the quoted bond price will go up, so the manager would profit from the deal. Otherwise, he would have to bear the loss.

Since the future seller has the option to deliver the bond from a wider list of bonds, the sellers choose the bond that minimizes the value of Quoted bond price - Quoted Future Price * Conversion Factor. Such a bond is called cheapest-to-deliver, or a CTD bond.

4.3.7.3 Interest Rate Swaps

An interest rate swap is a bilateral, over-the-counter agreement between two parties to exchange a series of interest payments without exchanging the underlying debt. An interest rate swap can be viewed as a series of forward rate agreements. In a plain vanilla fixed-to-floating rate swap, the first party, also known as the fixed-rate payer, promises to pay to the second at specified intervals a stipulated amount of interest calculated at a fixed rate on the notional principal amount, while the second party, also known as the floating-rate payer, promises to pay to the first at the same intervals a floating amount of interest on the same notional amount calculated according to a floating rate.

Interest rate swaps have become a very popular and effective interest rate hedging instrument and liability management tool. Interest rate swap transactions are based upon a simple economic principle of comparative advantage. For example, one party may prefer fixed interest rates due to the nature of his or her business but may not have a good credit rating. The other party may have a good credit rating but may prefer floating interest rates due to the nature of his or her business. This party comes to a bilateral agreement with a broker who can negotiate with banks and swap the rates. Thus, their comparative advantage has been shared between two parties. Information inefficiencies and institutional restrictions are the major factors that contribute to the differences in transaction costs in both the fixed-rate and the floating-rate markets across national boundaries, which, in turn, provide economic incentive to engage in an interest rate swap.

Interest rate swaps are used to hedge against interest rate fluctuations. Arbitrage CDO managers receive interest rate payments on underlying securities and loans and then distribute them to CDO investors after deducting transaction costs and fees. The cash inflow should be greater than the cash outflow. The structure may have priced the premium for default, but since the underlying securities can be floating rate securities, the cash inflow may exhibit some uncertainties. In this case, managers enter interest rate swap agreements to hedge against interest rate risk.

Interest rate swaps can also be used as an effective tool for financial institutions to manage the basis risk in the balance sheets. Under a floating-to-floating interest rate swap, both parties pay floating rates of interest based on different floating-rate indices. Suppose that the bank has an asset yielding a return of the LIBOR rate plus 75 basis points, which has been financed with a floating-rate CD at a cost of the T-Bill rate minus 25 basis points. The counterparty has floating-rate funds at

25 basis points above the LIBOR rate. Under the floating-to-floating interest rate swap, the bank pays to the counterparty floating-rate interest equal to the LIBOR rate (reset every six months) and receives from the counterparty floating-rate interest equal to the T-Bill rate plus one-half percent (reset weekly). The economic implication of this transaction is that the bank has transformed its T-Bill-rate-based CD liability into a liability with a cost three-quarter percent below the LIBOR rate and has locked in a positive spread of 150 basis points against its LIBOR-rate-based assets. The effective cost of the floating-rate funds to the counterparty after the swap transaction is equal to the T-Bill rate plus 75 basis points.

4.3.7.4 Interest Rate Caps

Interest rate caps provide insurance against the interest rate rising above a certain level. The level is known as the cap rate and is similar to the exercise price in options. When the floating interest rate rises above the cap rate, the seller of the cap pays the difference between the floating rate and the cap rate. The interest rate cap can be considered as a floating-rate note, where the interest rate is reset periodically equal to LIBOR. The payoff in each tenor is called a *caplet*, and the payoff diagram to the cap buyer resembles that of a long call option. Therefore, a cap can be considered as a series of caplets.

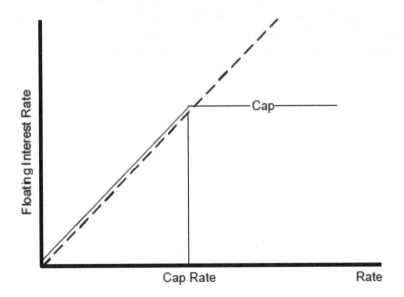

Consider an example where the principal amount is $1 million, the tenor is three months, and the life of the cap is three years with a cap rate of 5 percent. The cap provides insurance against the interest on the floating rate note rising above 5 percent.

Suppose that on a particular reset date, the three-month LIBOR interest rate is 4 percent. Since the interest rate is below e the cap rate, the cap seller does not need to make any payment.

Suppose that the three-month LIBOR rate on the next reset date is 6 percent. Now there is a 1-percent difference above the cap rate. But this is an annual rate, so the interest per quarter is 0.25 percent. The cap seller is obligated to pay 0.25 percent interest on the principal amount.

The payment to the cap buyer is 0.0025 * 1,000,000 = $2500. This amount is paid at the end of the tenor.

4.3.7.5 Interest Rate Floors

Interest rate floors provide insurance against the interest rate declining below a certain level. If a lender issued a floating rate loan and was worried about falling interest rates, he could buy interest rate floors to insure against losses. A floor provides a payoff when the underlying floating rate falls below a certain level. Similar to the interest rate cap, the interest rate floor is a series of put options on interest rates, each put option being referred to as a *floorlet*.

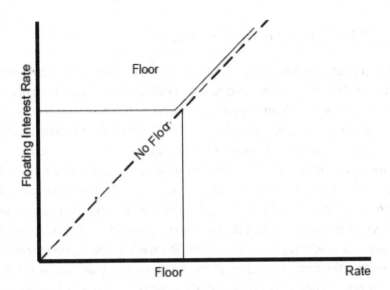

Consider an example where the principal amount is $1 million, the tenor is three months, and the life of the floor is three years with a floor rate of 5 percent. The floor provides insurance against the interest on the floating rate note declining below 5 percent.

Suppose that on a particular reset date, the three-month LIBOR interest rate is 6 percent. Since the interest rate is above the floor rate, the floor seller does not need to make any payment.

Suppose that the three-month LIBOR rate on the next reset date is 4 percent. Now there is a 1-percent difference below the floor rate. But this is an annual rate, so the interest per quarter is 0.25 percent. The floor seller is obligated to pay 0.25 percent interest on the principal amount.

The payment to the floor buyer is 0.0025 * 1,000,000 = $2500. This amount is paid at the end of the tenor.

4.4 Currency Risk

4.4.1 Importance of Currency Risk

As the markets become more and more efficient, investment managers are looking for new markets and reaching out to global markets to make profits. Therefore, the issue of protecting investment returns from currency risk is becoming critical. Let us take a very simple form of analysis, the measure of investment and returns in domestic currency. If the exchange rate remains constant from the time of investment to the realization of returns, then there would not be any currency risk. On the other hand, if the exchange rate changes, then the repatriation may either enhance the returns or may result in loss. If the foreign currency, where the investment was done, is devalued, then the conversion back to the home currency may reduce the profits in terms of the home currency or even result in loss. Currency fluctuation is essentially a noise, and every investor in foreign assets must make an explicit decision on whether to hedge the currency risk or embed the currency risk premium in expected returns.

Some experts argue that when viewed over a long investment horizon, currency movements cancel each other out and tend to revert to the long-term average. In other words, exchange rates exhibit mean-reversion and an expected return of zero. If the investment is intended for the long term, ignoring short-term dynamics of currency returns could be a perfectly valid strategy. However, hedge fund managers are accountable to show the performance to investors on a quarterly basis even if the manager intends to hold the investment for the long term. Under such circumstances, the fund manager is forced to take into account the impact of currency movements on the risk-return characteristics of his portfolio. Hedging the currency risk reduces the volatility of the return and makes the fund strategy attractive. Therefore, whether foreign investments are being held for the short or the long run, hedging can help fund managers to achieve stable performance and thus deliver value to investors. However, the decision to hedge or not to hedge is often dependent on the characteristics of the asset class and the risk and return objectives of the fund manager. While some international investors may be willing to accept some currency risk and a higher level of portfolio volatility in exchange for a greater potential return, for more defensive asset classes, such as property and fixed interest, hedging continues to be a prudent long-term portfolio management strategy.

4.4.2 Causes of Currency Crashes

The main factors that lead to major currency crashes are high inflation, a large current account deficit, and rising unemployment. Often these three may be interconnected. High inflation or expansionary macroeconomic policies can boost demand for imports and thus lower the current account balance. Also, a drop in foreign demand for a country's exports can create a current account deficit and rising unemployment.

High Inflation: High Inflationary policies put upward pressure on all prices of domestic goods, and as a result, the country depends on heavy imports. This will result in an increase in the price of foreign currency, which implies a depreciation of the exchange rate. Exchange rate depreciation can happen early or late in the inflationary process depending on factors like wage and price controls, trade barriers, controls on international capital flows, and the exchange rate regime. As asset prices are driven by information efficiency, the exchange rate tends to respond quickly to new information, including information on the future stance of macroeconomic policy.

Large current account deficit: The account deficit is caused by decreasing stock of foreign exchange reserves. When investors suddenly decide to pull their capital out or to stop financing the current balances, foreign exchange reserves will start diminishing. Diminishing foreign exchange reserves will put more pressure on foreign currency prices.

Rising Unemployment: Rising unemployment rates make central banks tend to ease monetary policy. The ease of monetary policy can take the form of devaluation or lower interest rates, which in turn pushes down the exchange value of the currency

4.4.3 The 1997 Asian Financial Crisis

In the early 1990s, the US economy began to experience a growth and so inflation as well. The US Federal Reserve had begun increasing its interest rate to tackle possible inflation and to reduce overall spending and price hikes. Since money always looks for a higher interest rate or return from financial and real investment, there had been a capital inflow to US assets that caused the US dollar to appreciate. Since many Asian currencies were maintaining a fixed or close alignment to the US dollar, their currencies were also appreciated with the appreciation of the US dollar. As a result, these Asian economies were losing export competitiveness and, hence, continued to face current account balance deficits. Rising interest rates in the United States attracted fund mangers' hot money to gain higher returns compared to East Asian assets. This caused a plunge in the demand for Asians in the security market.

The Asian financial crisis began on July 2, 1997, when the Thai Central Bank withdrew its support of its currency, the Thai baht, which resulted in the 20 percent depreciation of Thai currency within a month. Currency depreciation in Thailand brought a similar depreciation in all the neighboring Asian currencies and, hence, intensified the financial crisis. The first round of currency depreciation happened in the Thai baht, Malaysian ringgit, Philippine peso, and Indonesian rupiah. The second round of currency devaluation began with the Taiwan dollar, South Korean won, Singapore dollar, and Hong Kong dollar. To counter the weakness in currencies, governments started selling foreign exchange reserves and raised interest rates, which slowed economic growth. This made the interest-bearing securities more attractive than equities.

The contagion risk further sped to Russia. In August 1998, Russia unexpectedly defaulted on its debt, crushing the value of the ruble. The overall effect caused the yields on emerging countries' debt to increase and resulted in a flight to quality government bonds in developed nations. Yields on both high- and low-grade corporate bonds were increased. The increased credit spreads caused huge losses to LTCM, which was employing strategies based on relative value and credit spreads.

4.4.4 Hedging Currency Risk

It is often required to hedge currency risk that may be present in foreign investment strategies. Depending on the strategy, some fund managers may want to retain the currency risk expecting to earn premium while other managers want hedge the currency risk away. Various currency hedging techniques are discussed below.

Currency Forward is a contract to buy or sell a foreign currency at a fixed rate for delivery on a specified future date or period. If the date of the foreign currency usage and the maturity date of the foreign currency forward contract are matched up, the investor has in effect locked in the exchange rate payment amount. Foreign currency forward contracts are considered over-the-counter due to the fact that there is no centralized trading location and transactions are conducted directly between parties via telephone and online trading platforms at thousands of locations worldwide. Interestingly, unlike other forward contracts, currency forward contracts are more liquid than currency futures.

Currency Futures are similar to currency forwards in that the underlying asset is a currency exchange rate, such as the US dollar to euro exchange rate. However, there is a major difference: Currency futures are traded via exchanges, such as the Chicago Mercantile Exchange, and are therefore well controlled.

Currency Options are financial instruments that give the owner the right but not the obligation to buy or sell a specific foreign currency at a predetermined exchange rate. A call option gives the holder the right to buy the currency at an agreed price, and a put option gives him the right to sell it at an agreed price, irrespective of an unfavorable market price for the same.

Currency Swaps, similar to interest rate swaps, involve exchange rate transactions, where one party pays in one currency while the other party pays in other currency. Interests of currency swaps depend on the home country of the business, country regulation, and so on. Unlike interest rate swaps, a currency swap contract involves swapping of principal. Therefore, it involves a significant risk when the parties reside in two different time zones.

Circus stands for combined interest rate and currency swap. That is a fixed rate payments in one currency are swapped with floating rate payments in other currency.

Cross Hedging with Forwards: In less developed countries or frontier countries, capital markets are still in an infant stage, and foreign exchange markets are heavily controlled. Therefore, currency forwards and futures are either unavailable or are just starting to develop at a rather slow pace. International firms that are exposed to currencies of these countries should look for alternative currency hedging; such an exchange rate risk management technique is referred to as cross-hedging. Cross-hedging utilizes a triangular parity condition, which often exists among the home, foreign, and third currencies.

4.4.5 Risks of Currency Hedging

The main risk associated with currency futures comes from the level of leverage used. While the implicit leverage limits the initial amount of cash required, it exposes the hedger to the full amount. Leverage magnifies both the upside and downside movements and sometimes causes huge losses to the hedging strategy. While currency hedging may help to achieve stable returns and even to enhance investment returns, there are a number of risks that an investor should consider. There is the risk that the valuations for the hedging instrument may not accurately reflect the valuations for the physical securities on which they are based, due to timing or pricing variations. The volatile nature of foreign exchange markets may mean that the losses on a foreign exchange hedge vary from the foreign exchange related gains on the underlying physical securities in certain circumstances. Also, the use of hedging may affect the amount of any distribution payable.

4.5 Credit Risk

4.5.1 Components of Credit Risk

The five major components that constitute credit risk are exposure at default, probability of default, recovery rate, default correlation, and maturity of exposure. Recovery rate can also be expressed in terms of loss given default, which is equal to 1 – the recovery rate. Further, the credit risk can be measured in terms of credit VAR, which is the difference between unexpected loss and expected loss. Expected loss represents the decrease in the credit portfolio value subject to the probability of default. Unexpected loss represents the variability in expected loss.

Expected Loss or EL = EAD * LGD * PD

Where EAD = Exposure at default

LGD = Loss given default

PD = Probability of default

Unexpected loss can be modeled using the variance of LGD and EDF.

4.5.2 Implied Probability of Default

The probability of default (PD) can be extracted from the market value of the bond prices. The PD obtained using this procedure is called the implied probability.

Let us assume that market price of the bond is P and the face value of the bond is F.

Due to the exposure to default risk, the investor does not expect 100 percent of the face value to be returned. The expected face value at the time of maturity is face value – expected loss. The current market value of the bond reflects the present value of the expected face value.

Therefore, the market price of bond P = (F- EL)/ (1+r)

As we know that EL = F * PD * LGD

P = (F – F* PD * LGD)/ (1 + r)

=F (1 – PD * LGD)/ (1 + r)

Market price can also be expressed in terms of face value and yield.

So P = F / (1 + y)

Equating both the equations,

1 – PD*LGD = (1 + r)/ (1 + y)

PD*LGD = 1 - (1 + r)/ (1 + y)

= (y-r)/ (1+y)

Where y –r is equal to the credit spread of the bond yield over the risk-free rate.

Therefore, PD * LGD = CS/ (1+y)

For small values of y, the above expression can be simplified as:

PD = CS/LGD

4.5.3 Transition Matrices

Rating agencies like Moody's, Standard Poor's, and Fitch provide ratings for various bonds. The importance of ratings as a source of information to investors has been increasing as bond markets are including a wider range of obligors, products, structures, and geographies. Supervisory authorities have made regulatory requirements for financial institutions contingent on ratings. Over time, credit products are liable to move from one rating category to another depending on changes of the obligor's credit quality. Therefore, it is understood that a bond is subject not only to default risk but also to rating transition risk. Rating transition is also referred to as credit rating migration. Ratings volatility is likely to change across the ratings spectrum, that is, the probability of downgrade or upgrade of a speculative bond can be higher than that of an investment-grade bond. Rating transition probabilities are useful input for estimating loss distribution, preparing credit scenario analysis, and computing credit VAR measures.

Transition matrices can be used to observe various non-Markovian behaviors. According to Markov properties, the next period's distribution is only dependent on the present state and not on any developments in the past. The Markov assumption, while convenient, may be unrealistic. A Markov process has no memory: to compute future ratings, only knowledge of the current rating is required, not the path of how the firm arrived at that rating. However, the basic belief is that issuers that have experienced prior downgrading are prone to further downgrading, while issuers that have been upgraded before are less frequently downgraded. In other words, rating transition does depend on the path, which contradicts with the Markov property. Industry heterogeneity and time variation due in particular to the business cycle are some of the causes for non-Markovian behavior in rating transitions. In order to determine whether the rating transition depends on their previous state or not, path dependency analysis can be performed on rating transition matrices. Path dependency analysis reveals whether any one year's rating action has any impact on the following year's rating movement. In other words, it reveals whether the frequency of upgrades in any year is conditional on prior upgrades, and likewise, whether the frequency of downgrades in any given year is conditional on prior downgrades. In order to perform rating path dependency analysis, for example, period upgrade condition, one can simply exclude all the ratings that were previously stable or downgraded for a given year.

The increased reliance on rating systems as risk measurement devices has further increased the need for focusing on statistical analysis and validation methodologies for rating systems. While the formal definitions of ratings by the major agencies do not formally employ a probability, or an interval of probabilities, in their definition of the various categories, any use of the ratings for risk management and capital allocation will have to assign default probabilities to each rating category and to probabilities of transition between non default categories. A typical transition table looks like the one shown below.

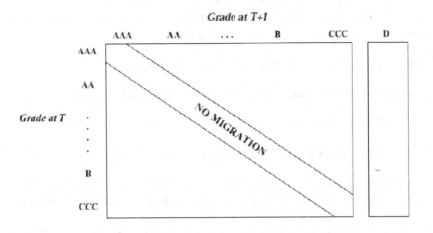

Typically, transition matrices exhibit higher default risk and higher migration volatility for lower-quality grades; more specifically, default likelihood increases exponentially with decreasing grade. A characteristic of all rating transition matrices is the high probability load on the diagonal: obligors are most likely to maintain their current rating. Considering the rating transition probability distribution of an obligor given its initial rating, the second largest probabilities are usually in the direct neighborhood of the diagonal. In general, the further away a cell is from the diagonal, the smaller is the likelihood of such an occurrence. Every year, major credit rating agencies publish rating transition matrices.

4.5.4 Credit Risk Models

Traditionally many banks and corporations were using internal models in order to measure default risk. Over the time many third party Risk Management specialty companies developed standard models and extended them to their clients according to the needs of clients. Some of the credit risk models are discussed below.

The Merton Model

The Merton model uses the Black-Scholes option pricing theory to evaluate a firm's equity value, debt value, probability of default, and loss given default. Merton models assume that the firm contains a single zero-coupon bond and shareholders. Any value of the firm above a zero-coupon bond will be equal to the equity that shareholders claim, and the value up to the face value of the zero-coupon bond belongs to the debt holders. The value of debt resembles a short put + a risk-free bond with face value F.

Therefore, the total value of the firm V can be expressed as follows:

Firm value V = Present value of risk-free bond + Short put + Long call

$$V = F * e^{\wedge}(-r*(T-t)) - Pt + Ct$$

From the above equation, we can also observe put-call parity.

If the firm value falls below the debt value, then the firm is said to be at default. This will happen when the call value is zero and the put value is in the money.

From the Black-Scholes option pricing theory, N(d2) gives the probability of exercising the put option or, in different words, the probability of moneyness.

Therefore, the probability of default PD = 1- probability of moneyness of put

$$PD = 1 - N(d2)$$

When the firm value falls below the face value of debt,

$$V = F * e^{\wedge}(-r*(T-t)) - Pt$$

Therefore, the loss to the debt holders is equal to the value of the put option. Since the loss is realized at the time of expiration, the loss corresponds to the future value of the put option.

Therefore, loss given default LGD = Pt * e^rt.

Drawbacks of the Merton Model:

1. The Merton model assumes that the firm contains only one debt in the form of a zero-coupon bond.
2. The bond can only default at the time of maturity.
3. The value of the firm is observable and follows a lognormal diffusion process.
4. Volatility and the risk-free rate are constant.
5. There is negotiation between debt holders and shareholders.
6. The Merton model does not consider illiquidity of assets.

Moody's KMV Model

In contrast to the Merton model, KMV models assume that the firm contains two forms of debt—one long-term and the other short-term. The KMV measures the default in terms of distance to default, which is calculated as follows:

The distance to default DD = (Firm asset value – Default threshold) / Standard deviation of assets

The default threshold is a linear combination of both the short-term bond and the long-term bond and can be calculated as follows:

Default threshold = Short-term debt + Threshold factor * Long-term debt.

The threshold factor = 0.7 – 0.3*short-term debt/long-term debt

or 0.5, whichever is higher.

More precisely, the distance to default can be calculated from the Black-Scholes model by replacing the face value of the zero-coupon with the threshold value. The distance default is nothing but the moneyness of the put option.

The expected default frequency is calculated using the steps provided below:

1. Calculate DD for each firm, say, 1000.
2. Group the firms by the value of DD.
3. Find out how many of the firms defaulted in each group.
4. EDF is calculated as the ratio of the number of firms that defaulted with DD of X and total number of firms with DD of X.

Credit Metrics

Unlike market risks, where daily liquid price observations allow a direct calculation of value-at-risk (VAR), Credit Metrics seeks to construct the volatility of value due to credit quality changes. This constructive approach makes Credit Metrics less an exercise in fitting distributions to observed price data, and more an exercise in proposing models that explain the changes in credit-related instruments. Credit Metrics was built on the fact that the credit risk does not rely on the assumption that returns are normally distributed. Credit Metrics looks to a horizon and constructs a distribution of historically estimated credit outcomes or rating migrations, including potential default. Each credit quality migration is weighted by its likelihood using transition matrix analysis. Each outcome has an estimate of change in value. Credit Metrics then aggregates volatilities across the portfolio, applying estimates of correlation. Thus, although the relevant time horizon is usually longer for credit risk, Credit Metrics computes credit risk on a comparable basis with market risk.

Credit Risk+

Credit Risk+ models default risk by considering aa portfolio of obligors, size, maturity, credit quality, and the systemic risk of an obligor. It makes no assumptions about the causes of default. The Credit Risk+ model considers default rates as continuous random variables and incorporates the volatility of default rates in order to capture the uncertainty in the level of default rates. The probability of default of each obligor is calculated as proportionate values of a scaled risk factor; from the default probabilities of all the obligors, the loss distribution for the portfolio can be estimated to assess the credit risk in a portfolio.

Credit Portfolio View

The credit portfolio view is developed based on the empirical evidence that default and credit migration probabilities are linked to the economy. As credit cycles follow business cycles, as the economy worsens, downgrades and defaults increase; when the economy becomes stronger, upgrades will increase and defaults will decrease. The credit portfolio view is a multifactor model that employs various macroeconomic factors, such as GDP growth rate, unemployment rate, long-term interest rates, currency rates, government expenditures, aggregated saving rates, and fiscal policy and simulates the joint conditional distribution of default and migration probabilities for various rating groups. The models use transition matrices of economic cycle data. This model applies better to speculative-grade obligors.

4.5.5 Sources of Credit Risk

Concentrated portfolios are the major sources of credit risk in a portfolio. Some of the concentrations are discussed below.

Name and Credit Concentration

While name concentration tells how much outstanding there is to a name or counterparty, credit concentration tells the maximum proportionate exposure to securities of a particular credit rating, for example, BBB credits.

The combination of name and credit concentration is dangerous to a portfolio. When the counterparty is downgraded or the market quality of securities of credit ratings is downgraded even at the other counterparty, the value of the portfolio will be impacted severely.

Industry Concentration

Industry concentration tells how much exposure there is to an industry, and what the impact is if the industry sector is undergoing cyclical changes, economic downturn, and so on.

Country or Region Concentrations

Country or region concentrations deal with what the country mix of the portfolio is and how it is exposed to regional concentrations. It considers such questions as: What is the likely impact of credit downgrades by country and the rollover effects in the region? How linked are countries in that region?

4.5.6 Credit Derivatives

The main difference between credit derivatives and other off-balance sheet products, such as equity, currency, or bond derivatives, is that the latter can be priced and hedged with reference to the underlying asset; such pricing and hedging can be problematic when applied to credit derivatives. Credit products pricing involves statistical data on the likelihood of default, the probability of payout, level of risk tolerance, and a pricing model.

Credit Default Swaps

A credit default swap is a bilateral agreement between two parties, in which one party offers the other party protection against a credit event by a third party for a specified period of time. In return, the protection buyer pays a premium periodically. The protection buyer is sometimes called a CDS buyer or swap buyer, and the protection seller is sometimes called the CDS writer. The third party is nothing but a bond issuer or the reference name or the reference entity. The contract can be viewed as the CDS buyer selling the credit risk and the CDS writer buying the credit risk.

CDS contracts are off-balance sheet and are structured as over-the-counter products. The ISDA documentation specifies the key contract items, such as maturity, premium, reference name, event triggers, and so on. The events that trigger the capital payoff on the CDS contract are negotiable and are wider than bond default.

The key credit events are

- Failure to pay
- Bankruptcy
- Repudiation
- Material adverse restructuring of debt
- Obligation acceleration or obligation default

A contingent payment is only made if a credit event occurs. If the credit event does not occur, the protection seller has no obligation. The premium can be thought of as the credit spread an investor demands to take the default risk of a given reference asset. The protection can be purchased on a loan, a bond, sovereign risk, or even on credit exposure due to a derivative contract, such as a counterparty credit exposure in a cross-currency swap transaction.

The settlement can be either cash or physical. In a cash settlement, though rare in a vanilla CDS contract, upon a credit event the seller pays par less the market value of the defaulted debt of the reference name less any accrued premium. The market values are typically determined by taking an average of independent valuations from dealers. In a physical settlement, the buyer delivers a reference entity, or equivalent that is specified in the contract, to the writer in exchange for par minus the accrued premium. Unlike the insurance contract, the buyer of protection does not have to own the reference entity at the time a claim is made.

Credit protection can be linked to an individual entity or to a basket of entities. A basket CDS is CDS on a portfolio of entities, where the payoff occurs based on a predetermined credit event. A basket CDS can be a first-to-default or nth-to-default CDS. In a first-to-default CDS, the first reference entity default triggers a payoff either in cash or by physical delivery. As in the case of a regular CDS, the payoff typically equals1 − recovery rate - accrued interest. There are then no further payments or payoffs. In the case of an nth-to-default CDS, the payoff does not occur for the first n-1 default and the buyer continues to pay the premium. When the nth default triggers the payment from the writer for that bond, the contract gets terminated. Correlations among the assets in the basket are the main determinant factor for the swap premium. The higher the correlation, the higher the premium. The premium on the first-to-default CDS is usually less than that of the nth-to-default. However, as the correlation among the assets increases, the premium for the first-to-default CDS approaches the premium value of the nth-to-default. In a basket where all the assets in the basket are perfectly correlated, the premium for first-to-default and nth-to-default will be the same.

Total Return Swaps

A total return swap is a bilateral agreement between two parties that exchanges the total return from an asset between them. This is designed to transfer the credit risk from one party to the other. In addition, total return swaps are also used as synthetic repo instruments for funding purposes. The total return swap (TRS) is sometimes called a total rate-of-return swap, or TR swap. In a TRS, the total return of an asset or credit-sensitive security is exchanged for some other cash flow, usually tied to LIBOR, or some other asset or credit-sensitive security. The maturity of the underlying asset does not need to match with the contract maturity. In a TRS, the total return from the underlying asset is paid over to the counterparty in return for a fixed or floating cash flow. This slightly distinguishes the TRS from a credit default swap, as the payments between counterparties to a TRS are connected to changes in the market value of the underlying asset, as well as changes resulting from the occurrence of a credit event. So the TRS is used to transfer both credit risk and interest rate risk or any other risks that influence the market value of the asset. In a TRS, the total return buyer receives the complete cash flows of an underlying asset without actually buying the asset, which makes it a synthetic bond product and therefore a credit derivative. An investor may wish to receive such cash flows synthetically for tax, accounting, regulatory capital, external audit, or legal reasons. This concept is especially useful for illiquid assets.

The total return on the underlying asset is the interest payments and any change in the market value. A positive change in market value, which is called *capital appreciation*, makes the cash to flow to the total return receiver, whereas a negative change in market value, which is called *depreciation*, makes the cash to flow to the total return payer. The swap is usually paid on a quarterly or semiannual basis, with the underlying asset being revalued or marked-to-market on the resetting dates. The asset price is usually obtained from an independent third-party source, such as Bloomberg, or as the average of a range of dealer quotes. If the obligor of the reference asset defaults, the TRS may be terminated immediately, with a net present value payment changing hands according to what this value is. Alternatively if a secondary market exists for the underlying assets, then the contract may be continued, with each party making appreciation or depreciation payments as appropriate. Upon termination of the swap, counterparties will be liable to each other for accrued interest plus any appreciation or depreciation of the asset.

In a TR swap, one party purchases and retains rights of the underlying asset and transfers the total return of the asset to another party in return for a floating return, such as LIBOR + spread. The spread is a function of the credit rating of the swap counterparty, the amount and value of the reference asset, the credit quality of the reference asset, the funding costs of the beneficiary bank, any required profit margin, and the capital charge associated with the TR swap

Credit-Linked Notes

A credit-linked note (CLN) is a credit derivative under which a coupon or price of a note is linked to the creditworthiness or performance of a specific financial asset. It offers issuers a hedge on credit risk, and gives investors a higher yield on a note for accepting exposure to a specified credit event. Credit-linked notes are backed by collateral that is highly rated, such as treasury securities. CLNs are created through special purpose vehicles (SPCs), or trusts, which are collateralized with AAA- rated securities. Investors buy securities from the trust, which pays a fixed or floating coupon during the life of a note. The holder of a CLN has credit exposure to the issuer of the notes, as well as to the reference entity or entities as defined in the terms and conditions of the CLN. By purchasing a credit-linked note, the investor is effectively selling credit protection in relation to the reference entity. In return, the investor receives a higher coupon representing the premium paid by the buyer of credit protection. While an investor bears the credit risk of the issuer of the debt instrument, he physically holds a credit-linked note, which gives him a synthetic exposure to the occurrence of predetermined credit events in relation to the underlying entity. If no credit event occurs during the term of the CLN, it is redeemed on its maturity date at its nominal amount. If the referenced entity defaults or declares bankruptcy, the CLN buyer receives an amount equal to the recovery rate.

Credit-linked notes became increasingly popular from 1997, as banks tried to reduce their exposure to the risk of default in loans to emerging markets. A credit-linked note allows an investor to obtain credit exposure to a wide variety of underlying entities in order to enhance the return on the fixed-income investment portfolio. Since the characteristics of a CLN resemble those of a regular corporate bond, institutional investors, who are typically restricted from investing in other credit derivatives like a CDS or TRS, show interest to invest in credit-linked notes. In addition, due to the size of the minimum investment, they also attract retail investors. The presence of both institutional investors and retail investors increases the market for CLNs. In essence, there are more parties willing to write insurance against default.

Issuers may also issue a note that is linked to the credit of one or more reference entities. Such CLNs are called basket CLNs or nth-to-default CLNs. A basket credit-linked note is a note that references a basket of reference entities. Investors will receive a coupon until the earlier of the maturity date of the CLN or the date on which credit events have occurred in respect of every reference entity. If a credit event occurs, the nominal amount of the CLN will be reduced by the same proportion as the relevant reference entity bears to the basket, and the investor will be paid an amount equal to the recovery value of outstanding obligations issued by the relevant reference entity. Thereafter, as the nominal amount of the CLN has been reduced, coupon payments will be reduced proportionally and the coupon rate may be reset. As the basket CLN is not terminated following a credit event, the remaining nominal capital continues to be exposed to potential credit events throughout a remaining term.

An nth-to-default note is a note that also references a basket of reference entities. The difference between a basket CLN and a nth-to-default CLN is that upon occurrence of a predetermined number of credit events in relation to reference entities, the entire nth-to-default CLN terminates, whereas a basket CLN continues with a reduced nominal amount. An nth-to-default CLN would terminate after n reference entities suffered a credit event, that is, a first-to-default after one reference entity, a second-to-default after two reference entities suffered a credit event, and so forth.

Collateralized Default Obligations

A special purpose vehicle (SPV) assembles an entire portfolio of credit risk exposures, segments that exposure into different tranches with unique risk, return, and maturity profiles, and then issues collateralized default obligation securities transferring the risk to investors. The reference pool can be assembled with physical cash flow assets, such as bonds, loans, MBS, or ABS, or with synthetic credit risk exposures. A collateralized debt obligation (CDO) structure can have any number of tranches depending on attachment points. However, a typical CDO structure comprises three tranches—senior, mezzanine, and equity tranches. The equity tranche, or first-loss tranche, absorbs the losses up to a predefined percentage of the sum of the notional on a portfolio of reference names. Once the equity tranche is exhausted, the mezzanine tranche starts to absorb the additional losses. The senior tranche is considered to be least risky and typically gets AAA rating. The senior tranche performs well until both the equity and mezzanine tranches exhaust. At this time, the senior tranche will experience losses.

CDOs can be either funded or unfunded. In a funded structure, investors pay the principal amount of their tranches to the CDO manager, who in turn invests the capital in risk-free collateral, such as treasury securities. Counterparty risk is eliminated with a funded structure. However, the CDO structure is still subject to market fluctuations and reference default risk. In an unfunded structure, investors make no up-front payments. Instead, they receive periodic spread (coupon) payments in return for making a payment when a default in the reference portfolio affects their tranche. Credit risk transfer by an unfunded structure thus exposes the CDO manager to additional counterparty risk that must be managed.

Depending on the source of the funding for the tranche payment, CDOs can be classified as two types. Cash-flow CDOs pay interest and principal to tranche holders using the cash flows produced by the CDO's assets. Cash-flow CDOs focus primarily on managing the credit quality of the underlying portfolio. Market-value CDOs enhance investor returns through the more frequent trading and profitable sale of collateral assets. The CDO asset manager seeks to realize capital gains on the assets in the CDO's portfolio. There is greater focus on the changes in market value of the CDO's assets.

Cash-flow CDOs can be either balance sheet or arbitrage transactions. Balance sheet transactions are primarily motivated by the issuing institutions' desire to remove loans and other assets from their balance sheets, to reduce their regulatory capital requirements and improve their return on risk capital. Arbitrage CDO managers attempt to capture the spread between the relatively high-yielding assets and the lower liabilities to the investors. The popularity of arbitrage CDOs has been declining.

CDOs are available as single-tranche CDOs as well. Single-tranche CDOs represent the vast majority of all new synthetic CDO issuances. The CDO manager sells only a single tranche, usually at the mezzanine level, of the structure to an investor and retains the other tranches. This particular CDO structure, which may be funded or unfunded, has several advantages. The single tranche is tailored to the specific investor's needs with regard to name composition, subordination level, and size. It is not necessary for the CDO manager to find investors across the entire capital structure simultaneously.

When pricing the credit risk of an entire portfolio, it is necessary to take into account the fact that the default of a given name in the reference portfolio may affect the default risk of other names too. A high correlation of defaults within the reference portfolio implies a higher risk of many names defaulting at the same time, with the potential to inflict losses on the senior tranche. Therefore, a high correlation makes the senior tranche more risky. Since a default would be interpreted as a systemic event, a high implied correlation within the portfolio might be read as an indicator of perceived systemic risk by investors. A high correlation not only increases the likelihood of many assets defaulting at the same time but also the likelihood of no defaults occurring across the board. The valuation of the equity tranche rises accordingly when correlation is high. Conversely, the value of the equity tranche falls with low correlation. The effect of correlation on mezzanine investors is subject to extensive research on the nature of the assets.

4.6 Sovereign and Country Risk

Sovereign risk is a risk that a foreign government will default on its loan or fail to honor other business commitments because of a change in national policy. A country asserting its prerogatives as an independent nation might prevent the repatriation of a company or a country's funds through limits on the flow of capital, tax impediments, or the nationalization of property. The difference between sovereign risk and credit risk can be explained as follows: When a domestic party borrows money, then he would either pay the entire promised principal or interest as per the agreement if the financial situation is good or would seek to work out the loan with the lender by rescheduling part or all of the balance or would likely proceed with bankruptcy filing and eventually liquidating the firm's assets. Suppose that a high-grade corporation in a foreign country borrows funds from, for example, a US financial institution. If the foreign country's government's dollar-reserve position runs into bad shape after lending, then the foreign government will refuse to allow any further repayment to be made in dollars to outside creditors. This will put the foreign borrower automatically into default, even though the corporation maintains good credit. Therefore, the sovereign credit rating acts as a ceiling for the ratings of that country's borrowers regardless of the health of the borrower and makes the lending decision to a foreign-country corporation a two-step process. Lenders must assess the credit risk of the borrower and make necessary adjustments to credit spreads and credit limits, and then again readjust them by assessing the sovereign risk of the country in which the borrower resides. Sovereign risk events may take one of the following two forms:

- Debt repudiation: Repudiation is an outright cancellation of all of the borrower's current and future foreign debt and equity obligations.
- Debt rescheduling: A foreign country, or a group of creditors in that country, may declare a moratorium or delay on its current and future debt obligations and then seek to alter contractual terms, such as interest rates and debt maturity.

Though country risk and sovereign risk are related, they are two distinct phenomena. Country risk is associated with doing business in a particular country, and sovereign risk focuses only on the ability or willingness of debt repayment by government. In other words, country risk is the broadest measure and it includes sovereign risk, political risk, and transfer risk. Transfer risk is the risk that a transaction cannot take place because a government or central bank will not allow currency to leave a country. Though there is a positive relation between sovereign and country risk, the sovereign credit profile can improve without necessarily expecting improvement in the business environment. Similarly, deterioration in country risk conditions does not necessarily imply a worsening in sovereign creditworthiness, though often that will be the case.

Sovereign risk can basically be evaluated using internal models, external models, and implied risk models. While these are basic models, credit-rating agencies will follow a rigorous evaluation process by applying a number of variables that will be discussed later in this topic. Due to the lack of historical data and because of the relatively small size of the statistical sample set, sovereign risk cannot be assessed as precisely as for corporations.

4.6.1 Internal Evaluation Models

Internal evaluation models evaluate various macro and microeconomic variables and ratios that forecast the country's probability of rescheduling. Internal evaluation models are statistical models that calculate credit score, similar to the z-score rating of probability of corporate bankruptcy. Some of the important variables that can forecast rescheduling probabilities are debt service ratio, import ratio, investment ratio, variance of export revenue, and domestic money supply growth.

Debt Service Ratio

A country's primary source of dollar inflow depends on the export of goods and services, and part or all of the inflow will be used to pay down any interest and amortization on debt. The larger the debt repayments in dollars proportionate to export revenue, the greater the probability of debt rescheduling.

Debt Service Ratio (DSR) = Interest plus amortization of debt / Exports

A higher value of DSR indicates a higher likelihood of debt rescheduling.

Import Ratio

Countries that depend heavily on imports for infrastructure development or consumer needs import goods from other countries and pay the required dollar amount from foreign exchange reserves. The greater the need for imports, the faster the depletion of its foreign exchange and the more likely to result in debt rescheduling.

Import Ratio (IR) = Total imports / Total foreign exchange reserves

A higher value of IR indicates a higher likelihood of debt rescheduling.

Investment Ratio

A country that invests heavily in infrastructure development and factory construction would likely see more production in the future. The investment ratio measures the ratio of real investment and the gross national product. The higher the investment ratio, the lower the probability of rescheduling.

Investment Ratio (INVR) = Real investment / GNP

A higher value of INVR indicates less probability of debt rescheduling.

Variance of Export Revenue

Variance of export revenue reflects the fact that export revenue may be highly volatile due to quantity risk and price risk. While quantity risk is the risk that the production of raw commodities that a country can sell in other countries depends on surplus and shortage, price risk is the risk that the export of commodities is subject to supply and demand in international markets.

A higher value of variance of export revenue indicates a higher likelihood of debt rescheduling.

Domestic Money Supply Growth

A country's inflation depends on the domestic growth rate of that country's money supply, and a higher growth rate will increase the inflation rate. Higher inflation will likely weaken the currency value. When a country's currency loses credibility as a medium of exchange, then the country must increasingly depend on hard currency for both domestic and international payments.

$$\text{Money Growth (MG)} = \frac{\Delta M}{M}$$

Where ΔM is the change in money supply and M is the initial level of the money supply.

A higher value of MG indicates a higher likelihood of debt rescheduling.

Disadvantages of Statistical Models:

1. The delay in collecting the economic variables makes the model stale.
2. Statistical models estimate rescheduling probability on both interest and principal amortization, but in reality, some countries may reschedule only one component and pay the other as scheduled.
3. Statistical models ignore political risk events, such as strikes, elections, corruption, and revolutions.
4. Statistical models are not always stable due to the fact that rescheduling that occurred in the past due to inefficient ratios is not necessarily indicative of the future.

4.6.2 External Evaluation Models

Various external agencies provide country risk analysis, either in the form of detailed reports or ratings or a combination of rating and report. The main criteria used by the majority of country risk analysis firms are as follows. This list gives a general picture about country risk assessment and does not include every factor, and some of these factors may not be applicable in certain situations.

Internal Political Risk Factors:

• Fractionalization of the political spectrum

- Fractionalization by language or region
- Willingness to compromise
- Potential social disturbances
- Political effectiveness
- Political instability
- Corruption

External Political Risk Factors:

- Influences of regional political forces
- External conflicts
- Foreign influence

Economic Risk Factors:

- GDP per head
- Real GDP growth
- Budget balance as percentage of GDP
- Inflation rate
- Level of economic development
- Fiscal and monetary policy
- Soundness of the banking system

External Debt Indicators:

- Debt service ratio
- Debt consumption
- History of default and rescheduling

Balance of Payment:

- Current account as percentage of GDP
- Terms of trade
- Export growth rate
- Import ratio
- Access to capital markets

The Economic Intelligence Unit rates countries by combining economic policy risk, political risk, economic structure risk, and liquidity risk. It provides detailed reports on country analysis, as well as democracy indices for major countries. The Economic Intelligence Unit belongs to the Economist Group and was founded in 1949. The EIU is known as the world's leading provider of country intelligence and covers more than a hundred countries. The EIU rates a company on a hundred-point scale. The higher the score, the riskier the country. It then divides the score into five bands from A to E. A indicates low risk, and E indicates high risk.

The US-based *Institutional Investor* magazine publishes institutional investors' credit ratings twice a year and covers about 150 countries. *Institutional Investor* specifically concentrates on the issue of the country's creditworthiness. *Institutional Investor* asks about a hundred global bankers to rate countries based on their perception of creditworthiness. All selected bankers are surveyed during the same window of two months that ends forty-five days before the publication date. Bankers are not allowed to rate their home country. The *Institutional Investor* ratings models employ both advanced quantitative techniques and subjective appraisals. The magazine finally provides scores on the scale of zero to a hundred, zero being the highest risk of default and 100 being the lowest risk of default.

Rating agencies, such as Fitch, Moody's, and S&P, have developed rigorous models that employ both quantitative and subjective analysis to calculate sovereign risk. They cover more than a hundred sovereigns and provide ratings. For example, Fitch's scale starts from AAA (lowest default risk) through C (high default risk) and to DDD, DD, and D (default). Fitch is primarily concerned with a country's external debt, government policy, standard financial and macroeconomic indicators, long-term factors, and internal and external political risk factors. The team of analysts runs stress tests to assess the economy's ability to overcome international exogenous shocks.

4.6.3 Implied Sovereign Risk Model

Similar to the way the implied credit risk can be calculated from market prices of bonds, implied sovereign risk can also be estimated from the secondary market prices of sovereign debt. The factors that lead to a secondary market for sovereign debt are:

1. Larger financial Institutions want to reduce their exposure to sovereign debt.
2. Financial institutions are willing to swap one country's debt for another's in order to rebalance the portfolio.
3. Wealthy investors and hedge funds seek to engage in debt-for-equity swaps.

Sovereign debt is available in the secondary market in four ways: Brady bonds, sovereign bonds, performing bonds, and nonperforming bonds.

Brady Bonds

Brady bonds are bond-for-loan swaps where US and other financial institutions exchange their dollar loans for dollar bonds issued by sovereigns. These bonds typically have a longer maturity and lower coupon than was originally promised. However, the principal is usually collateralized through the issuing country's purchasing US treasuries. In the event that the sovereign defaults on its Brady bonds, the buyers of the bonds can access the dollar bonds held as collateral.

Sovereign Bonds

Sovereigns issue sovereign bonds to repurchase the country's US-dollar-denominated Brady bonds. Since Brady bonds are collateralized by US treasuries, their value partly reflects the value of US treasuries. In contrast, sovereign bonds are uncollateralized, and their price reflects the credit risk of the country.

Performing Bonds

Performing bonds are original or restructured outstanding sovereign loans on which the sovereign is making payments to lenders. Sovereigns that have a potential for rescheduling of payments may sell the bonds at a discount.

Nonperforming Bonds

Nonperforming bonds are original or restructured outstanding sovereign loans on which the sovereign is currently not making payments to lenders. These bonds are typically traded at deep discounts.

4.6.4 Implied Country Risk in Market Prices

Market prices on sovereign loans are available on a monthly basis. Managers construct a statistical country rating analysis (CRA) model to analyze which key economic or political events have led to changes in secondary market prices. The CRA model involves regressing periodic changes in secondary market prices on a set of key variables.

4.7 Operational Risk

Hedge funds are very heterogeneous in nature and are exposed to various risks, such as liquidity risk, market risk, counterparty risk, and so on, thus acting as market makers. Hedge funds implement various arbitrage and nonarbitrage trading strategies, such as fixed-income arbitrage, distressed-security strategies that are potentially subject to large profits. These strategies require trading activities that can be considered less conventional than in the long-only universe and expose the manager to operational risk for which the manager does not receive premium.

Recent studies reveal the fact that operational risk greatly exceeds the risk related to the investment strategy, with at least half of hedge fund collapses directly related to a failure of one or several operational processes. A weak operational environment will increase the impact of an external event, such as tough trading conditions or brutal changes in financing conditions. Indeed, few hedge funds failed purely because of operational issues.

While the main sources of observed hedge fund operational issues are misrepresentation, misappropriation, and deliberate fraud, they could have been prevented to some extent by using practices like position pricing and NAV calculation procedures, client reporting procedures, reconciliation capabilities, compliance controls, and risk management infrastructure. Not all hedge fund frauds were necessarily intentional; some may have occurred due to loopholes in the systems and processes that could have been found and prevented with a proper monitoring system.

Operational risk is as old as the industry, yet it has been neglected by firms. The banking industry has long recognized the importance of market risk and credit risk and developed various models to quantify them. Due to the broader nature of operational risk, there was no clear definition of operational risk, and every risk that does not fall under market or credit risk used to be treated as operational risk. Basel II came up with a definition for operational risk, and based on this definition, the sources of operational risk can be detected, monitored, and controlled.

According to Basel, operational risk is defined as "the risk of direct and indirect loss resulting from inadequate or failed internal processes, people and systems, or from external events. "Basel's definition includes legal risk but excludes business risk, strategic risk, and reputational risk where losses would be difficult to quantify. A few examples of operational risks are provided below.

Inadequate Processes: Systems with a lack of advanced features, missing functionalities, not enough automation, redundancy, and so on.

Internal Processes: Model error, availability of loss reserves, model complexity, transaction execution error, booking error, collateral confirmation, collateral netting error, erroneous disclosure, limit exceeds, volume risk, position reporting error, and profit and loss reporting error.

People: Incompetency, inadequate resources, key personnel, management, communication, internal politics, conflicts of interest, lack of cooperation, fraud, and organized labor activities.

Systems: System failures, network failures, system inadequacy, compatibility risk, supplier risk, data corruption, disaster recovery risk, system age, system support, hacking damage, and theft of information

External Events: Political, taxation, regulatory, social tensions, competition, theft, forgery, check kiting, and natural disaster losses.

Understanding of operational risk is more important in the modern era of investments due to the growing sophistication of financial technology and rapid deregulation and globalization of the financial industry. While it may not be feasible to eliminate operational risk failures completely, the sound operational risk management framework must focus to minimize the occurrence of events and potential losses. At a minimum, the following objectives should be considered by the operational risk management framework:

- To define and explain the operational risk from the context of the institution
- To avoid potential catastrophic losses
- To educate all the employees at all levels and business units on enterprise-wide operational risk
- To motivate all departments to anticipate all kinds of risks, thereby effectively preventing the failures from occurring
- To make the firm less vulnerable to any breakdowns
- To identify potential problem areas in the firm
- To prevent operational mishaps from happening
- To establish clarity of roles, responsibilities, and accountability
- To identify business units in the firm with high volume and high turnover
- To identify business units with high complex support systems

- To empower business units with the responsibility and accountability of the business risk they assume on a daily basis
- To monitor the danger signs of both income and expense volatilities
- To ensure that there is compliance to all risk policies
- To ensure that there is clear and concise measure of due diligence on all risk -taking and non risk-taking activities of the firm.
- To provide the executive committee regularly with a concise report

The Basel Committee on Banking Supervision, under Annex -7, breaks down loss events into seven general categories:

Internal Fraud: Losses due to acts of a type intended to defraud, misappropriate property, or circumvent regulations, the law, or company policy, excluding diversity/discrimination events, which involve at least one internal party. Internal fraud is further classified as unauthorized activity, and theft and fraud. Examples of unauthorized activity include transactions not reported (intentional), trans type unauthorized (with monetary loss), and mismarking of position (intentional). Examples of theft and fraud include fraud, credit fraud, worthless deposits, theft, extortion, embezzlement, robbery, misappropriation of assets, malicious destruction of assets, forgery, check kiting, smuggling, account takeover, impersonation, tax noncompliance, evasion (willful), bribes, kickbacks, and insider trading (not on firm's account).

External Fraud: Losses due to acts of a type intended to defraud, misappropriate property, or circumvent the law by a third party. External fraud is further classified as theft and fraud, and systems security related. Theft and fraud include theft, robbery, forgery, and check kiting. Systems security related include hacking damage and theft of information (with monetary loss).

Employment Practices and Workplace Safety: Losses arising from acts inconsistent with employment, health or safety laws or agreements, payment of personal injury claims, or diversity/discrimination events. These events are further classified as employee relation matters, such as compensation, benefit, termination issues, organized labor activities, and environment safety issues, such as general liability (slips and falls, etc.), employee health and safety rules and events, and workers compensation.

Clients, Products, and Business Practice: Losses arising from an unintentional or negligent failure to meet a professional obligation to specific clients (including fiduciary and suitability requirements), or from the nature or design of a product. These events are further categorized into five types, described below:

Suitability, Disclosure, and Fiduciary: Fiduciary breaches, guideline violations, suitability, disclosure issues (KYC, etc.), retail consumer disclosure violations, breach of privacy, aggressive sales, account churning, misuse of confidential information, and lender liability

   Improper Business or Market Practices: Antitrust, improper trade or market practices, market manipulation, insider trading (on firm's account), unlicensed activity, and money laundering

   Product Flaws: Product defects (unauthorized, etc.) and model errors

   Selection, Sponsorship, and Exposure: Failure to investigate client per guidelines, exceeding client exposure limits

   Advisory Activities: Disputes over performance or advisory activities

Damage to Physical Assets: Losses arising from loss or damage to physical assets from natural disaster or other events. Disaster events include natural disaster losses and human losses from external sources (terrorism and vandalism)

Business Disruption and Systems Failures: Losses arising from disruption of business or system failures. These events include events related to systems, such as hardware, software, and telecommunications and utility outages and disruptions

Execution, Delivery, and Process Management: Losses from failed transaction processing or process management, and from relations with trade counterparties and vendors. These events are further classified as follows:

   Transaction Capture, Execution, and Maintenance: Miscommunication, data entry, maintenance, or loading error, missed deadline or responsibility, model or system misoperation, accounting error or entity attribution error, other task misperformance, delivery failure, collateral management failure, and reference data maintenance

   Monitoring and Reporting: Failed mandatory reporting obligation or inaccurate external report (loss incurred)

   Customer Intake and Documentation: Client permissions/disclaimers missed or legal documents missing or incomplete

Customer/Client Account Management: Unapproved access given to accounts, incorrect client records (loss incurred), or negligent loss or damage of client assets

Trade Counterparties: Nonclient counterparty misperformance or miscellaneous nonclient counterparty disputes

Vendors and Suppliers: Outsourcing vendor disputes

4.7.1 Measuring Operational Risk

Operational risk can be evaluated using top-down and bottom-up approaches. While top-down approach is easy to implement the bottom-up approach provides more accurate assessment as it involves gathering the information from micro level.

Top-Down Models

Top-down models use data that is readily available, such as the firm level financial performance or industry level performance, to calculate the implied operational risk. These models are relatively simple and give a general picture of the company's operational risk. The most common top-down models available to measure operational risk are the implied capital model, income volatility model, income pricing model, and analogue model.

Bottom-Up Models

In contrast to top-down models, bottom-up models analyze risk factors at the source level and calculate the firm level operational risk The Basel II encourages banks to develop bottom-up models. Among the commonly used bottom-up models, two most popular approaches are process approaches and the actuarial approach.

Loss Distribution Approach

The loss distribution approach (LDA) model, an actuarial type of bottom-up model, is one of the approaches used to model operational risk measurement. Under this approach, frequency of loss and severity of loss are modeled separately and then combined through a process called convolution to measure the operational loss. Unlike other models, the LDA uses both frequency of loss and severity of loss to measure the operational risk. Like market risk and credit risk measurement models, LDA also uses historical data to model the distribution. However, there is not adequate historical data available either internally or externally, as firms or data providers started recording operational risk data relatively recently. This poses some challenges in measuring operational risk. It is standard practice that firms use internal data to estimate the frequency of losses and both internal and external data to estimate loss severity. External data providers include Operational Risk data eXchange Association, Fitch Risk, and so on. External data may be biased due to the size and nature of the firm where the event occurred. A scale bias may be caused by the possibility that larger firms would have larger biases. A truncation bias may be caused when the firms do not capture loss data below a certain threshold level. The correlation between probability of loss and size also matters. Therefore, external data needs to be scaled when used in the loss measurement models.

Loss Frequency Distribution

The probability of loss event, which has no time dimension, is translated into the loss frequency, which represents the number of loss events occurring during the risk horizon. Risk horizon refers to a fixed time period over which the events are to be observed and is usually set as one year for regulatory purposes. LDA models often use Poisson distribution, negative binomial distribution, or binomial distribution to model the frequency distribution.

In the Poisson distribution, the mean and standard deviation are equal, and therefore only three parameters are required to measure the probability of losses. The three parameters are mean or standard deviation lambda, time horizon T, and number of losses.

The probability of n losses = (e^(-lambda * T) * (Lambda * T) ^ n) / n!

Severity Distribution

While a little data may be sufficient to model the frequency distribution, modeling loss severity distribution requires a huge amount of data, and there is not adequate data available either internally or externally. This makes the modeling loss severity more challenging. Loss severity is usually modeled using lognormal distribution. High frequency risks can have severity distributions that are relatively lognormal, but low frequency risks can have distributions that are too skewed and leptokurtic to be well captured by the lognormal density functions.

Common density functions are gamma density, generalized hyperbolic, lognormal mixtures, and general mixture distributions.

Some external databases that are constructed from public, newsworthy events will have very few but extreme losses. There is an implicit high threshold for the losses included. In order to get values in the tail, analysts attempt to model the body and tail separately. Tails are typically modeled using generalized Pareto or other distributions in EVT class o distributions.

Operational Loss Distribution

Loss frequency distribution and loss severity distribution will be combined into a single distribution called *operational loss distribution* through a convolution process.

As with other types of risks, correlation among various components of operational risk may reduce the combined risk. Various correlations observed in operational loss distribution modeling are provided below:

- Correlations among loss events within the cell
- Correlations among severity samples within the cell
- Correlation among loss events between cells
- Correlation among severity samples between the cells
- Correlation between frequency distribution and the severity distribution

For various practical reasons, only the dependencies of frequency distribution are taken into account and are often measured using Gaussian copulas.

4.7.2 Hedging Operational Risk

As operational risk is mainly related to the way of doing business operations and external events, it is certainly difficult to find the specific source of operational risk. Moreover, operational risk measurement is a highly subjective process requiring certain judgments. Even if various operational risks are identified, aggregated risk may not be reliable, as the correlations among risks are merely assumptions. For these reasons, it is difficult to price the operational risk and hedge it away. Nonetheless, there are certain products available in the market that can be used to hedge operational risk depending on its nature. Some of the operational risk-hedging instruments are insurance, catastrophe options like underwriting derivatives and weather derivatives, and catastrophe bonds like indemnified notes, indexed notes, and parametric notes. Firms willing to hedge operational risk may have to depend on multiple products as there is no single product that can protect or insure against firm level operational risk.

Insurance companies write policies to cover different types of operational risks. One of the operational risk insurance companies is Fidelity Insurance, which protects the firm from employees committing fraudulent acts. Directors' and officers' insurance company covers legal expenses resulting from litigations concerning the fulfillment of directors' and officers' fiduciary duties. The Chicago Board of Trade (CBOT) trades catastrophe options, which have payoff linked to an index of underwriting losses written on a large pool of insurance policies. These options have deductibles and maximum limits and closely resemble collar or cover below and above certain limits. Weather derivatives are linked to an index that is based on weather conditions, such as average temperature, precipitation, and wind speed. Indemnified bonds offer relief to the debt issuer based on internal events, such as a large underwriting loss. Indexed note payoffs are based on established insurance loss indices. The most commonly used index is the one produced by Property Claims Services. Parametric notes are linked to the magnitude of an external risk event, such as hurricanes.

4.8 Integrated Risk Management

Integrated risk management is the identification and assessment of the collective risks and the implementation of a firm-wide strategy to manage those risks. While tactic risk management focuses on narrow goals and views each risk as isolated, integrated risk management is strategic in nature and focuses on long-term goals of the firm. The integrated risk management approach departs from the standard practice of viewing each risk in isolation and develops a strategy to respond to the full range of risks a firm faces, taking into account that a risk management policy designed solely to respond to an individual risk may have other, unintended consequences on the firm's other business operations. A simple example is that a manager who buys a credit default swap cannot think the default risk of the bond has been hedged away. The newly purchased device (CDS) is actually exposed to counterparty risk, and the counterparty risk is mainly connected to the systemic risk, which in turn gets impacted by market risk. Integrated risk management brings benefit from new insights about the interplay among different types of risk and traditional financial decision areas, connections easily missed without a comprehensive framework.

Firms manage risk in three different ways: modifying the firm's operations, adjusting its capital structure, and employing targeted financial instruments, such as derivatives. Integration refers both to the combination of these three risk management techniques and to the aggregation of all the risks faced by the firm. Because the three ways to manage risk are functionally equivalent in their effect on risk, their use connects seemingly unrelated managerial decisions. For instance, because capital structure is one component of a firm's risk management strategy, effective capital structure decisions cannot be made in isolation from the firm's other risk management decisions.

Integration refers to both the integration of the risks and the integration of ways to manage the risk. Integrated risk management evaluates the firm's total risk exposure, instead of a partial evaluation of each risk in isolation, because it is the total risk of the firm that typically matters to the assessment of the firm's value and of its ability to fulfill its contractual obligations in the future. Furthermore, by aggregating risks, some individual risks within the firm will partially or completely offset each other. Thus, in implementing hedging and insuring transactions to manage the risk of the firm, one need only address the net exposures instead of covering each risk separately. This netting can significantly reduce transaction costs. Considering the firm's total risk exposure from all sources, however, saves more than transaction costs. Such an analysis is essential in charting an effective risk management strategy. By focusing narrowly on one specific risk, the manager may create or exacerbate other types of risk for the company. Such interactions between risks are not always obvious, especially when they occur among unrelated businesses within the firm.

4.9 Stress Testing and Scenario Analysis

As we discussed earlier, VAR does not tell the worst case loss beyond a certain confidence level. It can only predict the maximum loss over a specified horizon at a given confidence level. A stress test can help to gauge the worst case loss. However, a stress test cannot be viewed as a substitute for value-at-risk; instead, it is used as a supplement to VAR. A scenario analysis involves estimating the loss from extreme movements. A combination of stress testing and scenario analysis provides intuitive feedback regarding the extreme loss that can occur to the portfolio. In other words, stress testing is useful to explain how VAR can change in various sorts of scenarios, such as extreme market moves, abnormal events, and distress conditions.

In abnormal markets, unrelated markets can become linked quickly, and correlation breakdown occurs. Hedging mechanisms will not work, and orderly execution will become difficult. Markets will experience sudden drops in liquidity.

The need for funds may result in selling liquid assets, leaving concentrated illiquid portfolios.

Over the last century, markets have seen various abnormalities. The following are various extreme market movements in the recent past:

- 1987 stock market crash: Dow Jones Industrial Average (DJIA) fell 23 percent in a single day and caused contagion effects.
- 1990 Nikkei crash: Nikkei fell 48 percent over the year.
- 1992 European currency crisis: The European Rate Mechanism (ERM) prescribed set of currency bands broke down.
- 1994: US federal funds short-term target rate was raised.
- 1997 Asian crisis: The Thai baht fell 16 percent on July 2, 1997, leading to contagion risk.
- 1998 Russian crisis: Russia defaulted on its internal government debt, and as a result, the Russian ruble fell 41 percent from August 25, 1998, to August 27, 1998, with a one-day fall of 29 percent on August 27, 1998.
- 1998 LTCM: Failure of Long Term Capital Management.
- 1999: Brazil crisis.
- 2001: Internet boom was burst.
- 2007–2008: Global financial crisis.

A stress test involves both qualitative and quantitative analysis, and firms perform stress testing based on the characteristics of the investments. Regardless of the nature of the investment, the following are the most common scenarios for stress testing:

- Historical event analysis: This involves simulating past events, such as the 1987 Dow Jones crash and calculating the worst loss that can occur to the present portfolio.
- Tuning historical events: Repeating the above case, but by updating the events for current conditions.
- Portfolio specific analysis: Identifying scenarios based on the portfolio and identifying the vulnerabilities and the worst case loss events specific to the portfolio.
- Extreme standard deviation analysis: Measuring the portfolio value for the extreme moves of standard deviation, such as deviating by -2,-3,-4, and-5.
- Parallel shifts in the yield curve: Calculating the interest-rate risk and portfolio impact of a 1 percent shift in the yield curve.

- Yield curve twists: Identifying the impact of changes in the shape of the yield curve.
- Price jumps: Evaluating the impact of price jumps in equities, commodities, and other asset classes, such as real estate, and their impact on the portfolio.
- Currency devaluations: Estimating the impact to the portfolio of currency devaluations and the effect on related markets and currencies.
- Liquidity: Testing what happens when market liquidity dries up so that hedging techniques no longer work.
- Contagion: Evaluating the portfolio impact of all positions and markets moving in the wrong direction.
- Modifying covariance matrix: As the correlation changes dramatically during abnormal markets, it is helpful to modify the correlations in covariance matrix and recalculate the portfolio risk. In this approach, first change the correlations of assets for which the underlying returns on any two factors change relative to each other and then find out how the correlations of other assets change with respect to the change. The correlation modification method involves both quantitative and qualitative judgments.
- Sensitivity analysis: Sensitivity analysis involves finding the uncertainty in the output of a model to different sources of uncertainty in the model input.
- Factor-push method: This method involves pushing each individual risk factor in the direction that results in a loss for the portfolio.
- Prospective scenarios: Based on subjective analysis and past experience, hypothetical and reasonable events that have not yet occurred should be predicted and applied to portfolio risk analysis.
- Extreme value theory: As discussed in the Extreme Value Theory section, the theory applies to extreme observations in a sample.

4.10 Other Risks

4.10.1 Beta Expansion Risk

Most hedge fund strategies are built based on convergence theory, anticipating that price movements of long and short positions cancel each other out. Some strategies calculate net exposure based on value, while other strategies are built based on net beta exposure. When there is change in beta of either long or short positions, then the manager readjusts the long or short positions to achieve the desired net beta exposure. The beta expansion risk is the risk that beta of long and short positions change unproportionately.

When many managers short sell the stock at the same time, then there will be an added downward pressure on that stock that will make the stock price more volatile. The increased standard deviation increases the covariance with the stock market. This will cause the beta to be expanded more than the manager anticipates. The increased beta of a short position will require more positions to be added on the long side in order to achieve the previously desired net beta exposure. The other source of beta expansion is that there will be increased demand for hedging when the markets start declining. In order to protect from downside risk, managers who have not yet hedged the portfolio will start selling the stock short, which will result in downward pressure. This will reduce their anticipated profits. In other words, risk management will become expensive during market declines.

Beta expansion risk is more common in small capacity strategies, such as convertible arbitrage strategies. In a convertible arbitrage strategy, managers purchase convertible bonds or preferred stocks and then short the same company's or a similar company's stock. As more and more managers implement the same strategy on the same company's convertible bonds or preferred stocks, there will be more shorting of the stock. This will add downward pressure on the stock, and the beta of the stock will expand.

4.10.2 Short Volatility Risk

Short volatility risk is quite common in insurance strategies where the returns are consistent in terms of premium. However, the sale of insurance contracts is a short volatility investment strategy that can result in occasional large losses. Short volatility risk appears in any traditional or nontraditional strategies that closely resemble insurance strategies. For example, an option seller receives up front premium when he writes either a put option or a call option. If the option expires, then the profit will be the premium that was received up front. However, if the market moves in an unfavorable direction, then the losses can be large. If the price of the underlying asset on which the put (call) option was sold goes down (up), then the option seller has to bear the losses. Since the exposure is synthetic and off-balance sheet, the transparency of the position is not apparent. The strategy makes the manager attractive in nonvolatile markets but brings huge losses if occur. In other words, the received premium shows short term profits but the volatility increases the chances of option execution demanding the option writer to purchase the underlying securities at unfavorable prices and deliver to the option buyer. Unfortunately, short volatility strategies are exposed to negative events only; they are not exposed to positive events. And therefore the upside potential is either limited or zero. Short volatility risk is quite common in fixed-income investments as well. The returns are consistent with limited or no upside potential. If the issuer defaults, then the investor loses the money that is equivalent to par value minus recovery value. Experts describe relative-value hedge fund strategies and event-driven hedge fund strategies as selling economic disaster insurance.

Short volatility risk has been practically demonstrated below using the merger arbitrage strategy. Consider the merger announcement that company ABC will merge with company XYZ in a one-for-one stock swap. After the announcement, company ABC's stock price is $10, and company XYZ's stock price is $8. The merger spread is $2.This is the premium that the hedge fund manager expects to earn. The hedge fund manager will short company ABC's stock at $10 and buy company XYZ's stock at $8.At the closing of the deal, the stock prices of the two companies must converge. Convergence occurs either from the drop of company ABC's stock, making money on its short position, or the rise of company XYZ's stock, making money on its long position. Alternatively, the merged company may end up with a stock price between $8 and $10, and the hedge fund manager will make money on both its short position and its long position. However, the maximum profit the merger arbitrage manager can earn is the merger spread of $2.Merger arbitrage managers take a bet that the merger will be completed. They analyze antitrust regulations, consider whether the bid by the acquiring company is hostile or friendly, and check on potential shareholder opposition to the merger. If the merger is completed, the merger arbitrage manager will earn the spread that it previously locked in through its long and short stock positions. However, if the merger falls through, the merger arbitrage manager may incur a considerable loss that cannot be known in advance. From this perspective, merger arbitrage hedge funds can be viewed as merger insurance agents. They insure against the risk of loss should the merger deal collapse. By buying the stock of the target company and selling the stock of the acquiring company from investors who do not have as much confidence in the merger deal, merger arbitrage hedge funds accept/insure against the risk of the deal collapsing. If the merger is successfully completed, the merger arbitrage manager will collect a known premium. However, if the merger fails to be completed, the merger arbitrage manager is on the hook for the loss, instead of the shareholders from whom he purchased or sold shares to. In essence, shareholders of the two companies can "put" their losses back to the merger arbitrage manager if the deal falls through.

Similarly, the risk of senior tranches in a CDO can be compared with short volatility risk. The returns are consistent in the form of the coupon and have no upside potential. However, if the correlations among the pool assets increase and the losses exceed the junior tranches, then the investor in senior tranches faces large losses. Therefore, the buying of a senior tranche resembles an insurance contract in systemic economic risk. Many hedge fund strategies use a short volatility strategy to enhance their returns. However, as explained earlier, the key issue is that short volatility strategies are often synthetic, off-balance sheet, and not apparent from position transparency. This will result in a reasonable return as long as the insurance premiums continue to be collected. However, when a volatility event occurs, the results can be disastrous. Investors, in effect, "put" their losses to the hedge fund manager, resulting in large declines in value. This exposure can be hedged by buying put options on the VIX index equivalent to the short volatility exposure embedded in strategies. This is an active strategy that requires the rolling of put options to maintain a continuous hedge against the strategies. In addition, the amount of put options to purchase will change as the delta of the short put option changes. This requires a form of dynamic hedging known as *portfolio insurance*. As explained in the section on beta expansion risk, chasing deltas as the market declines rapidly can lead to a downward spiral of stock prices from which it is difficult to recover. Therefore, the alternative hedge against short volatility risk is to diversify the portfolio by including funds that tend to be long volatility. Prior empirical studies have indicated that managed futures, or commodity trading advisors, have investment strategies that tend to be long volatility.

4.10.3 Basis Risk

Basis risk typically arises from hedging inaccuracy and appears in multiple forms. Basis risk is also called *spread risk*. Basis risk is the market risk related to differences in the market performance of two similar positions. The effectiveness of hedging depends on the level of correlation between two assets. The more the instrument to be hedged and the underlying used are imperfect substitutes, the bigger the basis risk is. The basis risk may result in reduced profits during favorable markets and fail from unfavorable market conditions. Therefore, the basis can also be defined as the risk that remains after the hedging mechanism has been established. For example, a portfolio manager who wants to temporarily eliminate the market exposure of a diversified stock portfolio might short S&P 500 futures. If the composition of the portfolio does not exactly mirror the S&P 500, the hedge will not be perfect, and the portfolio manager will be taking basis risk. This hedge might result in losses in either direction of the market. As another example, a foreign exchange trader who is hedging a long spot position with a short forward position is taking basis risk. While the spot position is sensitive only to changes in the exchange rate, the forward position is also affected by yield curve shifts. Accordingly, the two positions do not perfectly hedge one another, and the trader is taking basis risk.

Any major risks, such as market or credit risk, can have implicitly embedded basis risk. For example, the market risk of corporate bonds can be described as comprising treasury yield curve risk as well as the spread risk between treasury yields and corporate yields.

The higher the correlation between two positions, the higher the effect of hedging.

If asset 1 is hedged with asset 2 and sigma 1, sigma2 are the volatilities of the two positions, then the volatility of the resulting portfolio is:

(Sigma P)^ 2 = sigma 1 ^ 2 + sigma 2 ^ 2 – 2 * sigma 1 * sigma 2 * rho

Where rho is the correlation between two assets.

When rho tends to perfect correlation, that is, 1, then sigma 2 will tend to sigma 1, and sigma P will tend to zero.

Therefore, the basis risk can be defined as the volatility of the basis over time and is usually represented as the variance of the basis. With a perfect hedge, the loss on a hedged position will be perfectly offset by the gain on the hedging position. The most common sources for basis risk are described below:

Interruption in the Convergence of Two Positions

Normally, long and short positions will converge as the time-to-maturity decreases. For example, a manager may have a long position in off-the-run bonds and short positions in on-the-run bonds and expects both the prices to converge to the same at maturity. An economic shock might result in sudden increase in the spreads and a flight to quality and can cause both on-the run and off-the run bonds to decrease in value.

Maturity Mismatch

Risk of bonds varies based on the maturity of the bonds. For example, with all other things equal, a seven-year bond may be more risky than a three-year bond. Therefore, hedging the seven-year bond will result in basis risk.

Liquidity Mismatch

Illiquid assets will have wider bid-ask spreads, especially in troubled markets. An asset that was hedged with an illiquid asset may often see greater swings in spreads. The higher the liquidity of the hedged asset, the higher the basis risk.

Sensitivity to Other Risks

A bond with the same credit rating may have different risk exposures. For example, an AAA corporate bond may be more exposed to corporate-related risk or idiosyncratic risk, and an AAA mortgage bond may be more exposed to the general economy or systemic risk. Hedging a corporate bond with a mortgage bond may not work, especially when the economy deteriorates.

Convexity Effect

Convexity refers to the rate of change of delta. If a delta-neutral hedge is established, then the rise in delta of one position should be offset by the fall in delta of the other position. However, if one of the bonds exhibits negative at some point in time, then the changes in deltas may not offset each other. Falling interest rates result in higher prepayments and make mortgage bonds exhibit negative convexity at lower interest rates. Therefore, hedging a corporate bond with a mortgage bond will result in basis risk.

4.10.4 Contagion Risk

Contagion risk is defined as the risk that financial difficulties at one or more bank(s) spill over to a large number of other banks or the financial system as a whole. Contagion risk is also called *systemic risk*. Prior to the Asian and Mexican crises, structural adjustment problems in one country remained within its borders. The Asian crisis of 1997 was originally started with devaluation of Thai currency and spread to other countries at a surprising speed, causing contagion. After the Asian crisis episode, the literature on systemic risk and contagion grew at a rapid pace as researchers and analysts scrambled to explain the nature of the events that led to the massive system breakdown. There are mainly two issues that intensify contagion. They are interconnectedness and runs on banks.

Interconnections between banks speed up the transmission of losses from affected banks to many other banks. Suppose bank A loaned funds to bank B and is now facing a problem with a downgraded credit rating. In order to meet the required capital reserves, bank A either has to sell its assets, probably at discount, or force the other bank to repay the borrowed funds. In the latter case, bank B may need to sell assets, which may result in losses. Though bank B is not facing a credit problem, it was forced to sell assets and see the losses. The resulting loss may result in a downgrade of credit rating. The interconnectedness among more banks will intensify the problem even more.

The illiquidity of investments provides the rationale for the existence of banks and for their vulnerability to runs. Excessive withdrawals of deposits would force a bank into costly liquidation. Hence, if a depositor expects that others will withdraw, he will also withdraw to avoid losses from such liquidation. This is called a *run on the bank*. Contagion can be either pure or noisy. Pure contagion occurs when negative information, such as fraud or losses on specific risky investments, about one bank adversely affects all other banks, including those that have nothing in common with the first bank. Noisy or firm-specific contagion arises when the failure of one bank reveals a bad signal regarding other banks with common characteristics. If one bank fails, then other banks with a similar asset and liability structure may also face a run. In a world with imperfect information, runs on other banks can be triggered by perceived, not necessarily actual, similarities with the failing bank.

There are numerous potential channels for contagion from one country to the other. Notably, external linkages could stem from direct and indirect equity exposures of local banks in overseas banks or, conversely, share holdings of local banks by foreign banks; direct exposures through loan books; deposit and funding sources from overseas or from foreign banks; payments and settlement systems; and holdings of credit risk transfer instruments written on assets held by local or overseas institutions.

Contagion risk is more pronounced in the banking and investment sector than any other sector. However, contagion risk resulting from the banking and investment sector may have an impact on other sectors due to their systemic exposure. Contagion risk can better be analyzed using the extreme value theory (EVT) framework. The EVT approach to contagion better captures the information that large, extreme shocks are transmitted across financial systems differently than small shocks. Multivariate EVT techniques are used to quantify the joint behavior of external realizations of financial prices or returns across different markets.

4.10.5 Transparency Risk

In the world of competition, hedge fund managers think that revealing more information about the fund may impair them from competition. They also claim that the information may not be simple enough to interpret and is of less use to investors. On the other hand, investors want to make sure that their money is safe and earns enough risk premiums. As the investment world is becoming complex with many influencing parameters, investors demand information beyond the positions. Information that the investors typically expect are portfolio positioning (both long and short), usage of derivatives, operational reports, asset pricing valuation models, stress test analysis, portfolio volatilities, correlations, counterparty exposures, and other portfolio characteristics. Investors are mainly concerned with how the manager is achieving expected goals. For example, a fund manager who claims that he implements a long/short equity strategy may in fact be utilizing long and short options. While the risk is limited to the premium paid for long options, the risk of short options can occasionally be large due to the exposure to short volatility. Investors expect to know what percentage of the fund invests in derivatives. Investors may want to monitor the style drift. And investors may want to know the exposure to major events.

Due to the complexity of the hedge fund industry and its strategies, it is not clear that large volumes of fund data necessarily benefit investors. Individual investors may not possess the staff and expertise to digest, analyze, and comprehend vast new aggregations of investment information. Investors may not want to assume the complex and expensive challenge of sorting through the databases of multiple hedge funds. Many institutional investors consider this job to be precisely what they are paying for when they hire hedge fund managers.

Since the global financial crisis, regulatory authorities have come up with many rules and regulations dealing with hedge fund reporting. Implementation of the Dodd-Frank Wall Street Reform and Consumer Protection Act will force the largest hedge funds, which pose the most risk to the system, to register with the SEC and make active compliance an important element in the growth and sophistication of the overall private fund industry. Hedge funds and other private funds complying with Dodd-Frank must actively assess their operations, identify potential risks and conflicts, and tailor their own procedures to the new regulatory requirements.

Dodd-Frank addresses the following regarding reporting and administration:

- The accuracy of disclosures made to investors and regulators, including account statements and advertisements
- Safeguarding investor assets from inappropriate use by advisory personnel
- The accurate creation of required records and their maintenance in a manner that secures them from unauthorized alteration or use and protects them from untimely destruction
- Marketing advisory services, including the use of solicitors
- Safeguards for the privacy protection of client records and information; and
- Business continuity plans

4.10.6 Correlation Risk

Correlation risk refers to the risk of a loss when correlations in the market change. It plays a central role in risk management and the pricing of a single, paired, or portfolio of assets. Under stressed market conditions, correlation breakdown and divergence occur. Two uncorrelated asset classes may become correlated, and two oppositely correlated asset classes may tend to move in the same direction. This is partly because more investors become risk averse during stressed markets and may even prefer to forgo profit opportunities. For example, historically, commodities are negatively correlated with stocks and bonds or positively correlated with inflation. This was true even during the first half of 2008: when bonds were falling off, commodities were rising. However, with the collapse of Lehman Brothers, more investors, including commodity investors, moved to risk-free assets, such as treasuries. Since the market was facing a lack of investor base, commodity prices started falling off in correlation with bonds and stocks. This was mainly due to the fact that the same class of investors started investing in multiple and heterogeneous asset classes. For example, institutional investors now invest in both capital markets and commodity markets. When the investor faces losses in capital markets, he may be forced to sell even profitable and uncorrelated asset classes, such as commodities, in order to meet margin calls on capital markets. This will result in the breakdown of traditional relationships, and negative correlation will become positive correlation.

The important component of fluctuations in correlations is linked to liquidity risk. Market liquidity risk, funding liquidity risk, and correlation risk are all interrelated in a nonlinear fashion to the same underlying asset return uncertainty. These relationships between different dimensions of liquidity risk, and the seemingly unrelated correlation and asset return risks, have important implications on hedging strategies. Correlations work as expected, at least to some extent, in a normal market. This is because more lenders are ready to lend money and more investors are ready to borrow and participate in the market. In stressed markets, fewer lenders will be ready to lend money. Moreover, lenders try to withdraw loans. As a result, investors sell both performing and nonperforming assets. This will result in reduced market participation and increase the correlations among the asset prices. Therefore, the correlation risk is directly proportional to liquidity and is procyclical.

Correlation risk was one of the biggest risks that CDO investments have faced during the financial crisis. One of the determinant factors of credit quality of the tranches is the estimation of correlation of defaults in the asset pool. Lower default correlations will result in higher quality for senior tranches. At the beginning of and during the financial crisis of 2008, the default correlations increased dramatically above what was estimated. Some of the reasons for increased default correlations were common vintage year and credit quality characteristics of the underlying assets in the pool. The increased correlations resulted in large losses even to the senior tranches.

4.10.7 Headline Risk

Headline risk is loss to a portfolio due to a major event or story that spreads throughout various media publications. Even though the news may not be related to portfolio positions, it will show negative impact on the overall market. This risk is more pronounced especially in highly liquid assets or exchange-traded securities. Since the transactions are less frequent in illiquid assets, the news may have been digested before selling the illiquid assets and may not impact the prices.

4.10.8 Wrong-Way Risk

Wrong-way risk occurs when exposure to a counterparty is adversely correlated with the credit quality of that counterparty. Wrong-way risk, as an additional source of risk, is rightly of concern to banks and regulators. For example, party A may purchase a credit default swap from party B for the bond it owns. Let us say the bond was issued by party C. Now party C defaults, and party A wants to claim insurance from party B. If party B also defaults at the same time party C defaults, then party A will not be able to recover the par value. This is called *wrong-way risk*. Wrong-way risk increases with the correlation between the bond obliged and the protection seller.

The companion of wrong-way risk is right-way risk. Right-way risk is the risk that the counterparty defaults whereas the obligor does not. Right-way risk is less severe than wrong-way risk, as there are no pending claims from the counterparty. However, there is a risk that purchasing insurance from a new party may be subject to new terms and will depend on current market factors, such as interest rates and credit spreads.

4.10.9 Model Risk

Any model is only as good as the input. A model does not generate all the required input on its own. For example, the Black-Scholes options valuation model asks a user for an estimate of future volatility, and then translates that estimate into a fair option value. If the estimated volatility is not correct, the estimated option value may not be fair in reality. In other words, a model may be correct, but data like rates, volatilities, correlations, and spreads may be badly estimated.

An insufficient number of factors makes the model imperfect. For example, a one-factor model of interest rates may be reasonable for valuing treasury bonds, but much less reasonable for valuing options on the slope of the yield curve.

A model that was developed for one type of variable will not work for other variables. For example, assumption of a normal distribution of prices automatically makes the implicit assumption of returns to be lognormally distributed. A model developed on the assumption that bond prices are normally distributed for the sake of analytic simplicity, will not work for yield analysis, as the bond yields are more likely to be lognormal. Transforming the variable, for example, using exponents of yields in this case, may not work perfectly all the time. They may be approximate for the short term, but will be erroneous if used for long-term bonds.

A missing correlation factor, for example, ignoring the correlation between corporate credit spreads and corporate stock prices in valuing convertible bonds, leads to incorrect pricing.

The model developed may be inappropriate under current market conditions, or some of its assumptions may have become invalid. For example, interest rate volatility is relatively unimportant in currency option pricing at low interest rate volatilities, but may become critical during exchange rate crises.

Unexpected trading costs can make the model imperfect.

Market panic or sentiment can make the "theoretically correct model" imperfect, at least for a short time during the life of the model.

Programming mistakes can lead to widespread and hard-to-detect errors. Errors include, but are not limited to, logic, rounding, and miscounting the days between dates or the coupons to maturity. In addition, there are occasional hardware flaws, such as the widely publicized Pentium floating point error.

Controlling Model Risk

Model risk cannot be hedged. There is no single factor to which model risk can be mapped. There is no magic strategy for avoiding model risk. Developing sound risk management principles across the board and following general guidelines based on experience can *reduce* model risk, however.

A closer working relationship among model users, modelers, and model developers will reduce some of the potential errors. Model users are traders, salespeople, or capital markets personnel who may be physically and organizationally separated from the model creators. Furthermore, the model implementers are programmers, who are often similarly separated from the model theorists. To avoid risk, it's important to have modelers, programmers, and users who all work closely together, understand each other's domains well enough to know what constitutes a warning symptom, and have a good strategy for testing a model and its limits.

Highly complex models tend to model the noise rather than the information. They may sometimes mistakenly identify patterns. However, the simpler models tend to discard important information. Therefore, the model should be optimal to discard noise while detecting as much information as possible.

Test the model against simple and known solutions. Small disagreements often serve as warnings of potentially large disagreements and errors under other scenarios. Therefore, small discrepancies noticed by users or programmers cannot be ignored. Reevaluate models frequently to ensure the fitness of the model to current market conditions. Ensure the quality of data obtained from third-party vendors.

5. Hedge Funds

5.1 Long/Short Equity

5.1.1 Strategy

Long/Short equity hedge fund managers construct a portfolio whose returns are not intended to correlate with market performance; instead, they apply art and science to find undervalued and overvalued stocks. They buy the undervalued stocks and sell the overvalued stocks. The fund benefits from increased value of long positions and decreased value of short positions. Traditional investment funds, such as mutual funds, also employ a long/short strategy, but they typically have a constraint of 130:30 ratio of long and short, and therefore they are called *130/30 funds*. A 130/30 fund has a gross exposure of 160 percent but a net exposure of 100 percent, meaning they are effectively equivalent to 100 percent long.

Long/Short equity hedge funds do not have any constraints on net exposure, and so the long/short ratio can be anything, but typically they end up with a net long exposure. The advantage of the long/short equity strategy is that it provides greater gross exposure with a lesser exposure to systemic risk. Since the beta of the long/short equity portfolio is the weighted average of the individual betas and since short positions have negative beta, the net beta will be less.

Short positions generate profit as well as providing downside protection to the portfolio. Short positions also provide greater leverage. For example, if the portfolio is constructed with 80K of long and 40K of short, then, since the net exposure is 40K, the portfolio manager was able to establish 120K(gross) worth of positions using 40K.In this example, for simplicity, it has been assumed that the prime broker does not require any margin to be posted for the short position. In reality, fund managers may be required to deposit a portion of the funds received for the short position with the prime broker.

Long/Short equity hedge fund managers may also use derivatives for both long and short positions and are typically concentrated.

Typically, the payoff of the long/short strategy resembles a call option. The return profile of the long/short equity strategy has been shown in the diagram below. The long position usually outperforms in a bull market, and short positions generally outperform in bear markets, thus providing downside protection to the overall portfolio.

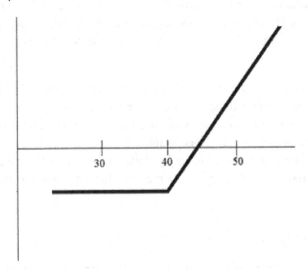

Typical payoff diagram of a long/short strategy

Since long/short equity funds normally tend to have long bias, they are exposed to market risk, or systemic risk. Therefore, returns are partially attributed to market risk premium, or beta return. Historical performance of long/short equity funds demonstrates significant excess returns, or alpha returns. Major sources of alpha are market inefficiencies, idiosyncratic risk (firm-specific risk), short selling, and use of leverage and derivatives.

The Capital Asset Pricing Model (CAPM) assumes that markets are efficient and states that idiosyncratic risk is not rewarded by excess returns. In reality, market inefficiencies do exist. Long/Short equity managers exploit market inefficiency using manager skills like stock-selection skills and trading talents. Various stock selection approaches engaged in by long/short equity managers are described in the following section. Long/Short managers earn excess returns from the risk factors not covered by CAPM, such as firm-specific risk, small-cap risk, liquidity risk, and event risk, such as merger announcements, possible bankruptcy protection filing, and so on. The other factors that commonly influence returns are long positions in high book-to-market stocks and short positions in low book-to-market stocks, long positions in small-cap stocks and short positions in large-cap stocks, and long positions in past outperforming stocks and short positions in past underperforming stocks.

Many institutional investors are not qualified for short selling due to internal or external compliance restrictions, and therefore they are not able to utilize the profit opportunities that arise from short selling. Since hedge fund managers do not have such constraints, they earn excess returns from short selling the stocks that are not performing well or are overvalued or have potential for bankruptcy.

Long/Short equity fund managers follow a variety of approaches to find stocks suitable to build the portfolio. Some of the most common approaches are the bottom-up approach, top-down approach, value approach, growth approach, large-cap/small-cap, sector concentration, trend and countertrend, activist approach, black-box trading, and equity market timing. Long/Short equity fund managers may also combine two or more of these approaches in portfolio construction.

Bottom-Up Approach

This is the most common approach employed by many long/short equity fund managers. They engage their researchers to perform ground-level research on companies that have limited analyst coverage to analyze company-specific information that is not yet known to the public. Company-specific information includes product offerings, intellectual rights, competitive advantage, regulatory compliance, slots in major retail stores, traffic to retails, and so on. They do not concentrate on macroeconomic trends and relative performance. In summary, they focus on strengths, weaknesses, opportunities, and threats, which is called the *SWOT framework*. Long/Short equity fund managers following this approach typically build concentrated portfolios.

Top-Down Approach

In contrast to the bottom-up approach, the top-down approach focuses on macroeconomic metrics, such as business cycle, monetary and fiscal policy, purchasing power, consumer confidence, and inflation forecast. Fund managers have a clear understanding of the interdependencies of macroeconomic factors and their impact on sector returns. They pay little attention to firm-specific analysis. Long/Short equity fund managers following this approach may also invest in sector ETFs and build diversified portfolios.

Value Approach

In the value approach, hedge fund managers use both fundamental and technical analysis. They conduct fundamental analysis of book-to-market, P/E ratios, dividend yield, and earnings growth by often sitting with the firm's management and comparing with competitors to look for undervalued firms. Managers usually pick firms that are temporarily unfavorable and use technical analysis, such as volatility of stock, to determine when to open the position.

Growth Approach

In the growth approach, managers look at past and current behavior of the stock and analyses to see if there is a potential for growth. To forecast potential growth, managers often look for the most recent sales and forecasted sales. Managers prefer small-cap companies, as they usually offer higher potential for growth than matured companies.

Large-Cap/Small-Cap

Small-cap companies typically have less analyst coverage and are less liquid in nature. However, they will have higher growth potential. Hedge fund managers gather private information. Large-cap companies typically have higher trading volume and analyst coverage, and so much of the company-specific information is known to the public. Long/Short equity fund managers using this approach usually go long in small-cap and go short in long-cap.

Sector Concentration

Long/Short equity fund managers following this approach utilize domain experts or research analysts who have been following sectors, such as oil, bio-tech, healthcare, alternative energies, real estate, and so on. Portfolios are constructed by going long in strong performers and going short in weak performers.

Trend and Countertrend

Managers that follow the trend and countertrend approach typically wait for market momentum to be established and invest in individual stocks or sectors when the trend is detected and reverse the position before the trend reverses. Mangers following this approach believe in mean reversion, thus thinking that excess market value will be eventually wiped out, thus establishing the countertrend.

Activist Approach

Managers following the activist approach find companies with poor management and will deal directly or indirectly with the board of directors to engage in corporate governance. They involve themselves with company activities and will make recommendations to improve operating performance and dividend payout, thus increasing the shareholders' wealth.

Black-Box Trading

The black-box approach, also known as the quantitative approach, uses computer-automated tools to find undervalued and overvalued stocks. Managers typically use screeners to filter out certain groups of stocks based on predefined criteria and establish a weights scheme to short list the stocks. Managers may also use stratification in order to gain diversification.

Equity Market Timing

Equity market timing strategy managers look for various buy and sell signals in the market to enter or exit the positions. Some of the common signals employed by equity market timing funds are provided below:

- A buy signal is generated when the price is above the moving average.
- A buy signal is generated when a short-term moving average crosses above a long-term average.
- A buy signal is generated when a group of moving averages are all increasing.
- A sell signal is generated when the price is below the moving average.
- A sell signal is generated when a short-term moving average crosses below a long-term average.
- A sell signal is generated when a group of moving averages are all decreasing.
- A buy signal is generated when RSI crosses below 30.
- A sell signal is generated when RSI crosses above 70.

- When the price difference between two securities (Price of A – Price of B) crosses below 30, then buy security A and sell security B.
- When the price difference between two securities (Price of A – Price of B) crosses above 70, then sell security A and buy security B.
- A channel breakout strategy generates a buy (sell) signal when the price crosses above (below) the previous high (low) in a specific look-back period.

Some equity market timing managers employ the strategy across different time zones of the globe. If managers expect that the price will go up the next day, then they may buy the stock in their counterpart funds in Japan and then sell at market open in the United States. Risks involved in this strategy are trend reversals, wrong signals, failure of trade execution in time, and so on.

5.1.2 Risk Characteristics

The long/short equity fund is exposed commonly to the following risk factors: systemic risk, concentration risk, firm-specific risk, liquidity risk, event risk, and short-squeeze risk. A manager's skill and the firm's capabilities of managing these risks efficiently and tactically yield a higher alpha.

Systemic Risk: Though the long/short equity strategy is not intended to build a portfolio that is correlated with market performance, the net-long exposure causes the long/short fund to be exposed to systemic risk, or beta risk. To some extent, the short position of the fund acts as a long put option and provides downside protection during market declines.

Concentration and Firm-Specific Risk: Long/Short fund managers that usually follow bottom-up, sector concentration, or activist approaches for stock picking contain concentrated positions. These funds are exposed to concentration and firm-specific risks.

Liquidity Risk: Small-cap stocks exhibit market inefficiencies and are not traded actively, and so they are exposed to liquidity risk. So the long/short funds that follow either the growth approach or the small-cap/large-cap approach are usually exposed to liquidity risk.

Event Risk: Funds that invest in activist or concentrated strategies are exposed to event risk, such as merger announcements, management changes, or announcements like negative outlook. If the long/short fund has been built such that the stocks that are exposed to these event risks are shorted, then the fund will outperform in adverse conditions.

Short-Squeeze Risk: Since prime brokers lend stocks to long/short fund managers to open short positions, they have the right to revert the position if the short stock price is móving up. This may end up in closing the positions at unfavorable prices.

5.1.3 Risk-Return Distribution

CAPM assumes that returns are normally distributed, which is symmetrical in shape with zero skew and zero excess kurtosis. However, in reality, even S&P 500 returns do not follow the normal distribution, but may exhibit a distribution that is closer to normal. Historical performance says that the S&P 500 exhibits some negative skew value and a positive kurtosis value. According to Hedgefund.net statistics, their long/short equity index distribution exhibits a skew value of -0.03, which is very close to zero, and a positive kurtosis value of 1.95. As explained in chapter 1, the main goal of a hedge fund manager is to shift negative skew to either zero or positive. The close-to-zero skew of Hedgefund.net's long/short index shows that long/short equity fund managers demonstrate skill-based investing. The ability to short stocks at the appropriate time reduces negative outlier events and also acts as a long put, providing downside protection to the portfolio. Part of the credit of shifting the negative skew to close to zero goes to the strategic short position. Hedge fund managers create short positions not only to reduce systemic risk but also to generate profit, expecting that their value will go down. So the returns are attributed to two alphas, one from the long position and the other from the short position. This is called *double alpha*. This explains the why the long/short equity index has a higher excess kurtosis than the S&P 500 index.

The long/short index has a standard deviation of much less than that of the S&P 500, while yielding returns higher than the S&P 500. This gives a higher Sharpe ratio, or risk-adjusted returns. According to the Hedgefund.net database, the long/short equity index exhibits an annualized Sharpe ratio of 1.29, using the risk-free rate of 3.5 percent. The table below shows annual returns of hedge fund industry aggregated index and Long/Short index.

Year	Hedge Fund Industry Aggregated Index	Long/Shorty Equity Index
1991	28.76%	N/A
1992	16.92%	N/A
1993	29.93%	28.88%
1994	7.32%	4.20%
1995	28.10%	32.38%
1996	25.33%	28.15%
1997	23.25%	24.29%
1998	11.48%	15.61%
1999	36.22%	52.12%
2000	13.11%	16.86%
2001	9.04%	7.31%
2002	4.38%	-1.03%
2003	21.30%	24.86%
2004	10.78%	11.48%
2005	10.94%	12.24%
2006	13.74%	14.55%
2007	12.62%	12.83%
2008	-14.37%	-19.04%
2009	21.41%	24.67%
2010	10.48%	10.31%

Annual returns of long/short index (Data source: Hedgefund.net)

The technology boom and a general booming economy made the year 1999 the best-performing year for the long/short strategy. The recession in 2001 and 2002 lowered the returns, but the short-sale part of the strategy protected the funds from further downside. The severe global financial crisis made the year 2008 the worst-performing year for the long/short equity strategy. The short-sale halt by the SEC further intensified the losses as fund managers were unable to provide downside protection due to a temporary ban of short selling.

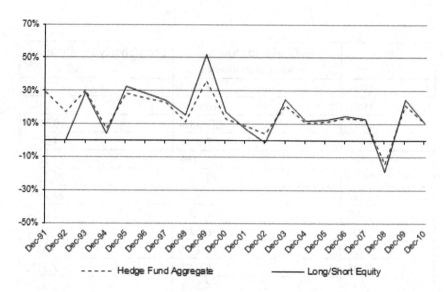

Annual returns of long/short index (Data source: Hedgefund.net)

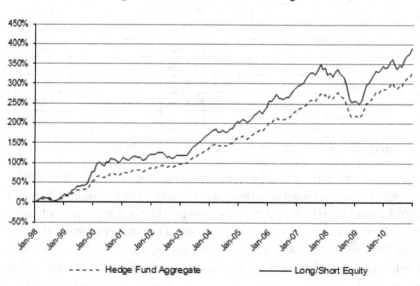

Cumulative returns of long/short strategy index (Data source: Hedgefund.net)

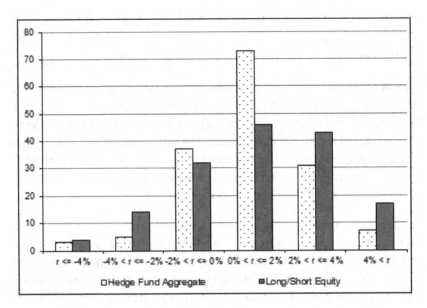

Distribution of returns of long/short index (Data source: Hedgefund.net)

5.1.4 Due Diligence

The following Due Diligence helps investors in choosing the suitable Long/Short Equity fund.

Substrategies: Various substrategies of long/short equity have been described in an earlier section. Investors should document if the fund managers follow one substrategy or multiple substrategies. If they follow multiple substrategies, are they being used simultaneously or switched from time to time? Investors should also know what the investment universe is. Does the fund invest in emerging-country stocks? If so, does the manager implement currency hedging, or is the manager anticipating profit from currency fluctuation?

Portfolio Construction: Investors should document if the manager builds the portfolio, implements the hedging, and then calculates the residual risk at the aggregated level. *Residual risk* is the risk that remains after the hedging has been implemented. Some fund managers take the industry sector as one unit and implement the hedging. Investors should also know if there is one short position for each long position.

Shorting Ability: In some cases, the ability to short depends on the long-term relationship with the broker and the good standing of the fund manager. Being unable to open short positions in time or getting pressure from the prime lender to close the position sooner than expected will have negative effects on the portfolio. Investors should assess the shorting ability of the fund manager.

Type of Shorting: Some fund managers short sell stocks that are not borrowed. This type of shorting is called *naked shorting*. Some fund managers short stocks by borrowing them from prime brokers. Such a shorting is called *covered shorting*. Naked shorting is dangerous to the fund, whereas covered shorting provides additional monitoring by prime brokers who revert the position when deemed necessary or if the fund manager is not responding. Investors should document the type of shorting the manager uses.

Range of Exposures: Long/Short equity managers have flexibility in maintaining net market exposure. However, the managers typically have net-long exposure and set upper and lower limits for net exposure. Investors should know what the limits are. Higher limits indicate higher market risk, and they should expect a higher premium. Investors should also document gross exposure limits.

Liquidity: While the long/short equity managers have flexibility in determining net exposure, an inability to maintain the desired level of exposure can lead to losses or reduced profits. If the manager cannot open or close long positions proportionate to short positions or vice versa, the manager may be tending toward a pure long or short portfolio. Investors should seek to know the liquidity capacity of the positions held.

Nonlisted Stocks: Investors should know if the fund invests in any regulated D stocks and pre-IPO stocks. If so, the investor should know if the manager has the relevant knowledge in dealing with private stocks.

Use of Derivatives: Use of derivatives provides implicit leverage and reduces explicit leverage. However, long options introduce counterparty risk, as most derivatives are OTC derivatives, and short options introduce short volatility risk. Investors should document how the derivatives are used and how they contribute to the portfolio.

Investment Restrictions: Investors should know if the fund manager sits on the board of any companies. If so, the fund manager may be restricted from trading the stocks of that company for a certain period. If the manager sits on a large number of boards, then he has to forgo certain trading opportunities.

Stop-Loss Rules: Investors should document stop-loss rules implemented by the strategy. Stop-loss rules provide both advantages and disadvantages.

Therefore, investors should carefully analyze them. In certain cases markets over react to any negative news. In such a situation the value of security may come down heavily and may instantly recover. If the stop loss rule is set then the security will be sold when the price hits below certain level and by the time the investor wants to repurchase it the price may have been recovered losing an opportunity.

Compliance with SEC: Form 13F filings reveal the positions of securities owned by the fund manager. Investors should know if the fund managers are filing them quarterly and should analyze them to know the positions owned. It may be the case that the positions opened and closed during a quarter will not appear in the Form 13F; however, not filing the Form 13F at all is a red signal for the investor. That is exactly what happened in the case of Madoff. Madoff claimed that he used to close the positions before the end of the quarter. However, investors should have gotten concerned about this pattern.

5.2 Short Selling

5.2.1 Strategy

While most hedge fund strategies employ short positions, this particular strategy depends purely on short sale and does not have any long positions. The short positions are established by borrowing the stocks from a third party, typically from a prime broker, and selling them in the market. It is required to deposit part of the funds received from a short sale with the security lender. The remaining funds are invested at the risk-free rate, which earns a short rebate. The fund manager is required to return any dividends received to the security lender. Some prime brokers demand that all cash received from a short sale be deposited with them. Some prime brokers even require the fund manager to pledge 30 percent to 50 percent of the market value of the stock to be deposited on top of any cash received from a short sale. In any case, little capital is enough to establish short positions. Some fund managers, though rare, short sell securities that are not borrowed. This is called a *naked short sale*. Some managers use derivatives, such as forwards, futures, and options, to execute the short selling strategy. Some managers will have little long exposure while maintaining net-short exposure. Managers unwind the positions by purchasing the stocks when the stock price goes down and returning the stock to the lender. The difference between the sale price and the purchase price is one of the components of the returns, the other component being the short rebate. Short selling strategy funds are typically concentrated with fewer funds. However, managers typically diversify across many sectors. Managers follow a bottom-up approach to evaluate the individual company's financial health and earning potential. Typical events that short selling fund managers expect are earnings downgrades, restructuring announcements, and potential bankruptcies. Some managers follow the mean-reversion theory and short sell securities that are overvalued, expecting that the stock price will be corrected back and return to the expected or long-run average value.

5.2.2 Risk Characteristics

Some risk factors are common in both short selling and long/short equity funds. A short selling fund is heavily exposed to short volatility risk, especially when the fund employs short options. A manager's skill and the firm's capabilities of managing the risks efficiently and tactically yield a higher alpha.

Systemic and Market Risk: The short selling strategy, though often correlated with the market negatively, is exposed to market risk in a reverse way.

Liquidity Risk: Stocks that are considered for short selling typically exhibit market inefficiencies and are not traded actively and so are exposed to liquidity risk. In other words, the manager may not find a good number of buyers at the time he believes is good for shorting.

Short Volatility Risk: Short selling funds may often employ short options, earning the premium and expecting options to expire. Short options provide instant cash inflow, and if options expire, then the managers keep the profit. If prices move in an unfavorable direction, then the losses from short options will be huge, and the premium earned may not be enough to cover these losses. This is called *short volatility risk*.

High Volatility: Securities selected for shorting typically have higher volatility than securities that are held long. This is mainly because securities selected for shorting tend to be companies without positive earnings or cash flows and that have underperformed their peers. These factors will lead to higher volatility. Some of the volatility of the portfolio can be reduced by holding many diversified securities.

Short-Squeeze Risk: Short sellers are required to return the borrowed stock to the lender when the lender demands it. Stocks that are heavily shorted experience more demand and the price may go up abruptly. This will either lead to reduced profit on the short sale or even negative returns. Short sale managers must review the lender's buy-in policy, which determines the time frame within which the short positions need to be covered.

5.2.3 Risk-Return Distribution

Short selling strategies are typically unhedged. This makes the strategy exhibit volatility higher than most other hedge fund strategies. Short selling strategies expect to perform better in falling markets. A manager's stock selection skill determines the returns during bull markets. Overall, short selling strategies earn returns closer to the risk-free rate, and therefore the share ratio of these funds is zero. Besides the global macro strategy, the short selling strategy is the only one that exhibits positive skewness. This strategy exhibits slightly positive excess kurtosis.According to the hedgefund.net database, short selling strategies exhibit positive skew of 0.6, excess kurtosis of 2.04, and an annualized Sharpe ratio of 0.21, using the risk-free rate of 3.5 percent. The Sharpe ratio is much less than that of the long/short equity fund, as shorted stocks do not earn dividends and upside potential is limited. The upside potential is limited to the value of the stock at the time of shorting, that is, when stock prices go to zero, the manager earns profit equivalent to the shorted value. Therefore, the maximum profit is capped. However, earning profit of up to the cap level is very rare.

Short bias strategies perform well in downward-trending markets, and a manager's skill yields positive returns even during normal market periods. From the stream of data provided in the table below, it is observed that short bias strategies performed well during the global financial crisis and yielded returns of 20 percent during 2008. However, on a risk-adjusted basis, short bias funds were not attractive, as their Sharpe ratio is 0.21(using the risk-free rate of 3.5%), which is somewhat closer to the long-only public market index. Since hedge funds themselves cannot be shorted, short bias hedge funds can provide downside protection for investors who hold a fund of funds. The perfect negative correlation with the S&P 500 makes short bias hedge funds attractive to investors to provide diversification.

Year	HF Aggregated Index	Short Bias Index
1991	28.76%	N/A
1992	16.92%	N/A
1993	29.93%	N/A
1994	7.32%	N/A
1995	28.10%	N/A
1996	25.33%	N/A
1997	23.25%	19.39%
1998	11.48%	7.57%
1999	36.22%	0.60%
2000	13.11%	21.50%
2001	9.04%	11.55%
2002	4.38%	23.43%
2003	21.30%	-11.76%
2004	10.78%	-0.94%
2005	10.94%	4.95%
2006	13.74%	-0.86%
2007	12.62%	10.52%
2008	-14.37%	20.22%
2009	21.41%	-10.16%
2010	10.48%	-10.87%

Annual returns of short bias strategy index (Data source: Hedgefund.net)

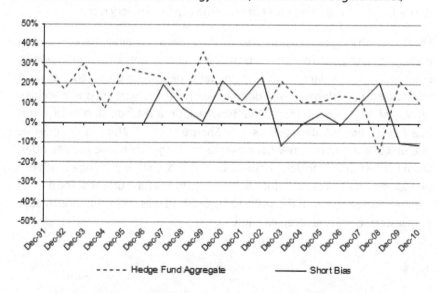

Annual returns of short bias strategy index (Data source: Hedgefund.net)

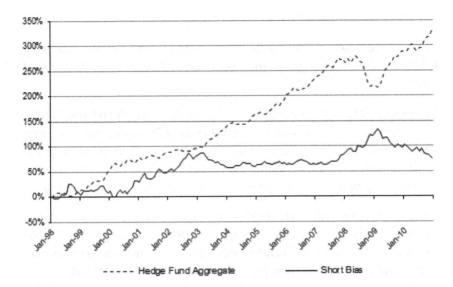

Cumulative returns of short bias strategy index (Data source: Hedgefund.net)

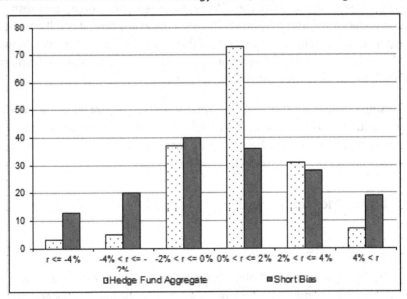

Distribution of returns of short bias strategy index (Data source: Hedgefund.net)

5.2.4 Due Diligence

Some parts of the due diligence for the short strategy overlap with that of the long/short equity strategy. The most common due diligence issues are listed below:

Shorting Ability: In some cases, the ability to short depends on the long-term relationship with a broker and the good standing of the fund manager. Being unable to open short positions in time or getting pressure from the prime lender to close the position sooner than desired will have negative effects on the portfolio. Investors should assess the shorting ability of the fund manager.

Valuation Methods: Short strategy fund managers short sell overvalued stocks. To determine if the stock is overvalued or undervalued, they follow various valuation methods. Some valuation methods may incorrectly select the stocks to short. Investors should know more about stock valuation methods.

Regulatory Changes: Investors should keep monitoring the regulatory changes pertaining to short sales. While the redemption agreements restrict the investors from withdrawing the investments at any time, it is still better to keep monitoring rules and regulations of short sales. In a case where withdrawal of funds is not possible, an investor may want to consider other techniques, outside the fund, to hedge the regulatory risk.

Shorting Criteria: Short strategy fund managers typically set their own criteria, such as number of stocks floating and size of the company to choose stocks for short sale. The best criteria help them to close the positions in time. Investors should find out what criteria the fund managers use.

5.3 Equity Market Neutral

5.3.1 Strategy

The equity market neutral strategy is similar to the long/short equity strategy in that both strategies take long positions in undervalued stocks and short positions in overvalued stocks. However, the equity market neutral strategy maintains net zero market exposure. In order to maintain zero market exposure, the equity market neutral strategy involves more frequent trading and positions may be held for shorter periods of time. Since more frequent rebalancing is required, equity market neutral funds tend to invest in more liquid securities and preferably in developed markets, though some fund managers who possess local knowledge invest in emerging markets. Equity market neutral fund managers typically follow a three-step process: initial quantitative screening to rank the stocks, fundamental research to select specific stocks, and portfolio construction. Some equity market neutral fund managers employ a black-box strategy, where a quantitative model detects security mispricing and selects the long or short positions. One such example of a quantitative technique is mean reversion of the price difference between two similar securities. Equity market neutral funds became more popular due to their consistent lower volatility, though the returns are much less than their peer strategy long/short equity.

Advantages:

- Since equity market neutral funds take equal long and short positions, their correlation with the market is very low compared to other hedge fund strategies.
- Equity market neutral funds exhibit lower volatility and generate stable returns over time regardless of market movements.
- Equity market neutral strategies demonstrate higher Sharpe ratios, or risk-adjusted performance.
- Equity market neutral managers do not typically engage in leverage, since most long investment comes from shorting the other stock in a pair.

Disadvantages:

- Lower returns when compared to other strategies.
- Higher transaction costs to fund managers due to the frequent rebalancing.
- May not be able to utilize trending markets efficiently.
- Since the managers maintain market exposure of net zero, equity market neutral funds produce single alpha only, while long/short equity strategies produce double alpha.

5.3.2 Risk Characteristics

Liquidity Risk: Since the strategy involves more frequent trading of securities in order to maintain net zero market exposure, the liquidity of securities is more important. If liquidity dries up unexpectedly, the strategy may experience short-term losses.

Event Risk: Though event risk will be diversified away somewhat due to a large number of securities, any surprise announcement, such as earnings revision, merger, or changes of management, may lead to significant losses.

Stock-Specific Risk: The equity market neutral strategy creates a peer position of every stock. That means market neutrality is maintained at a pair level, rather than at the entire portfolio level. If the stocks are not paired accurately or market characteristics are very different in the pair, then the strategy may not work efficiently.

Volatility Risk: Some quantitative models employ a strategy based on mean-reversion theory. If the stock experiences slowness reverting to the mean compared to its peer or volatility persists for longer than the expected time, then the strategy will experience loss.

Model Risk: Some stocks are selected based on internal valuation. Rapid changes in the market sectors or emergence of new sectors make it more difficult to value the stocks. Some emerging markets lack sufficient historical data to value the stocks. Rapid changes in market conditions make existing historical data irrelevant to current conditions. In that case, the model will become inefficient and may lead to incorrect selection of stocks.

Short-Squeeze Risk: The strategy has more exposure to short-squeeze risk than any other strategy since long and short positions are equal in dollar amount. A sudden increase in prices of the shorted security due to squeezing is dangerous to the strategy. Any halt in short trading by the regulatory authority will also hurt the strategy severely.

Operational Risk: Since the equity market neutral strategy involves heavy and frequent trading, the strategy is more exposed to operational risk arising from execution risk. A large number of positions require higher monitoring, which is prone to errors.

5.3.3 Risk-Return Distribution

When compared to long/short equity, the aggregated hedge fund industry, and the S&P 500, the equity market neutral strategy produces the lowest returns. However, it exhibits the lowest volatility and the highest Sharpe ratio among the four. The equity market neutral strategy produces returns higher than the S&P 500 with volatility of about 15 percent of that of the S&P 500. Since this strategy aims to produce consistent monthly returns regardless of market movements, the maximum drawdown exhibited is much less and is lower than that of the

S&P 500, long/short equity, and average hedge fund industry. Since the strategy involves only stocks, the credit risk is very minimal. Due to the large number of paired positions in the fund, even the minimal credit risk is diversified away. Less or no exposure to credit risk makes the strategy produce positive skewness and low positive excess kurtosis. According to the hedgefund.net database, equity market neutral strategies exhibit positive skew of 0.39, excess kurtosis of 2.81, and annualized Sharpe ratio of 1.51, using the risk-free rate of 3.5 percent.

Whether the strategy employs a pure quantitative or semi quantitative model to select the overpriced and underpriced stocks, the manager's ability of stock selection contributes to a major portion of the returns.

Year	HF Aggregated Index	Long/Short Equity Index	Equity Market Neutral Index	Short Bias Index
1991	28.76%	N/A	N/A	N/A
1992	16.92%	N/A	N/A	N/A
1993	29.93%	28.88%	N/A	N/A
1994	7.32%	4.20%	N/A	N/A
1995	28.10%	32.38%	N/A	N/A
1996	25.33%	28.15%	N/A	N/A
1997	23.25%	24.29%	17.42%	19.39%
1998	11.48%	15.61%	19.99%	7.57%
1999	36.22%	52.12%	20.36%	0.60%
2000	13.11%	16.86%	12.14%	21.50%
2001	9.04%	7.31%	9.34%	11.55%
2002	4.38%	-1.03%	5.76%	23.43%
2003	21.30%	24.86%	7.87%	-11.76%
2004	10.78%	11.48%	5.85%	-0.94%
2005	10.94%	12.24%	7.58%	4.95%
2006	13.74%	14.55%	8.30%	-0.86%
2007	12.62%	12.83%	8.12%	10.52%
2008	-14.37%	-19.04%	-3.15%	20.22%
2009	21.41%	24.67%	7.98%	-10.16%
2010	10.48%	10.31%	3.62%	-10.87%

Annual returns of equity market neutral strategy index (Data source: Hedgefund. net)

Between 1997 and 2009, there was only one year of negative returns. The negative returns during 2008 are much less compared to long/short equity, which proves that the equity market neutral strategies provide more downside protection than long/short equity due to its neutral exposure to the market. On an annual basis, the returns are less than long/short equity funds and higher than the S&P 500.The volatility is less than both long/short equity and the S&P 500, and therefore the risk-adjusted returns are higher than both long/short equity and the S&P 500.

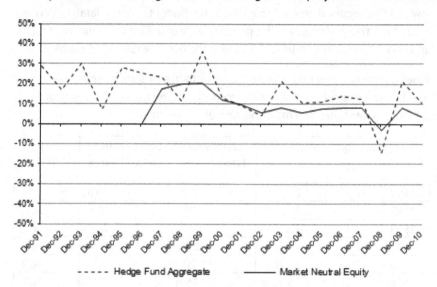

Annual returns of equity market neutral strategy index (Data source: Hedgefund.net)

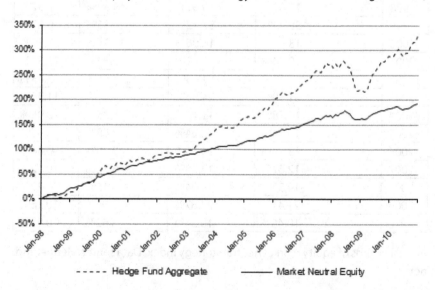

Cumulative returns of equity market neutral strategy index (Data source: Hedgefund.net)

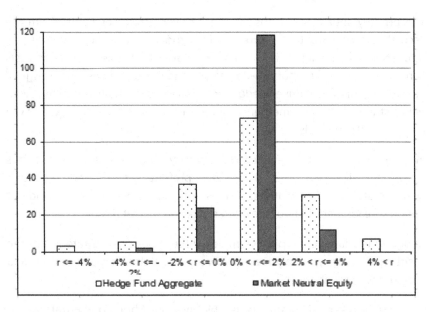

Distribution of returns of equity market neutral strategy index (Data source: Hedgefund.net):

5.3.4 Due Diligence

Due diligence issues pertaining to the equity market neutral strategy overlap with those of the long/short strategy. In addition, investors should seek details about dynamic rebalancing, the maximum time period of having nonzero exposure at any time, types of companies invested in, and so on.

5.4 Event Driven

5.4.1 Strategy

The event driven strategy is a non-directional strategy that fully employs events occurring in the corporate life cycle. Event driven strategy hedge fund managers utilize the broadest investment universe of any corporate event that acts as a catalyst for price movements. Therefore, the event driven strategy can be seen as a multistrategy approach. The events include, but are not limited to, mergers, acquisitions, spin-offs, business consolidations, special dividends, stock repurchase announcements, liquidation, capital restructuring, bankruptcies, addition or deletion to major benchmark indices, and legal disputes.

The primary source of returns for event driven strategies comes from the accurate prediction of the occurrence of a corporate transaction event, as well as the optimal time at which to commit capital to it. For this purpose, analysts conduct research using bottom-up analysis and utilize the best knowledge of industry sectors. Event driven hedge fund managers also build dedicated event driven strategies, such as merger arbitrage and distressed securities, which will be discussed separately.

In order to implement the event driven strategy, fund managers utilize various instruments like long stock, short stock, preferred stocks, debt securities, warrants, stubs, and derivatives, such as options, index put options, and put option spreads, hedging out the interest risk and market risk.

Hedge fund managers typically employ three types of substrategies of the event driven strategy: catalytic event driven, special situation event driven, and opportunistic event driven.

The catalytic event driven strategy is typically a long/short equity strategy that utilizes event analysis to determine the positions as the event acts as a catalyst in moving the prices up and down. The special situation event driven strategy uses distressed-type analysis and invests in companies that involve reorganizations and spin-offs but are not in bankruptcy. Managers employ the opportunistic event substrategy by utilizing multiple event strategies, including distressed securities, merger arbitrage, catalytic event driven, and special situation event driven strategies.

5.4.2 Risk Characteristics

Risk characteristics and risk-return distribution of dedicated event strategies has been discussed in individual strategies, such as merger arbitrage and distressed strategies.

5.4.3 Risk-Return Distribution

Event driven hedge funds are exposed to events like mergers, spin-offs, restructures, and many other events. Merger arbitrage strategies fall under the event driven category. However, event driven strategies invest not only in merger related but also in many other events, providing diversification. Though the event driven strategies provide wider diversification, the volatility is high compared to merger arbitrage. High volatility is attributed to the fact that event driven strategies may not always use arbitrage theory and tend to have direct exposure as well. The reason not to use arbitrage theory is a lack of companion positions due to the special nature of the event. In addition, event driven funds magnify small returns using leverage, which in turn magnifies the volatility. Due to the exposure to event risk and credit risk, they exhibit negative skewness. Excess kurtosis is also high positive. Returns are somewhat higher than merger arbitrage, but due to high volatility, the Sharpe ratio is less compared to the merger arbitrage strategy. Maximum drawdown is much higher compared to the aggregated hedge fund index. According to the hedgefund.net database, event driven strategies exhibit a negative skew of -1.16, excess kurtosis of 3.22, and an annualized Sharpe ratio of 1.15, using the risk-free rate of 3.5 percent.

Year	HF Aggregated Index	Event Driven Index
1991	28.76%	N/A
1992	16.92%	N/A
1993	29.93%	N/A
1994	7.32%	N/A
1995	28.10%	N/A
1996	25.33%	21.39%
1997	23.25%	27.44%
1998	11.48%	4.55%
1999	36.22%	24.11%
2000	13.11%	8.85%
2001	9.04%	12.82%
2002	4.38%	0.69%
2003	21.30%	23.40%
2004	10.78%	14.92%
2005	10.94%	8.04%
2006	13.74%	16.49%
2007	12.62%	7.25%
2008	-14.37%	-22.25%
2009	21.41%	33.69%
2010	10.48%	11.61%

Annual returns of event driven strategy index (Data source: Hedgefund.net)

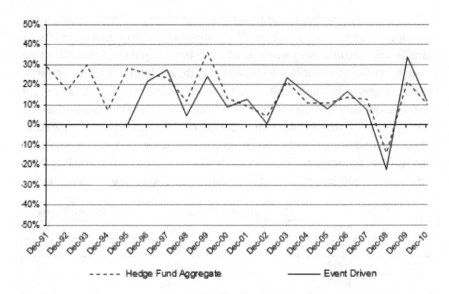

Annual returns of event driven strategy index (Data source: Hedgefund.net)

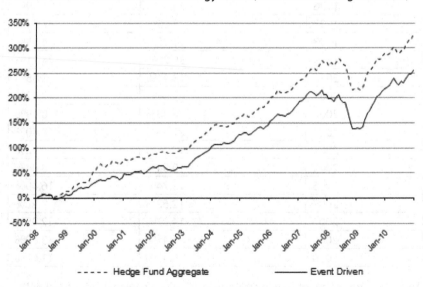

Cumulative returns of event driven strategy index (Data source: Hedgefund.net)

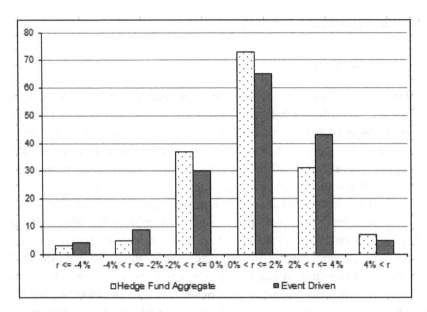

Distribution of returns of event driven strategy index (Data source: Hedgefund.net)

5.4.4 Due Diligence

Event driven strategies are information driven, meaning that the core part of the strategy depends on the manager's ability to gather timely information and his strong relationships with lawyers, bankers, proxy agents, journalists, and corporate managers. Investors should seek to ascertain the manager's information-gathering ability.

Due to a limited number of forecasted events, the event driven strategy is not scalable. During periods of market volatility, the number of event driven investment opportunities may be reduced for a period of time. Investors should know how the manager invests the funds in such cases.

Investors should know how the event driven fund manager achieves diversity. Investors should know what the various types of markets are on which the manager focuses, what geographies are considered, and whether the fund is business cycle independent.

Investors should know whether the event driven manager must ever drift out of his or her investment mandate and core competencies.

Investors should know how the fund performed in unpredictable markets.

5.5 Relative Value Arbitrage

5.5.1 Strategy

Relative value arbitrage strategies involve purchasing undervalued securities and simultaneously short selling overvalued securities. Relative value arbitrage fund managers maintain zero market exposure as they build the portfolio in such a way that market risk of long positions is cancelled out by that of short positions. Therefore, the relative values strategy is said to be nondirectional. Relative value arbitrage managers take advantages of price disparities caused by market inefficiencies that occur either because of lack of public coverage for the securities or because of market segmentation. Relative value arbitrage managers also employ dedicated arbitrage strategies, such as merger arbitrage, fixed-income arbitrage, convertible arbitrage, and volatility arbitrage, which will be discussed separately. Relative value arbitrage strategies are broad in scope in that they can involve a combination of any two securities including but not limited to stocks, bonds, options, forwards, futures, and swaps and may contain a combination of strategies, such as merger arbitrage, fixed-income arbitrage, convertible arbitrage, and volatility arbitrage. That is the why relative value arbitrage strategies are often called an "arbitrage smorgasbord."A special type of relative value strategy is a stub trading strategy that involves the piece of an equity security that is left over from a merger or recapitalization, which is called a *stub*.

5.5.2 Risk Characteristics

Risk characteristics and risk return distribution of dedicated relative value arbitrage strategies has been discussed in individual strategies.

5.5.3 Risk-Return Distribution

Relative value strategies have consistent returns with negative skewness and very high excess kurtosis. Volatility is less due to the relative positions in the strategy. Low volatility makes the Sharpe ratio attractive. According to the hedgefund.net database, relative value strategies exhibit a negative skew of -3.04, excess kurtosis of 17.30, and an annualized Sharpe ratio of 1.45, using the risk-free rate of 3.5percent. Higher excess kurtosis and negative skewness indicate that the relative value strategy is exposed to event risk and credit risk if debt securities are used as the underlying.

Year	HF Aggregated Index	Relative Value Arbitrage Index
1991	28.76%	N/A
1992	16.92%	N/A
1993	29.93%	N/A
1994	7.32%	N/A
1995	28.10%	N/A
1996	25.33%	15.63%
1997	23.25%	15.12%
1998	11.48%	5.99%
1999	36.22%	18.14%
2000	13.11%	14.34%
2001	9.04%	9.07%
2002	4.38%	7.27%
2003	21.30%	8.92%
2004	10.78%	5.47%
2005	10.94%	4.76%
2006	13.74%	10.33%
2007	12.62%	6.22%
2008	-14.37%	-14.35%
2009	21.41%	23.99%
2010	10.48%	10.21%

Annual returns of relative value arbitrage strategy index (Data source: Hedgefund.net)

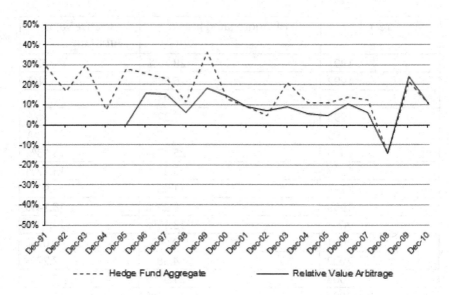

Annual returns of relative value arbitrage strategy index (Data source: Hedgefund.net)

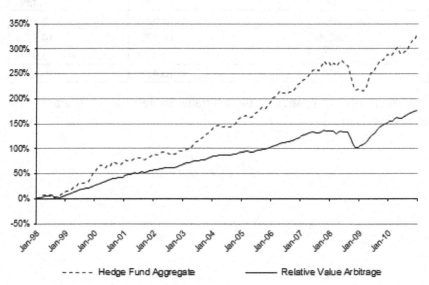

Cumulative returns of relative value arbitrage strategy index (Data source: Hedgefund.net)

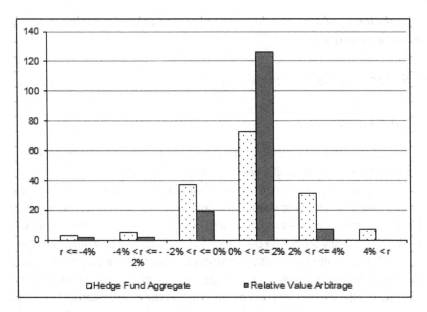

Distribution of returns of relative value strategy index (Data source: Hedgefund.net)

5.5.4 Due Diligence

The relative value arbitrage strategy is very broad, and a lot of specific relative value strategies exist. Some of the relative value strategies are fixed income arbitrage, capital structure arbitrage, and volatility arbitrage strategies. If the fund is especially called a relative value strategy fund instead of a specific type of relative value fund, then investors must perform additional due diligence to ascertain the more specific strategy.

Manager Experience: Investors should document the level of experience a manager possesses in various types of instruments. For example, a manager may be well versed in fixed-income securities but may lack skill in merger arbitrage, which is based on equity knowledge. Therefore, investors should ensure that the manager is expert in all the securities that the fund involves.

Concentration Level: Investors should know the relative size of each group of securities. While the general relative value strategy is well diversified, having concentrated positions will make the strategy tend toward a specific relative value strategy.

Correlations: Investors should know how each group of securities correlates with the other groups.

5.6 Convertible Arbitrage

5.6.1 Strategies

Companies with great potential for growth but with poor credit ratings or established companies with weak financial health often issue convertible bonds in order to avoid immediate stock dilution and to lower the coupon rate. Convertible bonds give the investor the right to convert the bonds into common stock. The right to convert the bond into common stock can be interpreted as the issuer implicitly selling the call option to the investor to purchase the issuer's stock. This call option reduces the coupon payment on the convertible bond. So convertible bonds comprise two components: a bond and an equity option. The option also acts as a long put on the bond, as the investor can put the bond back to the issuer with an exchange of stock. In this case, the stock price acts as the exercise price. Since the options are embedded and cannot be traded separately, pricing disparities occur, especially in volatile markets. Convertible arbitrage fund managers apply various quantitative techniques to price the bond and option and profit from arbitrage trading.

The convertible bond market is considered to be segmented, as most of the convertible bonds are typically issued by firms with noninvestment credit ratings or emerging firms. Many institutional investors have constraints against investing in these issuers, making the liquidity of the convertible bond market not so attractive. As a result, convertible bonds are undervalued. Convertible arbitrage fund managers take advantage of this undervaluation.

The most common arbitrage strategy is buying convertible bonds and selling the underlying stock, thus gaining profit from the convertible bond coupon, stock depreciation, and the short rebate. If prices move up, that is, in an unfavorable direction, then the loss from the short sale will be offset by the gain from the bond price.

Depending on the volatility of the stock, the manager builds various forms of convertible arbitrage strategies, such as static trading and dynamic trading strategies. The latter is also referred to as volatility trading strategies and takes various forms, such as the delta-neutral strategy, gamma trading, and skewed trading. Depending on the credit quality of the issuer, the manager builds various credit arbitrage strategies.

5.6.1.1 Static Trading

This is the basic form of convertible arbitrage strategy. A hedge fund manager buys a convertible bond or convertible preferred stock and short sells the underlying stock. The fund receives a coupon payment from the convertible bond or a dividend from the preferred stock. The fund invests the amount received from the short sale but pays the dividend back to the stock lender. Interest earned minus the dividend is called a short rebate. So the fund manager is compensated by a static return represented by the coupon payment and a short rebate even if gains from bond price appreciation are cancelled by loss on a short sale. Any transactions costs and leverage costs need to be subtracted from this static return.

5.6.1.2 Delta-Neutral Strategy

In contrast to static trading, volatility trading strategies are dynamic. In volatility trading, the fund manager re hedges the convertible bond positions according to stock price movements in order to maintain delta-neutral. The delta measures the sensitivity of an option price to the changes in the price of the underlying stock. Therefore, the delta of the convertible bond measures the convertible price sensitivity to the underlying stock price changes. The delta is used to calculate the hedge ratio, which gives the number of stocks to be shorted to achieve a delta-neutral portfolio of convertible bonds and short stocks.

Hedge Ratio = Delta * Convertible price/Conversion price

Where Conversion price = Underlying stock price + Conversion premium if any.

As the delta changes from time to time, the hedge ratio also changes, so the fund manager needs to adjust the stock position periodically in order to remain delta-neutral. This is called delta hedging. Delta is approximately one for deep in-the-money options, 0.5 for at-the-money options, and zero for out-of-money options. As the stock value increases, the delta increases; it decreases when the stock value decreases. The fund manager needs to sell more stocks as the delta increases and needs to cover the part of the short position when the delta decreases in order to maintain delta-neutral. If the gain (loss) from the convertible bond price is offset by loss (gain) from the stock price increase (decrease) due to portfolio rebalancing, then how will changes in the convertible bond price help the manager to gain profit? The profit comes from the convexity of the bond. Please see the fixed-income strategy below for the definition of convexity.

Due to the convexity effect, the convertible bond price will increase more rapidly than the stock price. So the gain from the bond is higher than the loss from the short position. Similarly, due to the convexity effect, the convertible bond price falls more slowly than the stock price decreases. So the loss from the convertible bond price is smaller than the gain from the short position. In other words, the fund manager gains from movements of the stock in either direction. This explains why the delta-neutral strategy can also be called a long volatility strategy.

5.6.1.3 Gamma Trading

Like the delta-neutral strategy, gamma trading is also dynamic in nature and is long volatility. In fact, gamma trading is an extension to the delta-neutral strategy and is built on top of it. This strategy requires more dynamic trading than the delta trading. Gamma measures the rate of change of delta with respect to changes in the underlying stock. Gamma is more sensitive for at-the-money options. The rate of change of delta or gamma increases as the stock value increases. As the gamma increases rapidly, fund managers of the delta-neutral strategy need to short more stocks. This will increase the short position value by the change in delta times the change in the underlying stock. Since the convertible bond market is relatively small, the heavy short selling will force the stock prices down. When stock prices revert back to their previous position, for example, then the fund manager needs to cover part of the short position due to decrease in delta. Since the fund manager can buy back the stocks at a lower price, he will lock in a profit of the change in delta times the change in the underlying stock. The higher the gamma, the higher the profit for the manager. Since gamma trading requires more frequent trading, the transaction costs will also be higher. Gamma traders prefer to buy at-the-money convertibles near to expiration, as gamma is more pronounced for at-the-money and near-expiration options.

5.6.1.4 Credit Arbitrage

Due to the embedded option, a convertible bond can fall into four sections of prices, known as deep-out-of-the-money, out-of-the-money, at-the-money, and in-the-money. As described earlier, delta and gamma are higher for at-the-money and in-the money, which helps the convertible fund manager profit from volatility trading strategies. For deep-out-of-the-money and out-of-the-money, the convertible bond hits the bond floor, acts more like a straight bond, and may not be useful for volatility arbitrage. Fund managers employ the credit arbitrage strategy when the convertible bond goes to either of these two stages. Convertible bonds deep-out-of-the-money are called *distressed convertibles*, and convertible bonds out-of-the-money are called *busted convertibles*. The issuer is said to be in financial distress in either case, and investors have concerns about payment of scheduled coupons and par value at maturity. At this stage, the bonds are exposed to both credit risk and interest rate risk. Convertible arbitrage fund managers profit by building credit arbitrage strategies using distressed and busted convertibles.

Distressed and busted convertibles come with a cheap equity option but are exposed to credit risk. Credit arbitrage managers strip out the fixed-income portion of the convertible and sell it to credit buyers at a discount price, typically entering into an asset-swap agreement. Credit buyers provide the credit arbitrager the option to repurchase the convertible at a slightly higher price. The difference between the repurchase price and the sale price is the premium that the credit arbitrage manager pays to the credit buyer or protection seller. An asset swap also provides protection against interest rate risk, as the credit arbitrager no longer needs to worry about interest rate fluctuations that will impact the bond price.

At a later time, if the credit quality of the issuer improves, then the distressed or busted convertibles will be at-the-money or in-the-money. At this juncture, the credit arbitrage manager buys the convertible back from the credit buyer at a predefined price and either sells it at a premium or converts it into common stock, gaining the profit from the strategy.

5.6.2 Risk Characteristics

Due to the complex nature of the convertible bond arbitrage strategy, it is often difficult to price the option component of the convertible accurately. Therefore, the model risk is considered to be the primary risk of the convertible arbitrage strategy. Other risks of the convertible bond arbitrage strategy are equity risk, credit risk, interest rate risk, volatility risk, event risk, liquidity risk, short-squeeze risk, and regulatory risk.

Model Risk: The biggest challenge of the convertible arbitrage strategy is model risk. Due to limited analyst coverage and segmentation of convertible bonds, market prices are not typically available. Therefore, managers use a mark-to-model approach to evaluate the convertible funds. Use of quantitative models, such as the binomial model, rely on the accuracy of predicting the probabilities of movements and therefore are exposed to model risk. Fund managers may not always realize mark-to-model prices when they want to liquidate a portion of the fund.

Equity Risk: Gamma is more pronounced for at-the-money convertible bonds and requires more dynamic hedging, and so at-the-money convertible arbitrage positions are more exposed to equity risk. If the hedging is not perfect, then the arbitrage strategy is exposed to market value fluctuations.

Credit Risk: Convertible bonds are typically issued by poorly rated firms, and therefore those bonds are exposed to credit risk. The intensity of credit risk is higher for convertible bonds that are in the busted and distressed phases. Managers who wish to retain only the equity component usually engage in asset swaps or other credit derivatives to hedge the credit risk.

Interest Rate Risk: Busted convertibles trade closer to the bond floor and behave more like straight bonds. Straight bonds are more exposed to interest rate risk. Rising interest rates will result in decreased bond prices, while the short stock position value decreases only slightly. This will result in loss to the convertible arbitrage fund. Decreased interest rates will result in increased bond prices, but if the convertible bond is callable, then the bond will reach an upper limit due to its negative convexity. Or the issuer may call back the bond to take advantage of the falling interest rates. In either case, the fund manager loses the opportunity from falling interest rates.

Volatility Risk: Convertible arbitrage strategies that employ volatility arbitrage are exposed to long volatility. Delta-Neutral and gamma trading strategies profit from increased volatility. As the stock price becomes stable, the volatility decreases, and so the embedded option price will decrease. Thus, the stability of stock prices may result in losses or reduced profits to the fund.

Event Risk: The convertible arbitrage strategy is exposed to certain corporate events, and some of the events can hurt the strategy, while some of the events can help the strategy to benefit. Volatility arbitrage strategies will be hurt when there is a rating upgrade from a rating agency. The improved creditworthiness may encourage the issuer to call back the bond. A credit upgrade may also result in lower volatility subject to volatility risk as explained in the volatility risk section above. An unexpected merger announcement will result in a sudden rise in stock price, which will result in loss from short positions.

Liquidity Risk: Convertible bonds are usually issued by noninvestment-grade issuers and so are least covered by analysts. These bonds are traded over-the-counter, and so the trading volume is less. Due to these reasons, the bid-ask spread widens, and the convertible arbitrage managers may not find a matching position for hedging in time. So the liquidity risk may result in loss to the manager or may lead to losing the opportunity to profit from pricing anomalies. The low liquidity also results in decreased volatility of the underlying stock, which in turn will decrease the value of the embedded option.

Short-Squeeze and Regulatory Risks: The strategy is more exposed to short-squeeze risk of shorted positions. A sudden increase in prices of the shorted security due to squeezing is dangerous to the strategy. Any halt in short trading by the regulatory authority will also hurt the strategy severely.

5.6.3 Risk-Return Distribution

Convertible arbitrage strategies performed better than any other strategy during 2009, with the emerging-markets strategy and the distressed-securities strategy being the second- and third-best performers. The best performance of the convertible arbitrage strategy can be explained by the following theory.

Credit cycles follow economic cycles and lead equity cycles both up and down. The four stages of economic cycles are beginning of recovery, bull market, late recovery/beginning of recession, and bear market. Credit spreads start tightening and bonds' prices start rising in the first phase and continue through the bull market. Equities, typically, start rising in the bull market and continue through phase three. Empirical studies reveal that credit spreads contract faster than they expand, as the credit spreads are more sensitive to liquidity. As liquidity returns to markets, bond prices rise (and credit spreads narrow) in advance of equity markets and the economy. Convertible arbitrage strategies typically take long positions in bonds and short positions in the same or similar companies' stock. During recessions, convertible bonds usually enter the distressed region or the busted region. In the distressed region, bonds are typically sold at 30 percent or below the par value, and in the busted region they are sold at between 30 to 80 percent of the par value. Convertible arbitrage fund managers who have established long/short positions in the bear market or at the beginning of recovery experience huge gains from long positions in bonds. However, the loss from increased stock prices is much less than the profit from longs in magnitude. This is because, as explained earlier, the credit market leads the equity market, which means that when bond prices start rising, equity prices are still falling or in oscillation mode. When distressed or busted bonds return to par value, the gain from bonds could be 20 percent to 25 percent. That means bonds that are selling below 30 to 80 percent of par value may reach 80 to 110 percent of par value. While part of that gain will be offset by loss from the short equity, the net gain will be substantial.

The above theory supports the 44.99 percent returns of convertible arbitrage strategies during the year 2009.The same theory can explain the losses during 2008. After the emerging markets strategies (loss of 33%), both convertible arbitrage and distressed-securities strategies posted an annual loss of about 25 percent. The amount of losses was also partially attributed to the fact that the SEC temporarily suspended the short selling of financial stocks after Lehman Brothers collapsed. This hindered the downside protection severely, and convertible arbitrage managers were left vulnerable to the effects of the tumbling global market. The fall and recovery of convertible arbitrage strategies were faster than other strategies due to their higher sensitivity to liquidity.

In the long term, the convertible arbitrage strategy performs between the S&P 500 and the average hedge fund industry returns. The returns are above the S&P 500 and below the average hedge fund industry, but volatility is lower than both the S&P 500 and the average for the industry. Due to the equity component of the S&P 500, the convertible arbitrage strategies are exposed to market risk, and as a result, the correlation with the S&P 500 is moderate, at about 0.43. The maximum drawdown is less than that of both the S&P 500 and the average hedge fund index. Since convertible arbitrage strategies are exposed to event risk, default risk, and credit risk, they exhibit negative skewness. According to the hedgefund.net database, convertible arbitrage strategies exhibit a negative skew of -3.52, excess kurtosis of 25.86, and an annualized Sharpe ratio of 0.92, using the risk-free rate of 3.5 percent. Higher excess kurtosis and negative skewness indicate that the convertible arbitrage strategy is exposed to event risk and credit risk. The figures following the table demonstrate the annual returns, cumulative returns, and return distributions.

Year	HF Aggregated Index	Convertible Arbitrage
1991	28.76%	N/A
1992	16.92%	N/A
1993	29.93%	N/A
1994	7.32%	N/A
1995	28.10%	N/A
1996	25.33%	15.71%
1997	23.25%	14.93%
1998	11.48%	6.10%
1999	36.22%	16.62%
2000	13.11%	12.98%
2001	9.04%	12.99%
2002	4.38%	9.69%
2003	21.30%	12.19%
2004	10.78%	2.61%
2005	10.94%	-0.57%
2006	13.74%	11.59%
2007	12.62%	5.34%
2008	-14.37%	-24.61%
2009	21.41%	44.99%
2010	10.48%	11.87%

Annual returns of convertible arbitrage index (Data source: Hedgefund.net)

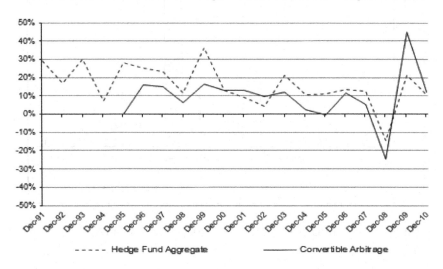

Annual returns of convertible arbitrage strategy index (Data source: Hedgefund. net)

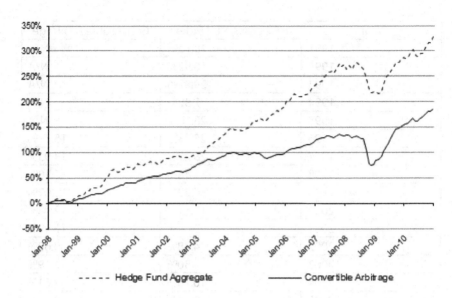

Cumulative returns of convertible arbitrage strategy index (Data source: Hedgefund.net)

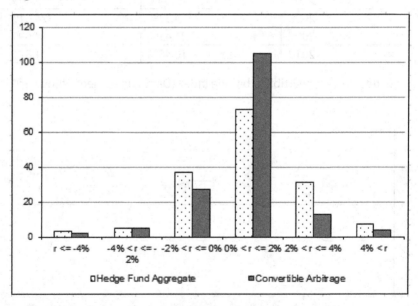

Distribution of returns of convertible arbitrage strategy index (Data source: Hedgefund.net)

5.6.4 Due Diligence

Types of Bonds: Convertible bonds are classified as four types depending on the credit spread and value of the embedded option. They are distressed or deep out-of-money bonds, busted or out-of-money bonds, hybrid or at-the-money bonds, and premium bonds or in-the-money bonds. Investors should document the types of bonds used in the strategy.

Substrategies: Convertible arbitrage includes various substrategies, such as static trading, delta-neutral strategy, gamma trading, credit arbitrage, and skewed trading. Return expectations and risk profiles vary for each substrategy. A different skill set is required for each strategy. Investors should document details of the substrategies and manager experience in the fund's substrategies.

Sophistication of Model: Convertible arbitrage strategies mainly depend on quantitative models to generate alpha. Due to the dynamics of convertible markets, models get outdated very frequently. Investors should know if the models employed by fund managers are sophisticated enough to react to changing market conditions and how flexible the model is to be altered.

Risk Parameters: Various risk characteristics are described in the previous section. While each risk is expected to earn premium, most convertible hedge fund managers hedge some risk and retain other risks. For example, the manager may hedge the credit risk and interest rate risk, and retain the equity option portion, expecting profit when the bond price goes up. Investors should document what risks are hedged and what other risks remain.

Hedging Mechanism: Investors should document how the fund manager hedges various risks. Hedging away certain risks may introduce other risks. For example, hedging credit risk using asset swaps may introduce counterparty risk. Therefore, investors should know if there are any residual risks.

Portfolio Rebalancing: Certain substrategies, such as gamma trading and skewed trading, require more dynamic rebalancing in order to achieve target levels. More frequent trading may require higher trading costs, which will substantially reduce profits. Therefore, fund managers set the intervals and tolerance level to re hedge or rebalance the portfolio. Inventors should document these details.

Liquidity: Since most convertible bonds are issued by small and midsize companies, convertible bonds become more illiquid after they are issued. That means off-the-run convertibles are more illiquid. If managers want to liquidate bonds of certain companies, then they may have to be sold at considerable discount, and the discount depends on the size of the position. Therefore, managers should diversify across multiple companies and impose limits on the size of exposure to each company. Investors should document the exposure limits and number of companies in the portfolio.

Leverage: Funds often employ both implicit and explicit leverage. Implicit leverage is obtained using options, with maximum risk of losing the option premium paid. However, implicit leverage also impacts overall volatility of the fund. Explicit leverage impacts overall volatility of the fund as well of risk of loss. Therefore, investors should document usage of both implicit and explicit leverage and the manager's experience at managing the leverage.

Shorting Ability: Convertible bonds are issued by small and midsize companies. Due to the small float of stocks, fund managers often find it difficult to borrow the stock for shorting. Some fund managers borrow the stocks of similar companies. A small float of stock is subject to short squeeze. The correlation between the convertible bond company and the company of shorted stock also matters. Borrowing the stocks also depends on the relationship with the prime broker. Investors should document all details pertaining to the shorting ability of the fund manager.

5.7 Fixed-Income

5.7.1 Strategies

Hedge fund managers build various arbitrage and nonarbitrage strategies using fixed-income securities by using term structure theories, by exploiting market inefficiencies, by using forecasting models, and by best utilizing the manager skill level. There are mainly three term structure theories, which are called the pure expectation theory, liquidity preference theory, and market segmentation theory.

The **pure expectation theory** states that the yield received in long investments is equivalent to the effective yield received by periodically reinvesting using short-term bonds. According to this theory, the rising term structure reflects that the market expects the short-term rates to rise in the future; the declining term structure reflects that the market expects the short-term rates to decrease in the future; and the flat-term structure reflects that the market expects the short-term rates to remain unchanged in the future. For example, if a one-year bond returns yield higher than that of a six-month bond, then investors anticipate that the yield six months from now should be higher than the six-month rate available now.

The **liquidity preference theory** states that long-term investments pose a higher interest rate risk than short-term investments, and therefore long-term bonds are less marketable and less liquid in nature. So investors either prefer short-term bonds or expect sufficient compensation for bearing interest rate risk and liquidity risk in long-term bonds. As a result, yield premium increases with maturity.

The **market segmentation theory** states that the bond market is segmented by maturities and thus, supply and demand are determined by bond maturities. Market inefficiencies also exist, as certain market participants are restricted from investing in noninvestment-grade securities.

Fixed-income strategies can use any of the following securities:

- US treasury bonds
- Corporate bonds
- Municipal bonds
- Sovereign bonds
- Asset-Backed securities
- Mortgage-Backed securities
- Fixed-Income futures
- Fixed-Income swaps
- Fixed-Income options
- Credit protection products

Using these theories and securities, fund managers build various arbitrage and nonarbitrage strategies. Arbitrage strategies involve two opposite positions profiting from pricing disparities. Nonarbitrage strategies involve investing using the mean-reversion theory and forecasting models, especially in structured products. Various possible arbitrage and non arbitrage strategies are described below. While each strategy has its own characteristics, fund managers often employ more than one compatible strategy in a portfolio.

Yield Curve Arbitrage: Yield curve arbitrage strategies employ the analysis of level, slope, and curvature of yield curve and trading bonds with different maturities and duration. Managers can use the yield curve of the same country or can use two yield curves across two countries.

Butterfly Strategy: This strategy also takes advantage of information that exists in the yield curve. This strategy involves taking one short position and two long positions one on each side of the short position, or one long position and two short positions one on each side of the long position.

TED Spread: TED stands for Treasuries over Eurodollars. Yield anomalies often appear between government bonds and the LIBOR rate with the same maturity. Fund managers profit from the disparity by taking two opposite positions.

On-the-run vs. Off-the-run: On-the-run bonds are bonds that are recently issued, and off-the-run bonds are bonds that were issued in the past. On-the-run issues are more liquid than off-the-run issues, so off-the-run issues require liquidity premium and therefore are cheaper than on-the-run issues with the same remaining expiration time. Both prices converge to their par value at maturity. Hedge fund managers take a long position in off-the run and simultaneously take a short position in on-the-run with the same remaining expiration time as that of off-the-run. At the time of maturity, the hedge fund manager will have captured profit that is equivalent to the difference between the basis points of the two positions. So the on-the-run vs. the off-the-run strategy profits from the noise level in the yield curve, rather than from the curvature of the curve.

Basis Trade: In a Treasury bond futures contract, the counterparty has the provision to choose the securities to be delivered from any government bond with more than fifteen years to maturity. This provision reduces the likelihood of market manipulation and produces a large supply of potential bonds that are deliverable on the contract. Fixed-income arbitrage managers profit from this embedded deliverable option on a future contract; technically speaking, the fund managers hold the long position in a delivery option.

The cash received by the short position = QFP*CF + Accrued interest

Where QFP = Quoted future price

CF = Conversion factor set by CBOT for the bond delivered

Cost to purchase the bond = Quoted bond price + Accrued interest

Arbitrage managers develop mathematical models that minimize the value of quoted bond price - QFP*CF to determine the cheapest-to-deliver Bond.

Structured Products Arbitrage: Fund managers employ a structured products arbitrage strategy by taking a long position in equity tranches of a CDO and a short position in mezzanine or equity tranches or selling a CDS. These strategies failed during crises due to the highly correlated nature of the underlying securities.

Barbell Strategy: The barbell strategy is a nonarbitrage strategy built on the concept of a core-satellite approach. Fund managers implementing this strategy take a long position in ultra-safe, high-liquid, short-term government bonds as part of their core position and a long position in high-yield, high-risk, long-term bonds. Short-term bonds have lesser duration, and long-term bonds have higher duration. This strategy does not invest in intermediate bonds. This strategy employs the principle that extreme shocks do not exist for a long time and things will revert to the normal condition; if the fund can survive the extreme event, the temporary losses in long-term bonds can be recovered by holding the position until recovery happens. Since short-term bonds are safe bonds, it is expected that they won't be affected by extreme events, and after expiration they can be rolled over to take advantage of market conditions that exist at that time.

Bullet Strategy: The bullet strategy is also a nonarbitrage strategy, but in contrast to the barbell strategy, this strategy invests in concentrated intermediate-term bonds by employing forecasting models. Since the duration is proportional to the square of maturity, the effective duration of the bullet strategy is less than that of the barbell strategy.

5.7.2 Risk Characteristics

Liquidity Risk: Most fixed-income arbitrage strategies earn liquidity premium by taking long positions in illiquid securities and short positions in liquid securities. Therefore, fixed-income arbitrage fund managers are said to be long liquidity risk. While the strategy can earn profit at the time of expiration or in the long term, temporary price divergence can occur before converging back to par value. The temporary divergence may lead to margin calls from prime brokers that require selling certain positions at unfavorable times if there is not enough capital reserve to meet the margin calls. This is called *funding liquidity risk*. In addition, the fund manager may want to close the positions either because of redemption demand from investors or because the fund manager foresees adverse price movements. This will affect the bid-ask spreads and may again lead to unfavorable trading. This is called *market liquidity risk*. As the profits in fixed-income arbitrage strategies are lucrative due to equity-like returns at lower volatility, competition has increased, and therefore many funds are utilizing the same kind of strategies. When it is really required to liquidate the fund due to economic shocks or extreme market conditions, the flight-to-quality will occur as many participants are trying to liquidate similar positions. This will eventually lead to unhealthy competition, which will lead to the loss of several standard deviations from the normal mean, as occurred in the case of LTCM.

Yield Curve Twist: Yield curve arbitrage strategies are built based on the term structure of interest rates. However, certain macroeconomic events may cause parallel shifts or twists in the yield curve. While parallel shift may not be risky to this strategy, twists will lead the prices of the positions in opposite directions, that is, prices of long bonds may decline and prices of short positions may increase. So arbitrage strategies, including butterfly strategies, built on the yield curve will face losses.

Convexity Risk: Due to embedded call or prepayment options, mortgage-backed securities (MBS) exhibit negative convexity at lower interest rates. At a lower level of interest rates, the price of MBS flattens, thus curbing the upside potential. Since arbitrage strategies employ long MBS and short treasury bonds and because treasuries have positive convexity, the prices of treasuries could rise faster than the price of the MBS securities, thus leading to loss from the short positions of the Treasuries.

Duration Risk: Fixed-income arbitrage managers often ensure that the net duration of the portfolio is zero, that is, the weighted average duration of the long positions is equivalent to that of the short positions. Due to embedded options in bonds, it may be possible to calculate the duration inaccurately, thus leading to losses due to interest rate fluctuations.

Credit Risk: Fixed-income arbitrage strategies that involve corporate or MBS securities are exposed to credit risk, as the issuers can default on bonds or mortgage borrowers can default on home loans. In addition, strategies that involve credit arbitrage or using credit default swaps are exposed to counterparty risk.

Short Volatility Risk: Some fixed-income arbitrage strategies use either long options or short options or both. Short options provide instant cash inflow, and if options expire, then the arbitrage managers keep the profit. If prices move in an unfavorable direction, then the losses from short options will be huge, and gains from long options may not be enough to cover these losses. This is called short volatility risk.

Event Risk: Fixed-income strategies are exposed to various events, such as fiscal policy changes, monetary policy changes, parallel yield curve shifts, changes in steepness of the yield curve, changes in yield volatilities, changes in key currencies, changes in swap spreads in the G-7 countries, and so on.

Correlation Risk: Structured products, such as CDOs and CDSs, are priced by estimating the correlations between securities that exist in the basket. In extreme market conditions, the correlation will increase, and the number of defaults will be more than that estimated by the model. This is due to the fact that most CDO and CDS baskets involve related securities, such as only RMBS related, CMBS related, ABS related, and so on. Even if the basket is diversified, the extreme market condition will have increased the correlations among the sectors, thus leading to more defaults in the basket than estimated by the model. The correlation risk is the biggest risk that influences the model risk.

Leverage Risk: Since arbitrage strategies exploit the small basis differences between short and long positions, it is required to use huge leverage in order to magnify the profits. The greater amount of leverage may also lead to enormous losses.

Regulatory Risk: Fixed-income strategies are exposed to regulatory risks. For example, a sovereign can impose a moratorium or repudiate loans, or a government can amend foreclosing laws. These risks can lead to potentially large losses to the strategy.

Prepayment Risk: Bonds that are issued with embedded call options exhibit negative convexity at lower interest rates. When the interest rates fall, issuers opt for calling the bond back and reissue the bonds at lower interest rates. In such cases, the bonds reach cap rate. This is especially true with mortgage loans, where the borrower has the option of prepaying earlier than the maturity date.

Reinvestment Risk: Reinvestment risk introduces some model risk, as the calculated duration assumes that the coupon payments are invested at the rate of the yield. However, the actual rates at the time of coupon payment may have fallen.

Event Risk: Since fixed-income securities are tightly coupled with interest rates and interest rates in turn depend on macroeconomic events, fixed-income funds are heavily exposed to monetary and fiscal policy events. The fund is exposed to internal events of the issuing firm as well.

Model Risk: The forecast of interest rates and prepayment probabilities are calculated using various quantitative models and are therefore subject to model risk.

5.7.3 Risk-Return Distribution

Fixed-income arbitrage strategies are exposed to event risk and short volatility risk, which will increase tail risk. As a result, the risk-return distribution of the fixed-income arbitrage index shows negative skew and larger excess kurtosis. Compared to convertible arbitrage strategies, fixed-income arbitrage strategies exhibit less negative skewness as the long and short positions are more similar infixed-income arbitrage strategies than in convertible arbitrage strategies, that is, hedging risk is less in fixed-income arbitrage strategies than in convertible arbitrage strategies. The fixed-income arbitrage strategy index showed negative returns during 1998 and 2008, reiterating that fixed-income strategies are heavily exposed to economic shocks. 2008 witnessed the credit crisis, and 1998 witnessed the Asian market crisis. The fixed–income, nonarbitrage strategy index had shown negative returns during 2008, but had shown the lower end of positive during 1998. Positive returns during 1998 demonstrated that fixed-income, nonarbitrage strategies are more flexible to generate alpha than arbitrage strategies and also that the 1998 crisis was not extreme compared to the 2008 crisis.

As explained in the convertible arbitrage strategy's risk-return distribution, credit spreads are more sensitive to reacting quickly to changing market conditions. However, the returns for fixed-income strategies were less than for convertible arbitrage and distressed-securities strategies because the sensitivity of the bond is directly proportional to the discount to par. That means the higher the discount at which the bond is trading to the par value, the higher the sensitivity. Since distressed and convertible arbitrage strategies typically deal with troubled bonds or deep discount bonds, they react more to the improved liquidity and as a result, yield higher returns during the recovery stage.

According to the Hedgefund.net database, fixed-income arbitrage strategies exhibit a negative skew of -3.55, excess kurtosis of 21.23, and an annualized Sharpe ratio of 1.19, using the risk-free rate of 3.5 percent. Fixed-income nonarbitrage strategies exhibit a negative skew of -1.44, excess kurtosis of 8.30, and an annualized Sharpe ratio of 1.19, using the risk-free rate of 3.5 percent.

Year	HF Aggregated Index	Fixed-Income Arbitrage Index	Fixed-Income Nonarbitrage Index
1991	28.76%	N/A	N/A
1992	16.92%	N/A	N/A
1993	29.93%	N/A	N/A
1994	7.32%	N/A	N/A
1995	28.10%	N/A	N/A
1996	25.33%	14.87%	14.48%
1997	23.25%	12.26%	14.96%
1998	11.48%	-0.84%	2.93%
1999	36.22%	16.65%	10.44%
2000	13.11%	7.67%	8.26%
2001	9.04%	10.51%	6.87%
2002	4.38%	9.91%	5.10%
2003	21.30%	10.10%	14.82%
2004	10.78%	7.55%	10.03%
2005	10.94%	6.62%	6.63%
2006	13.74%	9.11%	8.87%
2007	12.62%	5.77%	4.55%
2008	-14.37%	-13.85%	-11.92%
2009	21.41%	23.02%	22.97%
2010	10.48%	12.55%	12.23%

Annual returns of fixed-income strategy indices (Data source: Hedgefund.net)

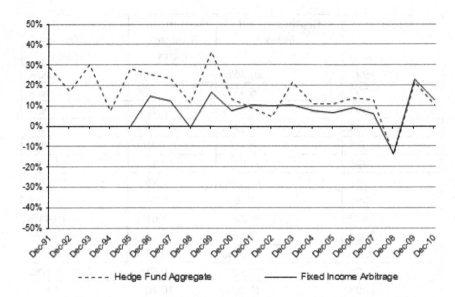

Annual returns of fixed-income arbitrage strategy index (Data source: Hedgefund.net)

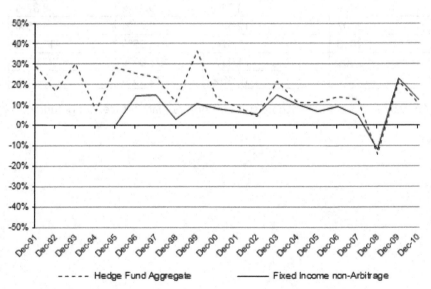

Annual returns of fixed-income nonarbitrage strategy index (Data source: Hedgefund.net)

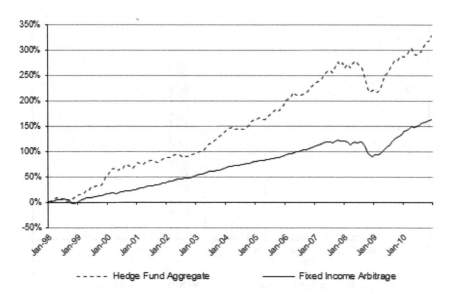

Cumulative returns of fixed-income arbitrage strategy index (Data source: Hedgefund.net)

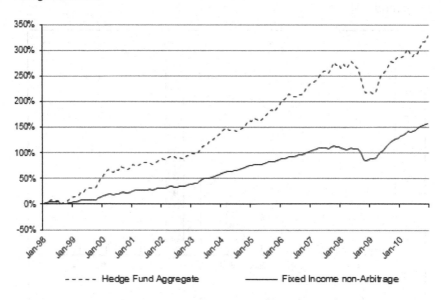

Cumulative returns of fixed-income nonarbitrage strategy index (Data source: Hedgefund.net)

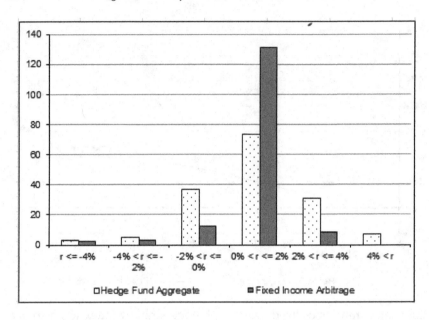

Distribution of returns of fixed-income arbitrage strategy index (Data source: Hedgefund.net)

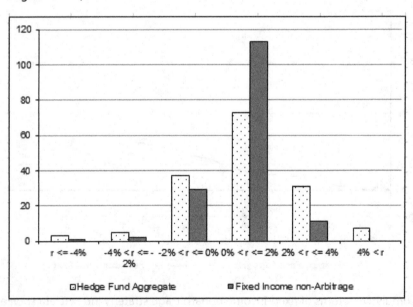

Distribution of returns of fixed-income non-arbitrage strategy index (Data source: Hedgefund.net)

5.7.4 Due Diligence

Fixed-income arbitrage strategies maintain neutral market exposure and depend on valuation models to earn profits. Investors should document at least the following details:

Investment Universe: Historically fixed-income strategies involved government securities and swap curves. Due to the popularity of mortgage securities and credit derivatives, fund managers started building strategies around high credit risk securities and even using emerging-market securities. Investors need to document the specific type of all instruments used in the strategy.

Leverage: Unlike equities, fixed-income securities produce little profit, and therefore fund managers magnify the fund size using leverage to enhance the returns. The risk of using leverage depends on the type of instrument and the maturity of the instrument. Investors should seek to know the leverage at various levels of exposure depending on type and maturity of instruments.

Fund Size: Investors should seek to know the size of contribution of the fund of each type of instrument and at various levels of maturity. In other words, investors should know if the fund is diversified across many types of fixed-income securities, maturity levels, and regions.

Loss Tolerance: Investors should know the exit strategy of the fund in difficult times. Investors should know if the fund retires only unfavorable instruments and replaces them with others or liquidates the entire fund. Investors should document the loss tolerance level.

Cash Reserves: Though high leverage is used in fixed-income arbitrage, it is quite common to have a significant amount of cash balance in the fund. A higher amount of cash balance is a good sign for the fund, as the redemption requests or margin calls can be fulfilled without liquidating any illiquid securities. Liquidating illiquid assets may incur substantial loss to the fund.

Cash Management: Cash reserves are usually invested in high liquid and short-term instruments. Returns from the cash reserves also contribute to the alpha of the fund. If cash is not managed properly or is invested in long-term instruments, then the fund will face issues during margin calls and redemption requests.

5.8 Merger Arbitrage

5.8.1 Strategies

Merger arbitrage strategy is considered as a combination of both relative value arbitrage and event-driven strategies, as it captures the spread between two positions and is mainly exposed to events, such as mergers, acquisitions, buyouts, and so on. Hedge fund managers employing merger arbitrage strategy look for merger or acquisition announcement events or anticipate such events, and then take long positions in the target company and short positions in the acquiring company. Announced mergers will need to go through various regulatory and non regulatory procedures, thus exposing to the risk of deal failure. Therefore, merger arbitrage fund managers are directly exposed to event risk. That is the reason why this strategy is also called *risk arbitrage*. Some risk-adverse hedge fund managers take positions in merger arbitrage only after seeing certain progress in the deal.

Immediately after the announcement, the stock price of the target company rises, but it will still trade at discount to the announced merger price. The discount reflects the premium that fund managers expect in order to bear the risk of the takeover not being completed. In the event the merger is called off, the target company stock will fall back to its pre announcement price. Prior to the deal completion, the stock price of the acquiring company falls, as the acquiring company is expected to pay a premium to the target stock and it is also expected that some level of capital needs to be set aside to integrate the two companies. This will earn the profit on short positions on acquiring companies taken by merger arbitrage managers.

The merger and acquisition can be a cash merger, stock-for-stock merger, or combination of both cash and stock merger. In the case of a cash merger, the acquiring company pays a fixed cash amount for each share of the target company plus premium. In this case, the merger arbitrage manager may not short the acquiring company stock, but will profit from the merger arbitrage spread, which is the difference between the announced price and the market price of the target company stock. In a case of stock-for-stock merger, the acquiring company offers a proportional share in the acquiring company in exchange for the shares of the target company. Therefore, the merger arbitrage fund managers take a long position in the target company and a short position in the acquiring company. Some merger arbitrage fund managers, who think that there is more probability of deal failure, take the opposite strategy that is, taking a short position in the target firm and a long position in the acquiring firm. After the merger is called off, the price of the target firm reverts back to its original value, and the acquiring firm stock will rise back to its original value, so the opposite merger arbitrage strategy earns profit to the manager.

Merger arbitrage fund managers conduct strong fundamental research on involved companies, which includes, but is not limited to, analysis of publicly available information, assessment of the acquirer's motivation, rationale for the merger, financial analysis, assessment of antitrust laws, and so forth.

5.8.2 Risk Characteristics

Merger arbitrage strategies are mainly exposed to event risk, regulatory risk, market risk, concentration risk, liquidity risk, leverage risk, short-squeeze risk, and interest-rate risk.

Event Risk: The merger arbitrage strategy is mainly exposed to event risk that an unfavorable event could cause the proposed merger to fail. Specific to the merger arbitrage strategy, event risk is also referred to as *deal risk*. There are many reasons why the deal can fail. Shareholders can refuse to approve the deal, two companies might not agree on the deal, there can be an unexpected decline in the target company earnings, or the economy may fall into recession. The deal can also fail if another potential acquirer enters into bidding with a more attractive offer, in which case the arbitrage will be shifted to the new acquirer. In the case of multiple bidders, arbitrage managers play with all bidders in order to seek profit from at least one bidder.

Regulatory Risk: Antitrust authorities and regulatory authorities may block the deal, or may ask the acquiring company to sell certain assets before approving the deal, distorting the terms of arbitrage. For example, in 2001,the European Commission declined the GE and Honeywell merger for antitrust reasons, which resulted in widening the spread from 5 percent to 36 percent within two days.

Market Risk: Merger arbitrage managers involving cash or tender offers do not take short positions in acquiring companies, and therefore the fund is exposed to a risk of market declines.

Concentration Risk: The number of deals at any period of time is limited, and therefore the fund manager may not be able to diversify the portfolio. It may be possible that a significant number of deals fail, especially in extreme market conditions, which will lead to major losses to the fund.

Liquidity Risk: Most of the mergers and acquisitions typically deal with small-cap companies, and if fund managers engage in arbitrage with multiple bidders, it may become difficult to unwind the failed target company position, which may increase the bid-ask spread.

Leverage Risk: Fund managers usually magnify the small basis arbitrage with huge leverage, and thus the strategy is exposed to leverage risk.

Short-Squeeze Risk: Since the merger arbitrage strategy involves short positions, the strategy is exposed to short-squeeze risk, as the lender may demand the covering of positions if price movement takes an unfavorable direction.

Interest-Rate Risk: Since an acquiring company uses a portion or all of the capital needed from borrowed funds, if interest rates rise before the merger is completed, then the acquirer may call off the merger.

5.8.3 Risk-Return Distribution

Since merger arbitrage strategies are exposed to event risk and managers magnify the event risk with the use of leverage, the return distribution exhibits negative skew and excess kurtosis than the aggregated hedge fund index. Even though the strategy is exposed to many risk factors, it has created a less volatile return stream overall. The diversification benefit of the strategy is limited, due to a limited number of M&A transactions and deals in the market. In addition, since merger arbitrage strategies are particularly tied to equity markets, the correlation with the S&P is more pronounced. Yet the strategy outperformed the S&P during both recessions of the decade. The years 1999 and 2000 became the best performance years for merger arbitrage strategies due to increased M&A transactions. Many small and medium-scale technology companies were merged with other companies during the Internet boom.

According to the hedgefund.net database, merger arbitrage strategies exhibit negative skew of -1.61, excess kurtosis of 6.60, and an annualized Sharpe ratio of 1.26, using the risk-free rate of 3.5 percent.

Year	HF Aggregated Index	Merger Arbitrage Index
1991	28.76%	N/A
1992	16.92%	N/A
1993	29.93%	N/A
1994	7.32%	N/A
1995	28.10%	N/A
1996	25.33%	N/A
1997	23.25%	17.81%
1998	11.48%	10.44%
1999	36.22%	21.27%
2000	13.11%	21.30%
2001	9.04%	3.51%
2002	4.38%	0.33%
2003	21.30%	6.89%
2004	10.78%	5.42%
2005	10.94%	6.02%
2006	13.74%	11.55%
2007	12.62%	5.11%
2008	-14.37%	-3.13%
2009	21.41%	9.09%
2010	10.48%	5.40%

Annual returns of merger arbitrage strategy index (Data source: Hedgefund.net)

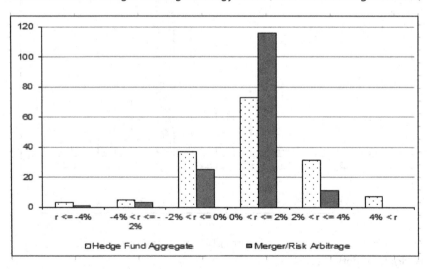

Annual returns of merger arbitrage strategy index (Data source: Hedgefund. net)

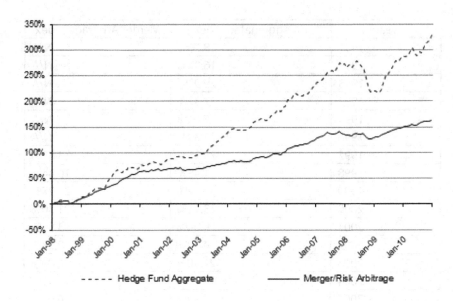

Cumulative returns of merger arbitrage strategy index (Data source: Hedgefund. net)

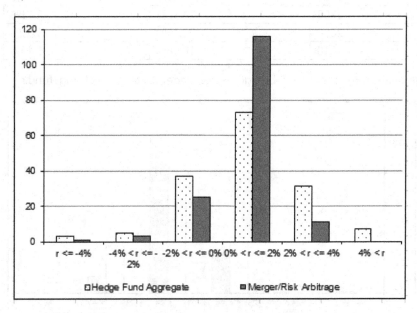

Distribution of returns of merger arbitrage strategy index (Data source: Hedgefund.net)

5.8.4 Due Diligence

Deal Types: Investors should know what types of deals the manager uses. Potential deals offer potential for huge profits, but at the same time, they are exposed to risk of deal failure. Losses can be substantial if the deals fail. On the other hand, taking positions in announced deals is safer, but is subject to lesser returns. Some managers take reverse positions, meaning they take long positions in the acquiring company and short positions in the target companies, expecting the announced deal will fail due to regulatory or other reasons. This strategy yields returns if the merger fails as expected.

Diversification: Since the merger arbitrage strategy is heavily exposed to event risk, unfavorable movement of the deal will cause huge losses to the fund. Part of the event risk can be diversified away by having a large number of positions in the fund. Investors should know the number of deals in the fund, relative size of each position, limit rules, and so on.

Cash Deals: Cash deals involve only long positions in the stock of target companies. Therefore, investors should know how the long positions are hedged against market risk.

Alternative Strategies: Hedge funds are typically held for the long term. Merger activity is cyclical, and fund managers may find reduced merger activity in the industry during the life of the fund. Investors should know how the manager invests available cash and what other strategies the manager possesses experience with.

5.9 Distressed Securities

5.9.1 Strategies

Companies with poor performance, excessive level of debt financing, accounting problems, or rating downgrades from major credit rating agencies are called distressed companies. Traditional institutional investors, such as pension funds and endowments, who have floors on the credit quality of securities, may be forced to sell distressed securities in order to be in compliance. These securities are often sold at discount due to the fire sale. Hedge fund managers employ various arbitrage and nonarbitrage strategies in distressed companies that are either already in the bankruptcy process or likely to file for bankruptcy protection. While private equity firms dealing with distressed companies take an active role in company activities, distressed-security hedge fund managers look for trading opportunities involving the troubled company's outstanding securities. However, most distressed-security hedge fund managers come from a legal background having experience with the bankruptcy process. Therefore, some distressed-security hedge fund managers build strategies that are slightly overlapping with private equity by having some involvement with company leadership. These hedge fund managers are called active distressed hedge fund managers. If an active manager takes a board seat or works on site with company management, then he or she is called an active control manager; otherwise, he or she is called an active noncontrol manager. Active distressed hedge fund managers are less correlated with the overall credit market, while passive distressed hedge fund managers have a higher correlation with the credit market. Distressed-securities fund managers employ various kinds of debt, which carry subinvestment-grade or noninvestment-grade credit ratings. Some of the most common instruments are mezzanine loans, busted convertibles, collateralized debt obligations, credit default swaps, credit default indices, distressed bank loans, equity stubs, high-yield bonds, preferred stocks, second-lien notes, and seller paper.

Depending on the type of the debt and the nature of the firm, distressed-security managers employ various substrategies.

Capital structure arbitrage involves pairing two levels of seniorities in long and short positions. Whether to take a long or a short position depends on the stage of the bankruptcy process. Before the bankruptcy process is declared, managers take a long position in a more senior security and a short position in a less senior security. Examples include taking a long position in senior secured debt and a short position in junior subordinated debt, or taking a long position in preferred stock and a short position in common stock. If bankruptcy is declared, the spread between the two securities will increase, allowing the manager to close out the positions with a profit. The manager's skill at analyzing the company's debt structure plays a major role in earning profits. Managers need to analyze the average yield, recovery rate, and coverage and leverage ratios. Managers need to understand legal issues, such as the rights of subordinated creditors, the status of off-balance sheet liabilities, and potential government intervention. In the late bankruptcy process, managers will take short positions in more senior securities and long positions in less senior securities in post-structured debt. If the company is successful, then the less senior securities are expected to rise in value, while the more senior either stay stable or decrease a little in value. Though the capital structure arbitrage strategy is considered as a substrategy of the distressed-security strategy, some fund managers implement the strategy as a standalone, not necessarily dealing with only troubled companies.

The outright short distressed strategy involves shorting the debt of the individual firm or buying credit default swaps on the debt of the firm. The value strategy involves buying undervalued debt. It focuses on buying debt before the bankruptcy filing, anticipating that the bankruptcy plan will result in a positive resolution with creditors. It also invests in post-restructured companies that are remerging with new management. Rescue financing involves investing in companies that are in deep trouble and bailing them out, avoiding the need of bankruptcy protection filing.

5.9.2 Risk-Return Distribution

The same theory that explains the performance of the convertible arbitrage strategy is also partially applicable to distressed-securities strategies. Credit cycles follow economic cycles and lead equity cycles, both up and down. The four stages of economic cycles are beginning of recovery, bull market, late recovery/beginning of recession, and bear market. Credit spreads start tightening or bond prices start rising in the first phase and continue through the bull market. Equities, typically, start rising in bull markets and continue through phase three. Credit spreads contract faster than they expand, as they are more sensitive to liquidity. As liquidity returns to markets, bond prices rise (credit spreads narrow) in advance of equity markets and the economy.

While both convertible arbitrage and distressed-securities strategies use the segmented section of the bond market, distressed-securities strategies can employ pure long bias, pure short bias, and arbitrage strategies. When arbitrage theory is used in distressed securities, the two positions in a pair contain either bonds or stocks. Combining bonds with stock in the distressed-securities arbitrage strategy is very rare, though not ruled out completely. Instead, different seniorities are used for the arbitrage purpose.

In 2009, distressed-securities strategies stood in third position in performance, with convertible arbitrage and emerging markets strategies being the first and second best performers. Higher sensitivity to liquidity and fast recovery ability account for the performance. Higher exposure to event and credit risk made distressed-securities strategies experience huge losses. The losses were higher than all the strategies except emerging markets and in par with convertible arbitrage strategies. As the economic cycle theory explains that credit markets lead equity markets both up and down, the year 2007 was a poor performance year compared to long/short equity. That means the credit market responded to illiquidity faster than the equity market. Similarly it recovered faster than long/short equity in 2009, demonstrating better performance than long/short Equity.

Distressed-securities strategies exhibit higher exposure to event risks, such as bankruptcy, liquidation, and foreclosure than any other strategies. This higher exposure causes distressed funds to exhibit high positive excess kurtosis and negative skewness, reflecting fat tails. Volatility is comparable with high-yield bonds due to similarities between high-yield bonds and distressed securities. Volatility is significantly less than the S&P 500. Therefore, the risk-adjusted performance is better than that of the S&P 500.

According to the hedgefund.net database, the distressed-securities strategy index exhibits negative skew of -1.92, excess kurtosis of 8.84, and an annualized Sharpe ratio of 1.04, using the risk-free rate of 3.5 percent.

Year	HF Aggregated Index	Distressed Securities Index
1991	28.76%	N/A
1992	16.92%	N/A
1993	29.93%	N/A
1994	7.32%	N/A
1995	28.10%	N/A
1996	25.33%	25.36%
1997	23.25%	18.81%
1998	11.48%	-5.74%
1999	36.22%	19.13%
2000	13.11%	0.15%
2001	9.04%	22.10%
2002	4.38%	5.38%
2003	21.30%	35.25%
2004	10.78%	19.17%
2005	10.94%	11.33%
2006	13.74%	15.04%
2007	12.62%	6.31%
2008	-14.37%	-25.23%
2009	21.41%	35.84%
2010	10.48%	16.92%

Annual returns of distressed-securities strategy index (Data source: Hedgefund. net)

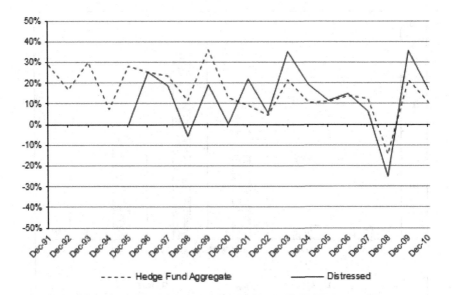

Annual returns of distressed-securities strategy index (Data source: Hedgefund. net)

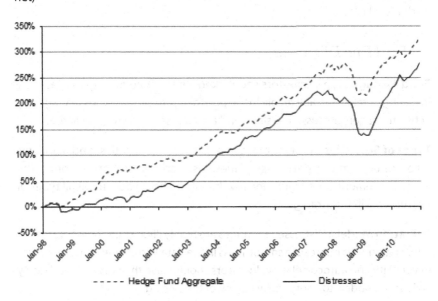

Cumulative returns of distressed-securities strategy index (Data source: Hedgefund.net)

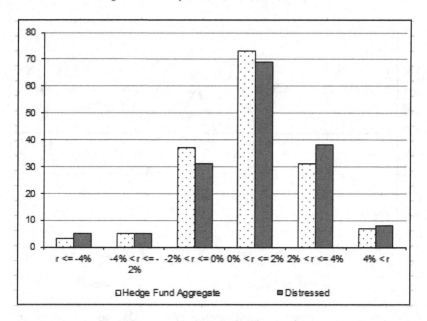

Distribution of returns of distressed-securities strategy index (Data source: Hedgefund.net)

5.9.3 Due Diligence

Fund Manager Type: Investors should know if the fund manager is passively investing or taking an active role in the portfolio companies. Funds managed by active managers are less diversified and are exposed to firm-specific risk.

Types of Securities: As described earlier, distressed-securities fund managers take positions in a variety of securities. Risk varies based on seniority. The lesser the seniority, the higher the risk. Investors should document all types of instruments in the strategy.

Valuation Models: Distressed securities are highly illiquid and possess a lack of information. This may cause smoothness in the data and creates downward bias in volatility and autocorrelation. Investors should have their own or third-party validation models to verify the accuracy of the pricing.

Liquidity: Investors should know how the liquidity of the fund is managed. Some funds offer flexible redemptions, but at the cost of other investors' returns. Therefore, investors should choose the funds depending on their redemption needs. Investors should know if the fund employs any side pockets. Illiquid assets are separated in side pockets, and a fund manager is required to liquidate them before liquidating liquid assets or sell them in proportion to liquid assets.

Leverage: Leverage is more dangerous with distressed-securities funds than any other funds. Use of high leverage is a red signal for the investor.

Credit Exposure: Distressed securities are highly exposed to credit risk. Some fund managers hedge part of the credit risk away, but at the compromise of returns. Investors should know the net credit exposure of the fund.

Diversity: Diversity is difficult for active distressed-securities fund managers due to limited opportunities. However, passive fund managers should diversify the portfolio well in order to reduce event-risk exposure. Investors should know the number of companies in the portfolio and gauge the diversity measure.

5.10 Mortgage-Backed Securities Hedge Funds

5.10.1 Strategies

Mortgage-backed securities (MBS) are securitized assets backed by a pool of residential or commercial mortgages. The three government-sponsored entities (GSE)—Fannie Mae, Freddie Mac, and Ginnie Mae—or private equities purchase loans from banks, mortgage companies, and other originators and then assemble them into pools. The entity then issues securities that represent claims on the principal and interest payments made by borrowers on the loans in the pool, a process known as securitization. The securities are primarily assumed to be protected because homeowners have equity in the house or have mortgage insurance, and also GSEs act as credit enhancers in the case of GSE securities.

Depending on the cash flow and risk distribution to investors, mortgage-backed securities exhibit three types of structures:

- Pass-Through securities
- Collateralized mortgage obligations (CMOs)
- Stripped MBS.

Pass-Through securities pass through prorata cash flows generated from the mortgage payments made by the underlying mortgage holders in the pool. Cash flows from borrowers come in three forms: interest, principal installment, and principal prepayment. One of the key drivers that determines the level of payment to the investor is prepayment rate, which increases the possibility of principal repayment in advance at any time with no penalty. Therefore, pass-through securities are exposed to prepayment risk and reinvestment risk.

Not all investors have the same level of interest to prepayment risk embedded in pass-through securities. Some investors prefer more exposure to prepayment risk and then expect higher risk premium, and some investors prefer little exposure to prepayment risk. **Collateralized mortgage obligations** (CMOs) repackage the cash flow generated by the mortgage pool into different tranches, each tranche having a different mixture of prepayment risk/reward. A CMO is fundamentally similar to a CDO in that the risk of a portfolio of bonds has been redistributed such that some investors are exposed to more risk and some are exposed to less risk, but the main difference is that the CMO is designed to redistribute prepayment risk, whereas the CDO is designed to redistribute default risk.

The most common type of CMO is a **planned amortization class (PAC),** which is amortized based on a sinking fund schedule that is established within a range of prepayment speeds, meaning that within a certain range of prepayment rates the payments to the PAC remain stable. PAC security is structured with a companion tranche called the support tranche, which provides prepayment protection for the PAC security. If the prepayment rate is higher than the upper prepayment rate, then the support tranche absorbs the excess payment, while the PAC receives payments as originally scheduled. If the prepayment rate is less than the lower prepayment rate, then payments to the support tranche are deferred and paid to the PAC. Therefore, the stability of the PAC security cash flows comes at the expense of increased risk to the support tranche. If the excess continues until the support tranche is paid off, then the PAC tranche will start receiving the excess payments. Similarly, if the payments are less than supported by the support tranche, then the PAC will receive lesser payments. At this stage, the PAC is said to be broken or busted.

In contrast to pass-through MBS securities, **Stripped MBS** do not distribute cash flows on a prorata basis. Stripped MBS receive either the principal component or the interest component of cash flow generated from the underlying pool. The strips that pay only the principal component are called principal-only strips or PO strips, and the strips that pay only the interest component are called interest-only strips, or IO strips.

Principal-Only (PO) securities are purchased at a considerable discount to par. The PO cash flow starts out small and substantially increases with the passage of time. Basically, the faster the prepayments occur, the faster PO securities receive their principal back and the higher the yield on the investment. PO tranches benefit from lower interest rates, where prepayments are much faster. This is because the borrowers who had borrowed at higher interest rate would like to take advantage of current low interest rates and so will prepay the loans through refinancing. That means the yield on PO price is inversely related to interest rates and exhibits negative convexity at lower levels of interest rates.

Interest-Only (IO) securities' cash flow starts out big and gets smaller as time passes. In contrast to POs, IO prices move in the same direction as interest rates. That is the reason why certain hedge fund managers prefer IOs during rising interest times. If interest rates are falling, then the underlying pool will be paid off faster than expected, and the IO investors will be left with no interest cash flows.

MBS prices are more volatile due to the prepayment option that is embedded in mortgage loans. In the United States, mortgage borrowers can prepay the home loan at any time without penalty, that is, the borrowers can avail themselves of the prepayment option at no explicit cost. However, mortgage loans include this option price implicitly. Since mortgage loans can be paid at any time, pricing MBS securities is a complex process, and therefore investors require a large premium for bearing prepayment risk. MBS arbitrage hedge fund managers develop various mathematical models and utilize Monte-Carlo simulations to calculate option-adjusted spreads. MBS arbitrage hedge fund managers take long positions in MBS with higher AOS values and short positions in treasury bonds to fund the long positions. Therefore, MBS arbitrage fund managers are said to be long prepayment risk.

5.10.2 Friction in Subprime Mortgage Securitization

Friction among various parties involved in mortgage securities were outlined in a research publication, "The Seven Deadly Frictions of Subprime Mortgage Credit Securitization" by Adam Ashcraft and Til Schuermann.

The securitization process involves various parties, beginning from mortgagor to investor. The main parties involved are mortgagor, originator, arranger, third parties, servicer, asset manager, rating agency, and investor. As information passes through various parties, it may be possible that a certain piece of information is lost or not gathered at all or misinterpreted, resulting in friction. As a result of friction, two parties will not have the same information. There are mainly seven types of frictions in the subprime mortgage securitization process, which are discussed below:

Mortgagor and Originator: This first of the seven frictions is caused by predatory lending. This may happen because mortgagors are not aware of all available financial options; and even if they were aware, they may not be able to make the right decision due to the complexity involved in loan structures. On the other hand, the lender may drive the mortgagor to products that are not suitable. Since a typical subprime borrower is typically financially unsophisticated, the borrower may become worse off after the loan than before because of increased interest rates, or he or she is not able to refinance due to inflated appraisals.

Originator and Arranger: The second friction in the securitization process involves the information problem between originator and arranger. The arranger, or issuer, purchases the loans from the originators for the purpose of securitization and will perform due diligence, but will still have an informational disadvantage. This is because either the originator has superior knowledge about the mortgagor and may have steered the borrower to his products, or the borrower himself may have misrepresented a certain piece of information in the loan application.

Arranger and Third Parties: The pool of mortgage loans is sold by the arranger to a bankruptcy remote trust, a special-purpose vehicle that issues debt to investors. This trust is an essential component of credit risk transfer, as it protects investors from the bankruptcy of the originator or arranger. Moreover, the sale of loans to the trust protects both the originator and arranger from losses on the mortgage loans, provided that there has been no breach of R&W (representations and warranties) by the originator. An important information asymmetry exists between the arranger and the third parties concerning the quality of mortgage loans. The fact that the arranger has more information than the third parties about the quality of the mortgage loans creates an adverse selection problem: the arranger can securitize bad loans (the lemons) and keep the good ones (or securitize them elsewhere). This third friction in the securitization of subprime loans affects the relationship that the arranger has with the warehouse lender, the CRA, and the asset manager.

Servicer and Mortgagor: The trust employs a servicer, who is responsible for collection and remittance of loan payments. The servicer makes advances of unpaid interest by borrowers to the trust. It accounts for principal and interest, provides customer service to the mortgagors, holds escrow or impounds of funds related to payment of taxes and insurance, contacts delinquent borrowers, and supervises foreclosures and property dispositions. The servicer is compensated through a periodic fee paid by the trust. A conflict of interest arises for troubled loans. The homeowner in difficulty does not have the incentive to keep up tax payments, insurance, or maintenance on the property and would prefer to foreclose the property.

Servicer and Third Parties: The servicer can have a significantly positive or negative effect on the losses realized from the mortgage pool. Moody's estimates that servicer quality can affect the realized level of losses by plus or minus 10 percent. This presents a problem similar to the fourth friction (servicer vs. mortgagor). In this case, the servicer has unobserved costly effort that affects the distribution over cash flows shared with other parties, yet has limited liability, with no share in downside risk.

Asset Managers and Investors: The investor provides the funding for the purchase of the MBS. As the typical investor lacks financial sophistication, an agent is employed to formulate an investment strategy, conduct due diligence on potential investments, and find the best price for trades. The investor, however, may not fully understand the manager's investment strategy, may doubt the manager's ability, or may not observe the manager's due-diligence efforts. The information gap between the investor and asset manager gives rise to the sixth friction. This friction between the principal/investor and the agent/manager is mitigated through the use of investment mandates and the evaluation of manager performance relative to a peer benchmark.

Investor and Credit Rating Agency (CRA): Arrangers, not investors, pay rating agencies. This creates a potential conflict of interest. If investors cannot assess the efficacy of rating-agency models, they are susceptible to both honest and dishonest errors. The information asymmetry between investors and the CRAs is the seventh and final friction in the securitization process. Honest errors are a natural by-product of rapid financial innovation and complexity. Dishonest errors may be driven by the dependence of rating agencies on fees paid by the arranger.

5.10.3 Risk Characteristics

Prepayment Risk: Mortgage borrowers have an embedded prepayment option in home loans. The embedded prepayment option gives the right to the borrower to pay an amount in excess of the required installment payment or even to pay off the loan entirely. This is essentially equivalent to a call option on corporate bonds. Prepayment can happen because of the following reasons:

Decline in Interest Rates: If the borrower is holding a high-interest mortgage loan and the interest rates fall, then the borrower will have a larger incentive to refinance the loan. If interest rates are decreased further or raised and then lowered, then the prepayment rate may be lowered. This is called refinancing burnout, as most borrowers who plan to refinance have already done so during the earlier drop in interest rates. This path dependency will lead to even more uncertainty in pricing mortgage securities.

Mortgage Age: The older the mortgage, the more likely it is to be repaid.

Season of the Year: More prepayments occur in summer, as homeowners tend to move in summer.

Loan Balance: The higher the principal balance, the more likely it is to be repaid.

Geography: Some parts of the country exhibit higher housing turnover, thus increasing prepayments.

Economic Activity: As the economy grows, personal income grows, and thus prepayments increase, in either installment payments or the entire loan.

The prepayment option also influences reinvestment rate risk. Fund managers should obtain the characteristics of the underlying mortgages from the issuers and then use them in pricing models to calculate the option-adjusted spread.

Liquidity Risk: Mortgage bonds that are rated as noninvestment-grade are typically segmented and therefore are illiquid in nature. If bond prices do not include sufficient premium to cover liquidity risk, then the bonds are typically at risk.

Interest-Rate Risk: Mortgage rates are driven by dynamics of interest rates. Market interest rates, in turn, influences prepayment rates.

5.11 Regulation-D Strategies

5.11.1 Strategy and Returns

In the United States, Regulation D of the Securities Act of 1953 allows public companies to issue stock or debt privately. Under Regulation D, the securities must be sold to sophisticated investors and must not be marketed to the public. The advantage to the issuer is the shorter time frame it takes to raise the capital, and the drawback is the limited number of investors to purchase the securities. Also, Regulation D minimizes the immediate dilution of company stock. Upon completion of the registration with SEC, investors are allowed to convert to ordinary securities of the issuer. The debenture agreement can be termed such that, if the registration cannot be completed in a certain time, the issuer has to pay the penalty to the investor. Hedge funds that employ the Regulation D strategy take advantage of the discount offered and build one or more substrategies, which are described below:

Value Strategy: The hedge fund manager purchases the privately issued securities at discount and uses leverage to enhance the returns.

Long/Short Strategy: The hedge fund manager takes a long position in privately issued securities at discount and shorts the public securities to minimize the downside risk. The return is limited to the spread between the public and private security.

Convertible Bond as Cheap Equity Strategy: The hedge fund manager purchases private securities that are offered as convertible bonds and convert to equity after a certain period of time.

Convertible Bond as a Cheap Debt Strategy: The hedge fund manager purchases private securities that are offered as convertible bonds and simultaneously shorts the public stock to gain exposure to cheap bonds.

5.11.2 Risk Characteristics

The most pronounced risk factors associated with the Regulation-D strategy are credit risk, registration risk, death spiral, and liquidity risk. Other risks include market risk and interest-rate risk.

Credit Risk: Credit risk comes in the form of default risk on the principal amount or coupon payment. Regulation-D securities usually do not include premium for credit risk. So the fund will face huge losses if the issuer defaults before conversion happens.

Registration Risk: While the typical registration process requires two to three months, significant delays in the process can occur if the company's financial condition is deteriorating or if the company is not providing necessary information in time. A Regulation-D fund manager may lose the expected profit opportunities due to lengthening of time.

Death Spiral: In toxic private placements, investors are allowed to receive greater and greater amounts of common equity as the price of the issuer's stock falls. This can create a death spiral for the issuer since the price of the publicly traded common stock tends to decline, which may lead to default. The potential default will cause investors to lose the rest of the investment.

Liquidity Risk: Regulation-D securities are usually issued by micro-cap or small-cap companies whose securities are considered illiquid in nature. Therefore, the strategy will face liquidity risk when it wants to close the positions after the registration is completed.

Market Risk: The strategy is exposed to equity market risk, and falling equity prices increase the number of shares received from conversion, which will increase the liquidity risk.

5.11.3 Risk-Return Distribution

Under Regulation-D, public companies issue private securities. The proceeds are typically used for company restructuring. Therefore, this strategy falls under the group of corporate restructuring. Regulation-D exhibits lowest volatility within this group and yields consistent returns. Returns distribution exhibits positive skewness and excess kurtosis. Higher positive excess kurtosis and positive skew indicate that the funds are exposed to positive events. Due to their lower volatility and higher consistent returns, Regulation-D funds have share ratio. This is the highest among all the strategies. Maximum drawdown is -12.37 percent and is lower than that of the average hedge fund index.

According to the hedgefund.net database, the Regulation-D strategy index exhibits positive skew of 0.68, excess kurtosis of 3.42, and an annualized Sharpe ratio of 2.16, using the risk-free rate of 3.5 percent.

Year	HF Aggregated Index	Regulation-D Index
1991	28.76%	N/A
1992	16.92%	N/A
1993	29.93%	N/A
1994	7.32%	N/A
1995	28.10%	N/A
1996	25.33%	N/A
1997	23.25%	N/A
1998	11.48%	36.07%
1999	36.22%	34.73%
2000	13.11%	22.47%
2001	9.04%	6.28%

2002	4.38%	21.24%
2003	21.30%	56.62%
2004	10.78%	33.42%
2005	10.94%	15.84%
2006	13.74%	25.76%
2007	12.62%	23.25%
2008	-14.37%	-6.78%
2009	21.41%	30.50%
2010	10.48%	6.55%

Annual returns of Regulation-D strategy index (Data source: Hedgefund.net)

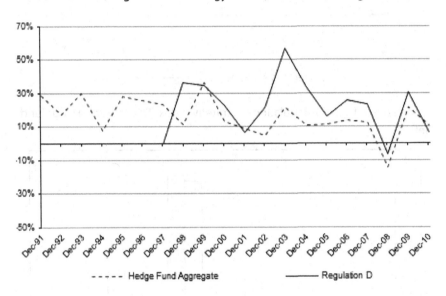

Annual returns of Regulation-D strategy index (Data source: Hedgefund.net)

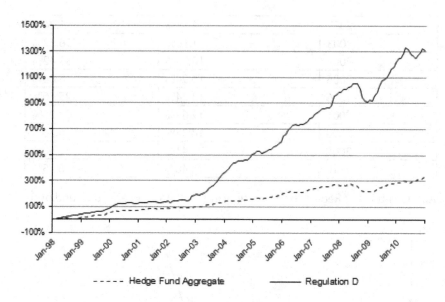

Cumulative returns of Regulation-D strategy index (Data source: Hedgefund. net)

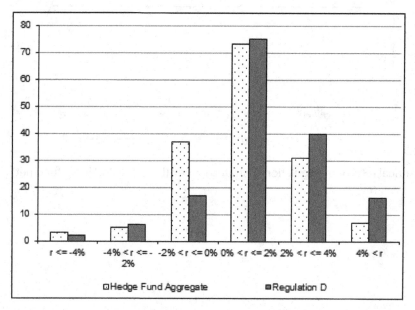

Distribution of returns of Regulation-D strategy index (Data source: Hedgefund.net)

5.11.4 Due Diligence

Investing in Regulation-D securities requires a special set of skills that is different from those of traditional equity investing. Investors should know the level of experience the manager possesses in the strategy. Investors should know what the various substrategies employed are, such as value strategy, long/short strategy, convertible bond as cheap equity, and convertible bond as cheap debt strategy.

5.12 Emerging Markets

5.12.1 Strategy

A country that is in the process of developing or is in the process of moving from a closed market to an open market is called an emerging market country. Such countries typically have per capita incomes on the lower to middle end of the world range. In fact, there is no exact definition for *emerging market country,* and there is no body that constitutes or represents emerging markets. It is a term that became popular over time. Emerging market countries include a wide range of nations in all continents. The most pronounced countries in the emerging market category are the BRIC countries, which are Brazil, Russia, India, and China. Emerging market countries constitute around 20 percent of the world's countries and 80 percent of the global population.

Emerging markets securities have higher beta or systemic risk, and as a result funds that invested in these securities became attractive for investors. While mutual funds were mainly interested in investing in traditional bonds and securities, emerging market hedge funds extended the investment spectrum to commodities, real estate, infrastructures, currencies, and derivatives. Emerging market hedge funds can also use leverage, offering significantly increased return potential. As a result, institutional investors, such as pension funds and endowments, who were looking for alternative investment options began pouring money into emerging market hedge funds. Emerging market hedge fund managers typically follow a long/short strategy.

Asian and Latin American countries encompass a wide spectrum of countries and investment opportunities. While some countries like South Korea and Taiwan are well on their way to becoming developed markets. There is huge potential for growth in the BRIC nations. The India and Russia markets are the fastest growing markets. Most of the Russia growth is attributable to energy focused companies. However, investment opportunities are not limited solely to large oil, electricity, and gas producers. When considering the emerging markets average index, more developed markets like Russia, India, and Brazil are strongly correlated with the returns of the emerging markets average, while less developed countries are not.

5.12.2 Risk Characteristics

Depending on the substrategies and instruments used in emerging markets hedge funds, they are exposed to the risks explained in individual strategy sections. The magnitude of risks lies heavily in contagion risk, political risk, sovereign risk, country risk, economic risk, default risk, currency risk.

Contagion Risk: From the emerging markets point of view, contagion risk is the risk that unrelated countries nonetheless suffer from a related crisis. For example, the currency devaluation in Thailand in 1997 caused a spillover that affected all markets within a matter of months. Contagion risk increases the correlation of movements among markets around the world and also increases the volatility and duration of market movements. As a result of increased correlation, the notion of diversification as a risk management strategy disappears as all assets and markets move in the same direction. So in market-neutral and relative value strategies, which are built on assumed correlations between long and short positions, instead of cancelling out the risks of each other, they reinforce each other. In addition, the magnitude of these movements tends to exceed historical levels. This is exactly what happened in the case of LTCM.

Political Risk: The most difficult risk to quantify in emerging market investments is political risk, as the information available is very subjective in nature and hard to obtain in a timely manner. Due to the larger role governments play in emerging market countries, it is very important for emerging markets hedge fund managers to conduct an in-depth analysis of political risk.

Sovereign Risk: Sovereign risk is a risk that a foreign government will default on its loan or fail to honor other business commitments because of a change in national policy. Even if the borrower is capable of repaying the loan, a country may impose restrictions on payment of debt, either in part or wholly.

Country Risk: Country risk is associated with doing business in a particular country, whereas sovereign risk focuses only on the ability or willingness of debt repayment by government. In other words, country risk is the broadest measure, which includes sovereign risk, political risk, and transfer risk. Transfer risk is the risk that a transaction cannot take place because a government or central bank will not allow currency to leave a country. Though there is a positive relation between sovereign and country risk, the sovereign credit profile can improve without necessarily expecting improvement in the business environment. Similarly, deterioration in country risk conditions does not necessarily imply a worsening in sovereign creditworthiness, though often that will be the case.

Economic Risk: Unexpected, adverse changes in the economic stability of a country can cause disruption in macroeconomic forecasts. Signs of economic risk can be found in inflation rates and fiscal and foreign account policy.

Default Risk: Default or major down grade of any country will result in contagion risk and effects investments even outside the troubled country. For example, a recent downgrade of Greece credit rating affected many international funds.

Currency Risk: Since investing in foreign funds involve multiple currencies the funds are exposed to currency devaluation risk.

5.12.3 Risk-Return Distribution

Due to the economic liberalization and globalization economy in emerging nations, hedge funds invested in those countries have been demonstrating superior performance. Between 1997 and 2010, there were only two years with negative returns. Poor performance in 1998 was attributed to the fact that several sovereign bonds were defaulted in 1998, led by the Russian Federation. This was added pressure on struggling financial markets, which started with the broad devaluation of Asian currencies in 1997. The other down year was 2008, which was a result of the global financial crisis. From the table below, it can be observed that both the profits and losses lie in extremes compared to other strategies. For example, emerging market strategy funds performed worse than any other strategies in 2008, and the same was reversed in year 2009 by demonstrating the best performance of all strategies. The maximum negative returns were partly attributed to the fact that emerging market nations provide fewer or no tools to protect assets from downward pressure. Most emerging nations either have banned short sale or have strict rules about them. The intensity of headline risk is higher in emerging markets than in developed markets. That means even though there is less perceived risk in a market, the market sometimes overreacts to event risk. This is true for even positive events. This analogy is also supported by the annual returns of years 1998, 1999, 2008, and 2009. While 1998 was a difficult year for the hedge fund industry as a whole, the emerging markets funds rebounded quickly in 1999, with its highest annual return of 63.11 percent. Similarly years 2008 and 2009 logged returns of -33.54 percent and 42.55 percent respectively. All four years stood in the extreme end of the return spectrum, either on the negative side or the positive side. This makes the returns distribution of emerging market funds exhibit high positive excess kurtosis, resulting in fat tails with returns concentrated either around the mean or in extreme tails.

According to the hedgefund.net database, the emerging markets strategy index exhibits negative skew of -0.99, excess kurtosis of 3.91, and an annualized Sharpe ratio of 0.82, using the risk-free rate of 3.5 percent.

Year	HF Aggregated Index	Emerging Markets Index
1991	28.76%	N/A
1992	16.92%	N/A
1993	29.93%	N/A
1994	7.32%	N/A
1995	28.10%	N/A
1996	25.33%	N/A
1997	23.25%	28.71%
1998	11.48%	-32.80%
1999	36.22%	63.11%
2000	13.11%	6.86%
2001	9.04%	26.48%
2002	4.38%	13.23%
2003	21.30%	41.34%
2004	10.78%	20.93%
2005	10.94%	23.46%
2006	13.74%	29.53%
2007	12.62%	31.32%
2008	-14.37%	-33.54%
2009	21.41%	42.55%
2010	10.48%	12.43%

Annual returns of emerging markets strategy index (Data source: Hedgefund.net)

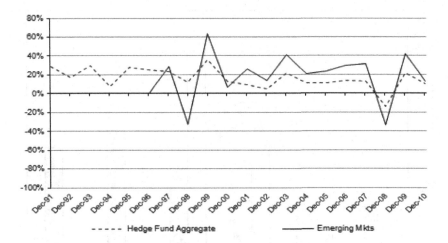

Annual returns of emerging markets strategy index (Data source: Hedgefund. net)

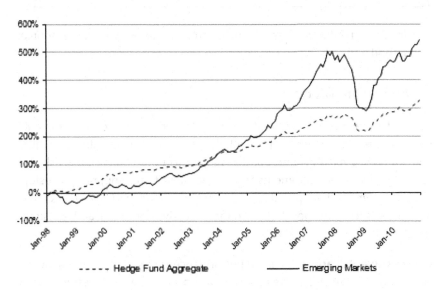

Cumulative returns of emerging markets strategy index (Data source: Hedgefund. net)

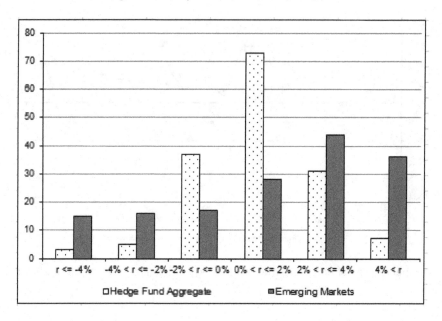

Distribution of returns of emerging markets strategy index (Data source: Hedgefund.net)

5.12.4 Due Diligence

Types of Instruments: The magnitude of risk depends on the type of instruments used. For the same type of instrument, the risk varies from country to country. For example, a fixed-income bond is subject to both counterparty risk and sovereign risk. Some instruments are more sensitive to currency rates. Investors should document the types of instruments used in the fund. Investors should also know if the manager deals with local securities or American Depositary Receipts.

Competitive Advantage: Funds' performance depends on the manager's knowledge of local laws and relationship with local businesses. Investors should document the manager's competitive advantage in proprietary research, dealing with senior management of local companies, and so forth.

Investment Style: Emerging markets fund managers employ various approaches, such as bottom-up, top-down, fundamental, and quantitative. The efficiency of the approach depends on the availability of historical data. In general, there is not enough historical data available for emerging markets' investments. Investors should know what style the manager is following. Funds that employ more than one style are considered to be good.

Investment Universe: Some emerging markets funds invest in advanced emerging nations, such as Brazil, Russia, India, and China (grouped and called BRIC), and some funds invest in frontier markets that are in the early stage of economic development. Frontier markets are associated with lack of information and liquidity risk, but offer the potential for huge profits. Investors should list all the countries that the fund is exposed to. Though there is correlation among emerging nations, country diversification is considered to be a good sign for the fund.

Liquidity: Investors should know how the liquidity of the fund is managed. Emerging markets securities are typically more illiquid and have wider bid-ask spreads.

Sensitivity to Contagion Risk: As explained in the previous section, emerging markets funds are more exposed to contagion risks. Investors should perform their own contagion risk analysis depending on the countries exposed and document all the details.

Dealing with Corporate Governance: Some emerging markets corporations are controlled by government, and some companies have minority shareholder protection. Investors should know how the manager deals with such companies.

Basis Risk: Some emerging countries prohibit short sale, while some countries have strict rules for short sale. Therefore, it is often difficult to hedge the portfolio perfectly, and emerging markets are exposed to long bias and basis risk. The investor should know how the fund is protected from any unfavorable market activities.

5.13 Global Macro

5.13.1 Strategies

A global macro hedge fund strategy is an opportunistic strategy and takes a macroeconomic approach on a global basis. Global macro hedge fund managers have the broadest investment universe and make leveraged bets on forecasted movements of equity, debt, currency, interest rates, and commodity prices. They employ a top-down approach and conduct analysis of macroeconomic variables associated with countries in which they invest. Global macro hedge fund managers can take directional positions or long/short, concentrated, or diversified positions. During the 1990s, legendary managers like George Soros's Quantum Fund and Jillion Robertson's Tiger Fund engaged in multibillion-dollar, aggressive, leveraged directional bets. A global macro hedge fund strategy depends heavily on the manager's skill, which is the most important source of returns. Based on the approach and strategies followed by global macro managers, they can be classified in two ways: discretionary global macro managers and systematic global macro managers.

Discretionary global macro managers employ a fundamental top-down approach and analyze information from different sources, such as central bank publications, survey data, confidence indicators, asset flows, liquidity measures, forecasting agencies, political commentators, and industry contacts. These managers think that asset prices are determined by fundamental economic factors that affect the supply and demand of an asset. While in the short run prices can deviate from their true economic equilibrium, in the long run they will converge to levels consistent with investor rationality as determined by fundamental economic factors. These managers spend an enormous time forming their views on likely market scenarios and alternative scenarios to identify the best risk/reward opportunities. From there, they determine appropriate entry points, often by applying traditional technical analysis. Discretionary global macro managers also borrow techniques from other strategies, such as fixed-income, long/short equity, and merger arbitrage strategies, and tend to use multiple techniques; as a result, there exists low correlation among these managers.

Systematic global macro managers develop sophisticated algorithms or quantitative models by replacing subjective macroeconomic analysis with highly structured, disciplined, and repeatable investment processes. They use these mathematical models to evaluate markets, detect trading opportunities, generate signals, and establish entry and exit points. The systematic global macro managers are said to be global trend followers, as their process leads them to long-term macroeconomic trends. Since systematic global macro managers build models on broad economic theory and tend to use the same techniques that many other systematic global macro managers use, the correlation among these managers is high.

Model-based global macro managers rely on financial models and economic theories, market movements, and detecting policy mistakes. They also use the models to compare the sensible estimate with implied market estimates.

The most commonly used models are carry trade, yield curve-related value trades, purchasing power parity models, valuation models, and option pricing models.

Carry trade involves short selling a financial instrument with a low interest rate, and then purchasing a financial instrument with a higher interest rate. Thus, the profit is the money collected from the interest rate differential. Yield curve-related value trades involve shorting the financial instruments at the lower-yield part of the curve and investing at the higher-yield part of the curve. Purchasing power parity models, also called "law of one price" models, are used to assess the relative value of currencies. Valuation models apply a bottom-up approach at each company level and then estimate expected returns and dividends. Option pricing models are used to derive the implied volatility of financial instruments and then forecast the future volatility.

Top-down macro strategies are generally opportunistic and directional. However, in order to achieve lower volatility as desired by hedge fund investors, macro managers also employ a long/short strategy, which is based on an outperformance bet on one asset versus another. While both directional and long/short macro strategies are subjective and are based on top-down macroeconomic views, a new strategy, called the macroeconomic arbitrage strategy, has become more popular in the recent era; it is based on detecting objective macroeconomic mispricing in markets.

Directional Macro

Directional macro trading strategies involve either buying or short selling assets based on views and expectations about underlying macroeconomic variables that influence the dynamics of that asset price. The existence of trend and pattern and the existence of normal relations between assets enable successful implementation of macro directional strategies. In addition, the fact that market forces dictate government actions also is an important factor for directional macro strategies.

One of the most effective directional bets was George Soros's bet. In 1979, the European Monetary System (EMS) was established in order to stabilize exchange rates, reduce inflation, and prepare for monetary integration. The system was initially started with France, Germany, Italy, the Netherlands, Belgium, Denmark, Ireland, and Luxembourg, followed by the joining of the United Kingdom later. One of the main components of the EMS was the exchange rate mechanism (ERM). The ERM gave each participatory currency a central exchange rate against a basket of currencies, the European currency unit (ECU). Each country was required to maintain its exchange rates within a 2.25 percent fluctuation band above or below each bilateral central rate. Some large countries, such as Italy and the United Kingdom, were given a band of 6.0 percent. The ERM appeared to be a success, and the disciplinary effect reduced inflation throughout Europe under the leadership of the German Bundesbank. Since mid 1992, international investors started worrying that the exchange rate values of several currencies within the ERM were inappropriate. As a result of German reunification in 1989, the nation's government spending surged, forcing the Bundesbank to print more money. This led to higher inflation and forced the central bank to increase interest rates, which in turn placed upward pressure on the German mark. This forced the central banks of other participatory countries to raise their interest rates as well, so as to maintain the pegged currency exchange rates.

In 1992, the United Kingdom was in recession, with an unemployment rate above 10 percent. George Soros, the Quantum Hedge Fund manager, realized that the United Kingdom's weak economy and high unemployment rate would not permit the British government to maintain the EMS policy for long. George Soros wanted to bet that the pound would depreciate because the United Kingdom would either devalue the pound or leave the ERM. Due to the progressive removal of capital controls during the EMS years, international investors at the time had more freedom than ever to take advantage of perceived disequilibrium. George Soros established a directional short bet in pounds. He also made great use of options and futures. In all, his positions accounted for $10 billion. Many other investors soon followed suit, selling pounds and placing tremendous downward pressure on the currency.

At first, the Bank of England tried to defend the pegged rates by buying 15 billion pounds with its large reserve assets, but its sterilized interventions were limited in their effectiveness. The pound was trading dangerously close to the lower levels of its fixed band. On September 16, 1992, a day that would later be known as Black Wednesday, the bank announced a 2 percent rise in interest rates in an attempt to boost the pound's appeal. A few hours later, it promised to raise rates again, to 15 percent, but international investors like Soros could not be swayed, knowing that huge profits were right around the corner. Traders kept selling pounds in huge volumes, and the Bank of England kept buying them. However, these efforts were ineffective, and ultimately the United Kingdom was forced to leave the ERM, resulting in steep depreciation in the pound's effective value. Soros's Quantum Fund made a profit of over $1billion by his directional bet against the British pound.

Long/Short Macro

The long/short macro strategy involves buying one asset and simultaneously selling short another asset, thus betting on the direction of the spread using macroeconomic views indicating that the former asset should outperform the latter. Long/short macro strategies work better in difficult markets. The idea is to replace directional views and expectations on an asset correlated with the direction of the market by macroeconomic information bet on a two-asset spread that is noncorrelated with the market. Directional macro strategy is hard to implement in a difficult market due to the lack of trend and pattern. For example, in 1994, the S&P 500 had no trend and no pattern after an upward trending in 1993. The S&P became a difficult market in 1994 as the Fed raised rates unexpectedly. Directional macro strategies, which were so successful in the previous year in a trending market with an upward channel pattern, faced difficulties in 1994. Long/Short strategies would have been more profitable during 1994.

After an incredible bull market period, Asian markets experienced difficulties in 1997. When Asian markets entered into a downtrend following the crisis and made short selling profitable, the United States and Europe experienced difficulties in implementing successful directional macro strategies. What made the situation worse for the United States and Europe was the collapse of the normal positive correlation between bonds and equities. Typically, weak noninflationary macroeconomic data is considered as a positive signal for both stocks and bonds. However, during the fall of the Asian markets, the weak noninflationary macroeconomic data was interpreted as negative for stocks, given the slow growth, thus decreasing the earnings prospective. At the same time, bonds were rallying. This caused the bonds and equities to become negatively correlated assets like commodities and equities. The negative correlation was further enhanced by investors switching out of equities into bonds. These market conditions made the long/short strategies more favorable, as the focus had been shifted from the direction of the market to the direction of new synthetic asset/spreads, whose direction had no correlation with the direction of the market.

Macro Arbitrage

Macro arbitrage strategies are based on detecting objective macroeconomic mispricing in global markets. A macroeconomic mispricing is an incorrect pricing of macroeconomic variables, such as interest rates, currency rates, and so on. Macro arbitrage strategies are also referred to as *relative value macro strategies*.

Relative value strategies are more heterogeneous than trend-following ones. The decision to trade is made in the context of other positions, potential trades either pair-wise or portfolio-wise. Many of these relative value strategies are based on an expectation of price convergence in the future. Since divergences can last longer or shorter than expected, risk control is the most important determinant of long-term success of a relative value strategy. Examples of relative value strategies include purchase power parity programs, currency carry programs.

Purchase Power Parity Theory

The purchase power parity (PPP) theory is based on an extension and variation of the "law of one price" as applied to the aggregate economy. It is a theory of exchange rate determination and a way to compare the average costs of goods and services between countries. This theory assumes that the actions of importers and exporters, motivated by cross-country price differences, induce changes in the spot exchange rate. The law of one price dictates that identical goods should sell for the same price in two separate countries when there are no transportation costs and no differential taxes applied in the two countries. The *Economist* magazine publishes the Big Mac Index. The *Economist* uses the price of the ubiquitous McDonald's meal to calculate the "Big Mac Index," a guide showing how far from fair value different world currencies are. The Big Mac theory, a flavor of purchasing power parity, says that exchange rates should even out the prices of Big Macs sold across the world. Global macro arbitrage managers detect if any violation of PPP exists and buy undervalued currencies and sell overvalued currencies. For example, if a McDonald's meal costs more in Euros compared to the United States in terms of dollars, then the Euro is said to be overvalued and managers buy US dollars and sell Euros, expecting the convergence of currency values.

Currency Carry Program

Currency Carry trade programs are built against uncovered interest rate parity (UIP) theory and covered interest rate parity (CIP) theory.

Uncovered interest rate parity theory states that the interest rate differential between two countries should be equal to the projected change in exchange rate between the respective currencies. If UIP holds true, then there will not be any arbitrage opportunities from the carry trade, as the gains from the interest rate side are offset by the loss from the currency side or vice versa.

However, in reality, the UIP does not hold true. This encourages fund managers to build arbitrage strategies that sell currencies with low interest rates and buy currencies with high interest rates. In other words, the strategy borrows from a country with low interest rates and invests in a country with high interest rates. Fund managers expect that high interest rates will go further up (currency appreciating further) and low interest rates will go further down (currency depreciating further) or both cases—in other words, low currencies will further depreciate and high currencies will further appreciate. At the end of the investment period, managers sell the investments and repay the funds. The expected profit is the difference between the difference of currencies at the time of rewinding and the difference between currencies at the time of investing. This strategy will be unfavorable in the following scenarios: if the funding currency appreciates by more than the appreciation in the target currency; if the target currency depreciates more than depreciation in the funding currency; the funding currency interest rates rise, which increases floating borrowing costs; or loss incurs in the invested country due to unfavorable market conditions. Liquidity of investments is also a determinant factor of profits. If the manager is not able to liquidate the investments in time due to the illiquid nature of investments, then the manager will have to forgo the arbitrage opportunity, which may not exist beyond a certain period.

Covered interest rate parity theory states that interest rate differentials between two countries are offset by the spot/forward currency premium, as otherwise investors could earn a pure arbitrage profit. However, in reality, deviations from CIP are neither rare nor short-lived in the long-dated capital market. Macro arbitrage fund managers employ a strategy that sells the foreign currency forward if the forward exchange rate is higher than the spot rate and buys the foreign currency if the forward exchange rate is lower than the spot rate. Typically, currencies with low interest rates are at forward premium, and currencies with high interest rates are at forward discount. Therefore, the strategy will be identical to selling currencies with low interest rates and buying currencies with high interest rates.

5.13.2 Risk Characteristics

Since global macro hedge fund strategies are opportunistic and involve investing anywhere in the world and in any type of financial assets, there is no unique set of risk factors associated specifically to this strategy. In fact, the global hedge fund is exposed to most typical risk factors that the underlying substrategy is exposed to. However, the magnitude of certain risk factors like political, currency, sovereign, economic, and interest-rate risks are high. Since global macro managers take bets against forecasted macroeconomic factors, a global hedge fund is exposed heavily to market risk. Market risk arises in the form of event risks, such as political developments, unexpected currency moves, unexpected earning revisions by major companies, and merger announcements. Governments can impose taxes on cross-border financial flows and payments, including certain types of reserve requirements, as well as quantitative limits and outright prohibitions. Investors might not have adequate information on global markets and on the financial health of the companies, the settlement systems might be inefficient and slow, accounting standards might be poor, and investor protection might be minimal. A significant portion of returns attribute to political risk premium, though it is hard to explain how much of the returns contribute to this premium.

5.13.3 Risk-Return Distribution

A broad investment spectrum of multiple countries and a variety of financial instruments allow global macro managers to achieve the highest level of diversification, and as a result, the return distribution of global macro hedge funds is very close to a normal distribution, with slightly positive skew and very little excess kurtosis. Positive skewness indicates a higher probability of large positive returns. Global macro hedge funds earn returns higher than the S&P 500 with volatility less than half of that of the S&P 500. Global macro hedge funds have a medium positive correlation with the S&P 500. The maximum drawdown exhibited by global macro hedge funds was significantly lower than the maximum drawdown for the S&P 500.

According to the hedgefund.net database, the global macro strategy index exhibits positive skew of 0.34, excess kurtosis of 1.56, and an annualized Sharpe ratio of 1.55, using the risk-free rate of 3.5 percent.

Year	HF Aggregated Index	Fund of Hedge Funds Aggregated Index	Global Macro Index
1991	28.76%	12.74%	N/A
1992	16.92%	12.49%	N/A
1993	29.93%	27.17%	N/A
1994	7.32%	-2.58%	N/A
1995	28.10%	13.52%	N/A
1996	25.33%	18.49%	N/A

1997	23.25%	17.43%	21.89%
1998	11.48%	2.53%	11.37%
1999	36.22%	25.93%	30.54%
2000	13.11%	8.89%	8.39%
2001	9.04%	4.93%	12.22%
2002	4.38%	1.94%	10.52%
2003	21.30%	11.67%	22.27%
2004	10.78%	6.89%	8.47%
2005	10.94%	7.73%	11.00%
2006	13.74%	10.07%	11.42%
2007	12.62%	9.76%	17.55%
2008	-14.37%	-18.85%	-1.27%
2009	21.41%	9.73%	13.45%
2010	10.48%	5.39%	8.56%

Annual returns of global macro strategy index (Data source: hedgefund.net)

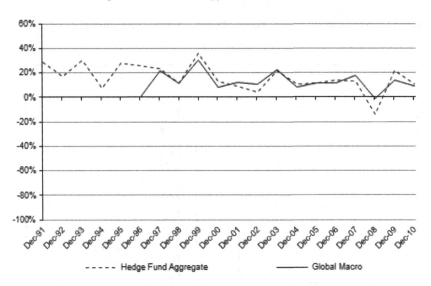

----- Hedge Fund Aggregate   ——— Global Macro

Annual returns of global macro strategy index (Data source: Hedgefund.net)

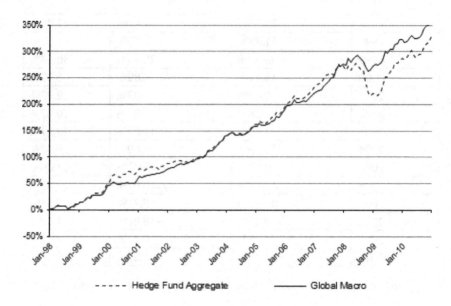

Cumulative returns of global macro strategy index (Data source: Hedgefund. net)

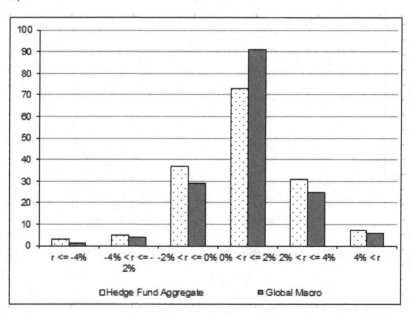

Distribution of returns of global macro strategy index (Data source: Hedgefund. net)

As per the HedgeFund.net research, total assets in funds employing a macro strategy increased by 11.80 percent from the end of 2009. At the same time, the percent of hedge funds employing fund of funds (FoF) declined to 38.2 percent in Q3 2010 from 48.4 percent in the prior year. The increased interest in global macro and decreased interest in FoF can be explained as follows: While both fund of funds and global macro achieve the highest level of diversification and are able to exhibit return distributions that are closer to the normal distribution, the FoF exhibits slightly negative skewness and global macro exhibits slightly positive skewness. Also, the FoF funds require a double layer of fees. As a result, investors are inclined toward global macro.

The other interesting observation from global macro index returns is that between 1990 and 2010, there were only two years of negative returns, the first one in 1994 and the second one in 2008. The negative returns during 1994were because managers in 1993 built long positions in European bonds, not anticipating that the Federal Reserve would raise rates subsequently, thus leading to a global bond market crash. Similarly the negative returns during 2008 can be explained by the global financial crisis. However, local or regional recessions during 1997, 1998, and 2000 could not impact global macro index returns even though few other hedge fund strategies have exhibited negative returns during 1998 and 2000 as well. From this study it can be inferred that global macro managers are exposed to macroeconomic and global markets, rather than local or regional markets, which explains the diversification benefit.

With capital reentering the hedge fund space after the 2008 global financial crisis and a surplus of market uncertainty going forward relating to issues like new financial reform, European economic turmoil, and natural disasters/ catastrophes, investors are looking for investment opportunities that offer absolute returns, transparency, liquidity, and proven success. Macro strategies appear to be emerging as one of the most qualified candidates. Several endogenous factors that are instrumental in producing global macros' over performance include flexibility, quick reposition, macroeconomic focus, global opportunity set, aversion to less liquid credit and other illiquid investments, and risk management.

Flexibility: Global macro hedge funds, by mandate, have the broadest investment scope of all hedgefund strategies, providing significant benefits when conditions driving individual markets are in transition. As opposed to individual security selection, global macro hedge funds have a greater focus on asset allocation, which has been shown to be one of the most important drivers of performance for long-only portfolios.

Quick Reposition: Macro funds provide investors with an actively managed strategy that can be quickly repositioned depending on the current market environment and future outlook. In the event of uncertain markets, macro funds might be the best option for mitigating risk while maximizing returns.

Macroeconomic Focus: Global macro hedge funds' focus on macroeconomics has achieved profits through increasing volatility of monetary and financial policy. Investment in foreign exchange and interest rate products allows for more direct exposures to central bank-driven changes than other asset classes. In addition, the extensive use of top-down economic analyses, as opposed to bottom-up company research, has provided an advantage for global macro hedge funds in changing macroeconomic environments.

Global Opportunity Set: The strategy's wide geographic scope enables global macro funds to dynamically shift exposures to markets that offer improved risk/reward profiles and expand efficient frontiers through more diverse and less correlated asset combinations. International diversification's portfolio benefits are combined with the flexibility of a mandate to reduce exposure to market-specific risks, allowing for performance through separate market dislocations. Country-specific emerging market risks have become pronounced in past financial crises, and the ability to both participate in and avoid this sector given changing geopolitical conditions has benefited global macro investments.

Aversion to Less-Liquid Credit and Other illiquid Investments: Though supported by global macro's broad mandate, credit allocations are generally lower than exposures to other asset classes. Global macro hedge funds mainly invest in listed securities and avoid less-liquid credit exposure. This results in less financing risk and higher levels of unencumbered cash, creating more of a "liquidity provider" profile than other, more capital-intensive, investment strategies. Thus, global macro hedge funds have access to a variety of these opportunities as they become attractive in post-dislocation environments; however, they do not rely on credit investments as a core part of their strategy.

Risk Management: In the early periods of global investing, macro fund managers used to follow naive approaches and were not using sophisticated risk management systems. However, in the modern era of investment, global macro managers are using various risk measurement techniques, such as VAR calculation and diversification of portfolios. This more disciplined investing is providing downside protection while not compromising returns. Since the peak of the financial crisis, most institutional investors have established new risk management practices. Macro funds most likely satisfy investors' risk appetites by offering steady liquidity and having a proven track record of performing well in both bear and bull markets.

5.14 Fund of Hedge Funds

5.14.1 Strategies

A fund of hedge funds or simply FoF is an investment vehicle rather than a strategy. FoF pools the capital of investors and allocates it to various hedge funds in an attempt to diversify across a range of styles, strategies, and managers. FoF is one of three possible ways for investors to gain exposure to the hedge fund world, the other two approaches being self-managed hedge funds and index investing. FoF is also known as a delegated approach, as investors buy shares in a fund of hedge funds, thus outsourcing manager selection, portfolio construction, risk management and monitoring, due diligence, and liquidity management. Funds of funds can employ various strategies, such as conservative, opportunistic, diversified, concentrated, and market defensive.

Conservative FoFs seek consistent returns by investing in conservative strategies, such as equity market neutral, fixed-income arbitrage, merger arbitrage, and convertible arbitrage strategies. The conservative funds earn consistent returns regardless of market conditions and exhibit lower volatility than the universal fund of funds index.

Opportunistic FoFs seek outsize returns by primarily investing in opportunistic and volatile strategies. For example, short-selling strategies may perform well before entering into a recession or during a recession, and fixed-income nonarbitrage strategies may perform well during the recovery stage of the economy. Opportunistic FoFs bend toward investing in emerging markets, long/short, short bias, and equity hedge. The opportunistic FoF exhibits a greater dispersion of returns and a higher volatility.

Diversified FoFs are the most popular FoF and seek returns by primarily investing in highly diversified strategies that are expected to be somewhat uncorrelated to each other and among multiple managers and geographies. Historical annual return and volatility are in line with that of the universal FoF and closely correlated with the universal FoF. On the other hand, a single strategy fund of fund managers invests in multiple funds of the same type of strategy.

Concentrated FoFs typically invest in five to fifteen hedge funds that are expected to be somewhat correlated to each other.

Market-Defensive FoFs seek profit by investing in strategies that are negatively correlated to equity markets, such as short selling, commodities, and managed futures.

Funds of hedge funds have become a large component of the hedge fund industry and contribute 20 to 25 percent of the assets under management of the hedge fund industry. Regardless of the type of FoF, whether it is called diversified or otherwise, a FoF by its nature provides diversification. While sophisticated investors might be inclined to invest directly in hedge funds, an investor who is new to the hedge fund world may well choose to invest through a fund of hedge funds. A fund of hedge funds is the preferred investment vehicle for high risk-averse investors.

A fund of Hedge Funds offers several advantages to investors, which are described below:

- Diversification
- Accessibility
- Economies of scale
- Information advantage
- Access to certain funds
- Compliance
- Leverage
- Liquidity
- Hedging
- Risk management
- Due diligence
- Consolidated reporting
- Fee structure
- Reduced survivorship bias
- No selection bias
- No instant history bias

Diversification: Hedge fund investing requires minimum capital, and therefore, a typical individual investor may not be able to diversify his intended funds across multiple strategies and thus may not be able to reduce the risk to a desired level. Prudent investing dictates that a portfolio should be well diversified. A FoF acts as a good investment vehicle for investors to gain exposure to a well-diversified portfolio in terms of manager, strategy, style, geography, and so on.

By combining a set of individual funds, the manager-specific risk or idiosyncratic risk is reduced, resulting in less volatile and more stable returns. A portfolio of five hedge funds can eliminate 80 percent of the individual manager-specific risk, while a portfolio of twenty funds can eliminate 95 percent of the individual manager-specific risk. The fund of funds portfolio diversification level also depends on the mix of strategies and correlation among managers underlying the portfolio.

Accessibility: The minimum level of capital required to invest in a single hedge fund is typically a million US dollars, which disqualifies a lot of individual investors. In contrast, the minimum investment level in a fund of hedge funds is relatively low. This allows more individual and small investors to gain access to hedge fund investing.

Economies of Scale: The work necessary to conduct due diligence, manager selection, research, risk management, risk monitoring, and administration of multiple investments is costly for individual investors. A fund of hedge funds shares these associated costs and provides a superior and more efficient way to invest in multiple funds.

Information Advantage: The depth of information available to individual investors and asset allocators varies significantly due to the private nature of the hedge fund industry. A fund of funds manager, as an asset allocator, has the ability to collect data from various channels, such as prime brokers, data providers, and industry contacts. The ability to access, collect, and interpret data gives them a competitive advantage over individual investors.

Access to Certain Funds: Some hedge fund managers report to database providers only if the performance is attractive. By the time the performance appears in a database, the fund might have been closed to new investors. Some hedge funds access additional investment only from existing investors. Investing in a fund of funds that is already allocated to these closed-end funds is a fast way to gain access to their superior performance.

Compliance: Some institutional investors, such as pension funds, are restricted from investing in hedge funds that are not registered with regulatory agencies like the SEC. In order to gain wider acceptance from their audience, most fund of funds managers register in their respective regulatory agencies. This allows institutional investors to gain access to funds that otherwise they could not have invested in.

Leverage: Though hedge fund managers use leverage to enhance returns, the end investor usually cannot use leverage to invest in individual hedge funds. Some fund of funds managers offer leverage to their investors, allowing them to earn higher returns at lower volatility.

Liquidity: Compared to traditional securities, such as stocks and bonds, hedge funds are illiquid in nature due to lockups, redemption gates, notice period, and limited redemption windows. Funds of funds offer relatively flexible liquidity— more than individual hedge funds—and offer monthly or quarterly liquidity in normal market conditions. Some funds of funds even offer daily liquidity.

Hedging: Since most hedge funds are available in US currency, individual investors of non-US countries face currency fluctuations, and hedging the currency may be costlier for them. Some funds of funds offer share classes denominated in currency of the investor's choice, with the currency risk hedged.

Risk Management: In addition to risk management provided by the underlying hedge fund managers, a fund of funds manager provides a second layer of risk management to investors. The top characteristic of funds of funds that investors like is the second layer of risk management. Funds of funds managers conduct a daily independent pricing, trade reconciliation, and risk exposure screening and have programs in place to take necessary actions to minimize adverse impacts.

Due Diligence: Due diligence is one of the important aspects of manager selection. Funds of funds perform professional due diligence before they are selected, as well as on an ongoing basis once investment is made. Fund of funds managers dedicate significant resources and expertise to conduct due diligence, including identifying and screening thousands of funds, selecting the qualified ones, and monitoring the managers.

Consolidated Reporting: The performance reports of individual hedge funds may often be biased due to self-selection, survival, or catastrophe biases. The data in reports can be lagged data. It may be that the reports are published at larger and irregular intervals. The information in reports may not be easily interpreted by individual investors. Funds of funds managers dedicate the staff to get the required information from the underlying hedge fund managers by conducting regular meetings and conferences and consolidate them to single and easily interpretable reports. This process reduces biases and ensures the most current information. The performance reports are then made available to investors at regular intervals. Funds of funds also prepare an audit as well as tax reporting each year.

Fee Structure: Even though the fund of funds charges double fees compared to an individual fee, the fee structure is still attractive, especially if the investor wants to invest in multiple funds, as the costs associated with due diligence, risk management, and research are shared among all the investors. Due to the power of their collective assets, some fund of funds managers successfully negotiate the fee with underlying managers and share the fee reduction with investors.

Reduced Survivorship Bias: Fund of funds managers maintain records for funds that stop reporting. This will either reduce or completely eliminate survivorship bias.

No Selection Bias: While individual hedge funds have a choice whether to report to an index database, the fund of funds will get the performance details. This will eliminate the selection bias.

No Instant History Bias: While adding new funds to its portfolio, a fund of funds typically does not backfill history in the database. This will eliminate the instant history bias.

5.14.2 Issues with FoF

Funds of funds have some disadvantages compared to individual hedge funds due to the commingled nature of a fund of funds and the extra layer between the investors and the hedge funds. The following are various disadvantages:

- Fee structure
- Taxation
- Lack of transparency
- Exposure to other investors' cash flows
- Lack of control
- Lack of customization

Fee Structure: There are two types of disadvantages related to fee structure: one is a double layer of fees, and the other is performance fees on portions of the portfolio. Fund of funds managers charge fees for their own work in addition to fees charged by the underlying hedge fund managers in their portfolio. The average fund of funds charges a 1.5 percent management and a 9.2% percent performance fee in addition to the average hedge fund management fee of 1.4 percent and an incentive fee of 18.4 percent. In addition, the investor must pay a performance fee for the funds that beat the hurdle rate, even if the overall portfolio does not beat the hurdle rate. For example, if half of the funds return more than the hurdle rate and the remaining perform badly such that aggregated returns are less than the hurdle rate, then the investor needs to pay performance on those funds that earn more than the hurdle rate.

Taxation: Many fund of fund managers register their entities offshore, and as a result, they may be tax inefficient for certain investors in certain countries.

Lack of Transparency: Some fund of funds managers do not disclose the details of their portfolio, claiming that it is their proprietary knowledge. As a result, it becomes difficult for investors to understand the risk and return characteristics beyond the stream of net asset values.

Exposure to Other Investors' Cash Flows: Since fund of funds managers pool the capital from individual investors and commingle the assets of a number of funds, there will not be any demarcation that distinguishes the individual investor portion of a portfolio. When there is demand from the investor for redemption, then the fund of funds manager may need to sell certain assets. This may involve transaction costs that will reduce the fund value, and thus the transaction costs will be shared among all the investors.

Lack of Control: Because of the commingled nature of the fund of funds portfolio, investors give up control over the portfolio.

Lack of Customization: Portfolio customization is not possible with a fund of funds.

5.14.3 Risk-Return Distribution

Although the fund of funds offers stable returns with a lower volatility, those returns are generally lower than those of an individual hedge fund and may even be lower than those of the aggregated hedge fund index. The return on FoFs is typically benchmarked as a margin over a cash return. According to statistics from HedgeFund.net, funds of funds have returned an average of 3.37 percent in 2010. This trails the hedge fund industry by nearly 400 basis points and lags the S&P 1200 Global by 100 basis points, but the FoF exhibited a small fraction of the volatility.

Because funds of funds invest in a variety of fund strategies and managers, thereby attaining the highest diversification level, they produce a returns distribution that is close to normal. However, the distribution of returns on the fund of funds index has slightly negative skewness and a large kurtosis.

Hedgefund.net estimates total FoF assets were $920 billion of the $2.407 trillion hedge fund industry at the end of Q3 2010, an increase of nearly 4 percent during the year. Hedge fund assets have risen over 10 percent in 2010.While funds of funds offer numerous advantages and remain the largest component of the hedge fund industry, their role has declined and will likely decline further for the following reasons:

- The hedge fund industry has grown and will continue to evolve.
- Large investors have become more sophisticated in their analysis.
- Investors are increasing the size of investments to the hedge fund industry.
- Lax due diligence, exposed by the Madoff scandal
- The lack of a liquidity plan in worst-case scenarios, exposed by the financial crisis
- The perceived mismatch of performance to fee structures, which is always evident when comparing FoF returns to hedge fund benchmarks

According to the hedgefund.net database, the fund of funds aggregated index exhibits a slightly negative skew of -0.66, excess kurtosis of 3.48, and an annualized Sharpe ratio of 0.99, using the risk-free rate of 3.5 percent.

Year	HF Aggregated Index	FoFs Aggregated Index	Multi Strategy Index
1991	28.76%	12.74%	N/A
1992	16.92%	12.49%	N/A
1993	29.93%	27.17%	N/A
1994	7.32%	-2.58%	N/A
1995	28.10%	13.52%	N/A
1996	25.33%	18.49%	20.09%
1997	23.25%	17.43%	24.73%
1998	11.48%	2.53%	8.06%
1999	36.22%	25.93%	29.68%
2000	13.11%	8.89%	14.48%
2001	9.04%	4.93%	9.19%
2002	4.38%	1.94%	6.38%

2003	21.30%	11.67%	18.51%
2004	10.78%	6.89%	10.49%
2005	10.94%	7.73%	10.17%
2006	13.74%	10.07%	14.16%
2007	12.62%	9.76%	11.21%
2008	-14.37%	-18.85%	-13.80%
2009	21.41%	9.73%	17.14%
2010	10.48%	5.39%	8.19%

Annual returns of fund of funds index (Data source: Hedgefund.net)

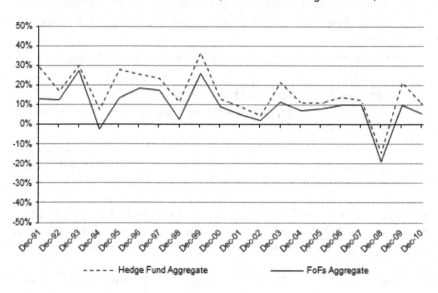

Annual returns of fund of funds index (Data source: Hedgefund.net)

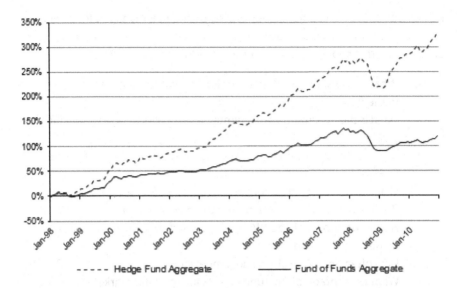

Cumulative returns of fund of funds index (Data source: Hedgefund.net)

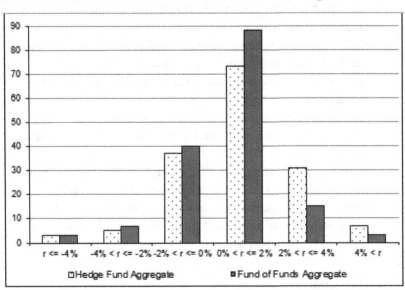

Distribution of returns of fund of funds index (Data source: Hedgefund.net)

5.14.4 Due Diligence

One of the main advantages of funds of funds is reduced risk due to the additional layer of due diligence performed by the fund of funds manager.

Regardless of the due diligence performed by the FoF manager, investors are required to perform their own due diligence for the fund of funds strategy. Fund of fund investors should, at the minimum, determine the following:

- What is the specified maximum and minimum number of funds in the fund?
- What is the maximum and minimum level of allocation to a specific fund?
- What is the minimum age of a fund to consider adding it to the FoF?
- What is the minimum or maximum number of sectors? The higher the number of sectors, the higher the diversification.
- How is the fee calculated? Will the badly performed funds penalized by netting the fund?
- How often does the FoF manager meet individual fund managers?
- What percentage of the fund invests in emerging market funds?
- When there are not enough top quintile funds in a particular sector, will the fund consider mid or bottom quintile managers or leave the sector with zero or less exposure?
- How is the risk measured and monitored for each fund? Does the FoF calculate both individual and aggregated risk?
- What are the redemption criteria that the fund establishes to invest in individual funds?
- How often does the fund rebalance the portfolio?
- On what basis does the fund define and change the asset allocation?
- Investors should note down all the underlying strategies that the fund invests in and assess the risks of individual strategies.
- What is the maximum percentage of nonstandard products?
- What are the qualitative and quantitative criteria used in the portfolio construction process?

5.15 Multistrategy

5.15.1 Strategy

Multistrategy hedge funds (MSF) are typically owned and managed in-house by one investment management firm or a large institutional investment firm and employ several strategies under a common organizational umbrella. Multistrategy funds may either represent multiple investment teams pursuing a similar trading strategy, or may diversify across different trading strategies. The latter setup has gained more popularity recently, while the prior one is slowly vanishing. Multistrategy funds are mainly compared to funds of funds. Funds of hedge funds are typically granular in nature, while multistrategy is typically a congregated strategy. Both multistrategy and funds of hedge funds have their own advantages and disadvantages. Due to the control in investments, multistrategy managers can easily switch to opportunistic trends. This is an advantage that multistrategy managers have over fund of funds managers.

Advantages

- There is a reduced fee when compared to the double layer fee of funds of hedge funds. However, multistrategy funds may charge a higher fee than single strategy funds. Therefore, part of the double layer fee of funds of hedge funds may get offset by the higher fee charged by multistrategy fund managers.
- There is more flexibility and nimbleness in reallocating capital. Because the underlying funds in an MSF are operated by a single firm, they may have the ability to more quickly reallocate investments within the various funds, and they also may have more control over the overall investment profile of the fund.
- There is a netting feature on excess performance. While funds of hedge funds charge an incentive fee on profited funds and do not penalize funds with negative returns, multistrategy funds net the profit before calculating the manager incentive.
- Improved transparency. Because of the common ownership structure, multistrategy funds typically offer improved transparency into the makeup of the underlying strategies.
- Improved liquidity. Multistrategy funds can better manage and control liquidity, as there are no restrictions on rewinding the investment.

Disadvantages

- Most multistrategy funds do not offer the same degree of diversification as most funds of hedge funds because each strategy requires a different level of manager's skill. Well-diversified multistrategy funds would be a more appropriate comparison to diversified funds of hedge funds, but they do not represent a significant percentage of the overall MSF market.

- Increased manager- or firm-specific risk.
- Potential for conflicts and subpar manager inclusion. There is a disincentive and perhaps an inability to fire an underperforming manager.
- Talent retention risk. When a manager with particular skills leaves the multistrategy fund, finding a new manager with the same level of skill may be difficult.

5.15.2 Risk Characteristics

Operational Risk: Since multistrategy funds are operated by a single firm, they are more exposed to firm-specific operational risk. Since most resources are common to all the substrategies, a single failure of system or human capital may lead to blow-up risk. Blow-up risk is the chance of catastrophic fund failure due to operational failures.

Cross-Collateralization Risk: Multistrategy hedge fund positions are cross-collateralized across portfolios and strategies, whereas each fund is considered as one unit in funds of hedge funds. The cross-collateralization may require closing of positions even from profitable substrategies.

Style-Drift Risk: Multistrategy funds may switch funds from low-performing substrategies to high-performing substrategy. The manager may also allocate more funds to a substrategy in order to recoup previously incurred losses. In this case, the multistrategy fund may behave more like a single-strategy rather than a multistrategy fund. This was one of the main reasons that lead to failure of the Amaranth Fund. The Amaranth Fund was originally a convertible arbitrage fund engaging in long gamma strategy. A few years later, gas traders were invited to the fund, converting the fund to a multistrategy fund. The fund manager may have thought that his long gamma experience might be helpful to natural gas trading. However, convertible arbitrage involves long gamma, while the natural gas trade is short gamma. Initially, the fund gained huge profits, partly attributable to the unexpected Hurricane Katrina. This profit encouraged the fund manager to shift more funds from the convertible arbitrage substrategy to natural gas spread trading. In later years, the fund experienced losses. In order to recoup the losses, the fund manager shifted even more funds to natural gas trading. At this stage, the Amaranth Fund was more correlated to a single-strategy energy fund rather than a multistrategy fund, though the fund was still described as a multistrategy fund.

5.15.3 Risk-Return Distribution

The multistrategy aggregated index exhibits less negative skew and little excess kurtosis. According to the hedgefund.net database, the multistrategy index exhibits slightly negative skew of -0.38, excess kurtosis of 3.05, and an annualized Sharpe ratio of 1.52, using the risk-free rate of 3.5 percent. Since multistrategy managers exercise full control on the fund investments, they can easily switch to opportunistic trends. This is an advantage that multistrategy managers have over funds of funds managers. This makes the multistrategy managers perform better than fund of funds managers, though both the strategies provide greater diversification. The additional layer of fee charged by fund of funds managers is also one of the factors for lesser returns compared to multistrategy managers.

Year	HF Aggregated Index	FoFs Aggregated Index	Global Macro Index	Multistrategy Index
1991	28.76%	12.74%	N/A	N/A
1992	16.92%	12.49%	N/A	N/A
1993	29.93%	27.17%	N/A	N/A
1994	7.32%	-2.58%	N/A	N/A
1995	28.10%	13.52%	N/A	N/A
1996	25.33%	18.49%	N/A	20.09%
1997	23.25%	17.43%	21.89%	24.73%
1998	11.48%	2.53%	11.37%	8.06%
1999	36.22%	25.93%	30.54%	29.68%
2000	13.11%	8.89%	8.39%	14.48%
2001	9.04%	4.93%	12.22%	9.19%
2002	4.38%	1.94%	10.52%	6.38%
2003	21.30%	11.67%	22.27%	18.51%
2004	10.78%	6.89%	8.47%	10.49%
2005	10.94%	7.73%	11.00%	10.17%
2006	13.74%	10.07%	11.42%	14.16%
2007	12.62%	9.76%	17.55%	11.21%
2008	-14.37%	-18.85%	-1.27%	-13.80%
2009	21.41%	9.73%	13.45%	17.14%
2010	10.48%	5.39%	8.56%	8.19%

Annual returns of multistrategy index (Data source: Hedgefund.net)

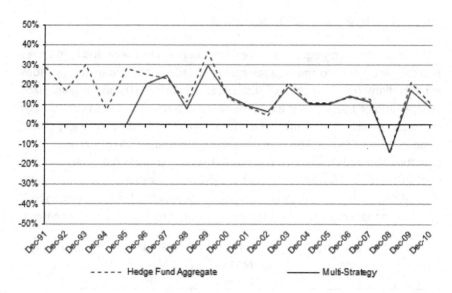

Annual returns of multistrategy index (Data source: Hedgefund.net)

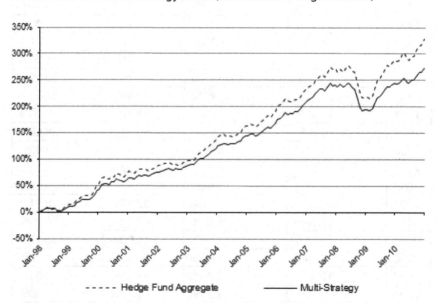

Cumulative returns of multistrategy index (Data source: Hedgefund.net)

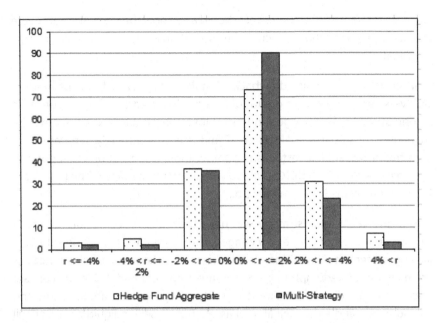

Distribution of returns of multistrategy index (Data source: Hedgefund.net)

5.15.4 Due Diligence

The most common questions during due diligence should include at least the following:

Substrategies: The investor should list and analyze the substrategies. There is some commonality across at least some hedge fund strategies. The commonality comes from either the types of instruments used or the style. For example, equity long/short and equity market-neutral strategies use the same type of securities and there is some similarity in portfolio construction. If a multistrategy fund states that the fund uses equity long/short, equity market-neutral, and short selling strategy, then from the consolidated portfolio point of view it is nothing but single strategy. Correlation among the substrategies also impacts portfolio level idiosyncratic risk. The lesser the correlation among substrategies, the higher the idiosyncratic diversification.

Risk Measurement: Due to the heterogeneity of substrategies, risk measures vary from substrategy to substrategy. The investor should seek to find out if the multistrategy is using common risk measures for all substrategies or has customized them for each substrategy. For example, the investor should know how each substrategy reacts to a stress test and how the entire portfolio reacts to the same factors. Investors should also know the risk at the aggregate level and should ask how effective the correlation analysis is when calculating aggregated risk.

Risk Culture: One major drawback of multistrategy over funds of funds is undiversified firm-specific operational risk. Most hedge funds fail because of operational risk of hedge fund firms. Investors should know how the risk management department is aligned and if it is completely separate from investment research. Investors should also know if the risk officer reports to the board or reports to the CEO along with investment officers. The higher the independence, the better the control.

Redemptions: A multistrategy will have both liquid and illiquid assets. If redemptions are not properly managed, then liquid assets may be sold first, leaving concentrated illiquid assets. Investors should know how the redemptions are managed, if redemption gates are implemented, and if side pockets are implemented. Side pockets allow the fund manager to separate the liquid and illiquid assets and either sell illiquid assets before selling liquid assets or sell liquid and illiquid assets proportionately.

Leverage: Leverage may be preferable to some strategies and dangerous for other strategies. The investor should know the leverage of individual and aggregated levels. The investor should also know if there is implicit leverage. Implicit leverage is a good sign for investors and the fund.

Subportfolio-Level Performance: Similar to measuring risk at the individual substrategy levels, investors should also know the performance and risk-adjusted performance at individual levels.

Capital Allocation: Multistrategy funds dynamically allocate capital among substrategies. Investors should know the rules of dynamic allocation. If one substrategy is allocated more funds, then investors should know if the higher allocation is because of its attractive performance or its capacity.

Impact of Collapsed Substrategy: Failure of one substrategy can impact the entire multistrategy fund. This could be either because the other subportfolios are liquidated in order to fulfill margin requirements of the failed strategy or the fund experienced huge loss and lost reputation. The investor should document the isolation level of each substrategy and the percentage of size of each subportfolio.

Fee Structure: Some fund managers charge the fee in fund of funds style. That is, the manager charges incentive for successful substrategies and does not penalize unsuccessful substrategies. Some multistrategy fund managers calculate the net profit of the entire strategy, which essentially deducts the losses. One of the main reasons why multistrategy attracts investors is the lower and single layer of fee. If managers are not applying the fee on net performance, then investors may have to rethink about investing in the fund.

5.16 Volatility Arbitrage Strategy

The volatility arbitrage strategy is an actively managed, derivative-based strategy that aims to generate absolute returns. Some volatility arbitrage strategies involve either short-lived positions, which typically range from a few hours to two days, while other strategies focus on long-term capital growth, minimizing short-term volatility. The strategies exploit arbitrage opportunities both within equity derivatives and between derivative and equity markets. Volatility arbitrage strategies are capable of generating returns that are negatively correlated with equity markets in a bear market while producing returns that are positively correlated during a bull market. The special advantage of volatility arbitrage is that, though it can generate returns that are negatively correlated with equity markets, it can also generate returns that are positively correlated with equities during a bull market. As a result, allocation to volatility arbitrage can significantly improve fund of funds performance during periods of high volatility without impacting performance in normal or bull market conditions. Various substrategies involving volatility arbitrage are gamma trading, volatility surface trading, skewed trading, and so on.

Volatility Surface Strategy

Options' future price volatility can be estimated using either backward- or forward-looking methods. Backward-looking methods forecast future volatility based on statistical measures, such as using time series models ranging from moving averages to GARCH models. Forward-looking methods estimate future volatility as the implied volatility obtained from observed option premiums by reverse engineering a theoretical option-pricing model, such as the Black-Scholes model. Forward-looking methods typically yield better predictions of future volatility than backward-looking methods, as it is believed that market prices quickly get adjusted to current market conditions.

The Black-Scholes option pricing model for European-style options assumes that volatility of the underlying asset, expressed as the standard deviation of its returns, remains constant over the life of the option. However, empirical research shows that the volatility of asset returns varies over. Therefore, the implied volatility may be different from the real volatility.

A term structure of implied volatility can be plotted as different implied volatilities are extracted from options with different maturities. Similarly volatility smiles present as different implied volatilities are extracted from options with different strikes. The combination of volatility term structure and volatility smiles, a three-dimensional plot, is called volatility surface.

When a volatility smile is detected, the manager buys the cheaper option in the volatility surface that is nearer the money and sells the more expensive option in the volatility surface that is further out of the money on the same underlying and at the same expiry. This type of spread trade can be constructed using either put or call options. If the manager has a negative view on the underlying market, a bear spread would be used, that is, long the put with a high strike and short the put with a low strike. Alternatively, a bear spread can also be executed by writing a call option with a low strike and buying the long with a higher strike. If the manager is positive on the market, a bull spread would be implemented using call options, that is, long the call with a low strike and short the call with a higher strike. Alternatively, a bull spread can be executed by selling the put option with a high strike and buying the put with a low strike.

Another form of surface trading is by using term structure according to which options further from expiry are cheaper than those near to expiry. In order to profit from this opportunity, the trader can sell near-to-expiry options in volatility terms and buy further-from-expiry options. This is called a calendar spread, and the trader aims to profit through time decay.

The third type of surface trading is using both the term structure and the volatility smile. Such a strategy involves taking a long position in an option far from expiry, with a high strike price, and a short position in an option near expiry, with a low strike price.

The above strategies can be implemented to be delta-neutral by buying and selling differing amounts of options, because the options for different expiries will have differing deltas on the same futures contract.

Straddles

The straddle strategy involves purchasing the same number of call and put options at the same strike price with the same expiration date. If both the call and put positions are long, then the straddle is called a *long straddle*; if both the positions are short, then the straddle is called a *short straddle*. In other words, selling a long straddle is nothing but a short straddle.

By employing a long straddle, the manager takes advantage of any sudden movement in the stock price regardless of direction. However, there is a risk of losing both the premiums if the stock price does not move enough to cover the premium paid. The maximum risk in the position is equal to the net premium. By purchasing both a call and a put, there are both upper and lower break even points. While the profit is unlimited from upside movement, there is limited profit from downside movement bound to the zero price of the stock, but such limited profit can still be high. Some managers employ a straddle if the implied volatility is low, anticipating that the option prices will go up when the implied volatility returns to the normal level, regardless of stock price movement. However, such a profit is very limited.

Managers expect profit from time decay of the option or from a stable price of the underlying stock. The profit on a short straddle is limited to the premium received on both the call and the put, but the losses can be huge if the stock price moves in either direction. If volatility falls for both or either option, the position could lose regardless of stock price movement.

Strangle

A strangle strategy is employed by taking a long position in a call option and a put option on the same underlying, and at the same maturity but at different strike prices. These positions are cheaper to implement, as the options with strikes further from the current underlying price will have a lower theta. Managers typically take a call position with a higher strike than that of the put position. The profit is not realized for slow movement of the stock. Large movements are required to lock in the profits. However, the cost of strategy establishment is low due to lower premiums.

Similar to a short straddle, managers expect profit from time decay of the option or from stability or little movement in the price of the underlying stock. The profit on a short strangle is limited to the premium received on both the call and the put, but the losses can be huge if the stock price moves in either direction.

If volatility falls for both or either option, the position could lose regardless of stock price movement. Within a certain band, the risk of a short strangle is less than that of a short straddle due to different strike prices.

Condor

As discussed above, the short straddle and short strangle strategies are exposed to short volatility risk, which can lead to huge losses. In order to limit the losses from higher movements of prices, two additional positions can be added to the short strangle or straddle. The two positions stay at the edges. As a result, there will be a total of four positions, as listed below. Such a strategy is called a *condor*. A condor provides downside protection from short volatility risk.

- One long put at the lowest strike in the range
- One short put at the next lowest strike
- One short call at the next highest strike
- One long call at the highest strike in the range

5.17 Summary of Strategies

The table below summarizes mean, standard deviation, skew, kurtosis, sharpe ratio, cumulative returns, and maximum draw down. The data has been gathered from hedgefund.net.

Strategy	Mean Monthly Return	Standard Deviation	Skew	Excess Kurtosis	Sharpe Ratio (3.5%)	Cumulative Return	Annualized Cumulative Return	Max Drawdown
Hedge Fund Aggregate	0.92%	6.81%	-0.19	2.04	1.16	316.52%	11.68%	-16.50%
Fund of Funds Aggregate	0.49%	5.56%	-0.72	3.79	0.48	114.79%	6.10%	-19.62%
Emerging Markets	1.19%	15.67%	-1.14	4.53	0.77	524.41%	15.24%	-39.88%
Long/Short Equity	1.01%	9.51%	0.10	2.26	0.96	374.47%	12.81%	-22.29%
Market-Neutral Equity	0.69%	3.47%	0.23	2.94	1.40	189.58%	8.58%	-6.24%
Short Bias	0.38%	12.21%	0.65	2.38	0.15	80.26%	4.67%	-22.99%
Event Driven	0.81%	7.32%	-1.16	3.20	0.89	247.32%	10.12%	-24.60%
Relative Value Arbitrage	0.65%	3.88%	-2.87	15.50	1.15	173.76%	8.11%	-14.70%
Convertible Arbitrage	0.67%	6.57%	-3.28	22.58	0.73	181.65%	8.35%	-26.15%

Fixed-Income Arbitrage	0.62%	4.27%	-3.32	18.56	0.96	160.77%	7.70%	-14.40%
Fixed-Income Nonarbitrage	0.61%	3.97%	-1.82	9.83	0.99	155.46%	7.53%	-13.04%
Merger/Risk Arbitrage	0.62%	3.77%	-1.65	6.65	1.08	161.22%	7.72%	-6.53%
Capital Structure Arbitrage	0.67%	4.27%	-2.98	18.65	1.10	182.34%	8.37%	-19.64%
Distressed Securities	0.84%	8.39%	-1.88	8.44	0.84	266.81%	10.59%	-26.86%
Regulation-D	1.73%	8.05%	0.68	3.48	2.19	1324.23%	22.83%	-12.37%
Global Macro	0.97%	5.53%	0.28	1.83	1.52	348.64%	12.32%	-7.78%
Multistrategy	0.84%	5.52%	-0.32	3.15	1.23	265.36%	10.55%	-15.19%
Commodity Trading Advisors	0.94%	7.87%	0.65	1.18	1.04	328.08%	11.92%	-6.97%

6. Commodities

6.1 Fundamentals of Commodities

Commodities are broadly categorized as grains, soft commodities, precious metals, industrial metals, and energy commodities. The following table shows examples of each category.

Commodity Category	Commodity Type
Grains	Corn, Wheat, Oats, Rice
Soft Commodities	Coffee, Cocoa, Sugar, Potatoes, Orange juice, Cotton
Precious Metals	Gold, Silver, Platinum, Palladium
Industrial Metals	Aluminum, Copper
Energy Commodities	Crude oil, Heating oil, Natural gas, Gasoline, Electricity

Commodities are different from traditional financial instruments in that they cannot be priced using the capital asset pricing model (CAPM) and net present values. Moreover, they typically perform well during the last stage of the business cycle, where both stocks and bonds start declining. Therefore, the commodity asset class is said to be countercyclical in nature. Commodities prices are driven by supply, demand, inventory levels, storage costs, and leasing rates. Commodity future returns are positively correlated with the inflation rate, and the positive correlation even increases as the time horizon increases. Positive correlation with inflation is good for investors in the sense that bonds and stocks are negatively correlated with inflation and so the negative correlation between commodities and bonds/stocks helps the portfolio manager to achieve greater diversification.

Historically commodities were used to hedge against inflation, thus achieving diversification. Now commodities have become a special class of assets and are widely used by hedge funds to enhance portfolio returns in addition to diversification. For example, oil prices are negatively correlated with both the S&P 500 and the FTSE 100. The negative correlation becomes even more negative as the time horizon increases. The addition of commodities to a portfolio of bonds and stocks will shift the efficient frontier upward and left, enhancing the return and reducing the overall risk. Within the commodity class, the returns of any commodity have low or even negative correlation with the returns of other commodities. This suggests that holding a diversified commodity portfolio can have significant benefits over holding a single commodity investment. Commodities provide a better inflation hedge than real estate. However the emerging markets bonds and stocks are positively correlated with commodities as the emerging markets are said to be net producers of commodities while the developed markets are said to be net consumers.

There are several ways of gaining exposure to commodity markets: spot market, pure play, commodity futures, and commodity indices.

Spot Market: Spot markets provide direct access to commodities and may deal with the producer directly or through an intermediary. However, the investor or fund manager has to deal with storage costs; and for some commodities, such as gas and electricity, the storage will be challenging. Spot markets are good for precious metals, which do not require much space to store. One other disadvantage of the spot market is that it requires full initial payment. If all the overheads can be managed properly, spot markets provide a better hedge against unfavorable movements of prices.

Pure Play: A pure play is a concept of buying stocks of desired commodity producer companies. For example, an investor who wishes to gain exposure to the copper market will purchase stocks of Freeport-McMoRan Copper & Gold Inc's stock, which moves in the direction of copper performance. However, the pure play is subject to operational risk of the company and depends on the effectiveness of company management.

Commodity Futures: Another way of gaining exposure to commodities is through the futures written on those commodities. Futures contracts are standardized agreements and are backed by the faith of exchanges and clearinghouses. They can be purchased through licensed futures commission merchants. In contrast to the spot market, futures purchases require little initial up front margin. Futures contracts may result in margin calls depending on the direction of spot prices. Investors can roll the futures contracts to future expirations if delivery is not required.

Commodity Indices: Commodity indices provide access to commodities or to a particular sector of commodities. Commodity-linked notes are also available, where prices are linked to total returns of commodities. Commodity indices are discussed in detail under the "Commodity Indices and Other Vehicles" section.

6.2 Structure of Commodity Market

The basic structure of the commodity market mainly involves four parties: exchange corporation, clearinghouse, Futures Commission Merchants (FCMs), and FCM customers. The exchange corporation has members in terms of clearing members and nonclearing members.

Exchange Corporation: Exchange corporations provide an organized marketplace with uniform rules and standardized contracts. Exchanges operate markets for spot commodities, options, futures contracts, and other financial securities. Exchanges are backed by membership fees and transaction fees paid on contracts. There were more than 1600 exchanges existing in the United States during the second half of the nineteenth century in the vicinity of harbors or railroad crossings; however, they are now limited to six. The Chicago Board of Trade (CBOT) was originally dedicated to agricultural commodities, trades futures, and options on corn, soybean, soy meal, wheat, rice, and precious metals like gold and silver. The New York Mercantile Exchange (NYME) trades crude oil, gas, copper, aluminum, and precious metals. The New York Board of Trade trades contracts on coffee, sugar, cocoa, cotton, and orange juice. Clearing members of an exchange are entitled to clear their own transactions and those of affiliated companies without a clearing license, as well as their clients' transactions. Nonclearing members of an exchange are not able to clear transactions on their own and pay clearing members to clear their trades.

Clearinghouse: The clearinghouse provides the facility to close out positions without having the buyer and seller interact each other. The clearinghouse supervises the delivery of commodities and guarantees each futures contract that it clears.

Futures Commission Merchants (FCMs): FCMs are the brokerage firms that execute, clear, and carry CTA-directed trades on the various exchanges. Some FCMs also act as commodity pool operators and trading managers, providing administrative reports on investment performance.

FCM Customers: FCM customers are end users who open and close the future positions.

6.3 Pricing of Commodity Futures

Since commodities do not yield any cash flows, they cannot be priced using the net present value of cash flow theory. Instead, they are priced based on expected future price, lease rates, convenience yield, and storage costs. Expected future value depends on factors like supply and demand. Agricultural commodity prices depend on weather conditions and production capacity, while energy commodities depend on season. Electricity commodity prices change even during the day, as storing of electricity possesses some challenges.

In a simple pricing technique, under a no-arbitrage assumption, the total cost of the commodity forward contract is equal to the present value of the expected future price.

Mathematically, $S0 = F0, t * e^{-rT}$ or $F0, t = S0 * e^{rt}$

The above equation illustrates that the commodity price at time zero is equivalent to the present value of a unit of commodity received at time t. The risk-free rate r represents the discount rate or opportunity cost. The above technique is simple and assumes that there are no storage costs or lease rates, which will be discussed later in this topic.

If the above equation does not hold, then arbitrage opportunities exist. There are two types of arbitrage opportunities: cash-and-carry arbitrage and reverse cash-and-carry arbitrage.

If $F0, t$ is greater than $S0 * e^{rt}$, then cash-and-carry arbitrage opportunity exists, in which case the present value of the expected future spot price is greater than the current spot price. Under this scenario, investors buy the commodity in the spot market and store and simultaneously sell the futures contract on the same. At contract expiration, they deliver the commodity and receive the future contract price. Investors may use borrowed funds to buy the commodities in the spot market, which will be repaid at the time of contract expiration by receiving the future contract price.

If $F0, t$ is less than $S0 * e^{rt}$, then reverse cash-and-carry arbitrage opportunity exists, in which case the present value of the expected future spot price is less than the current spot price. Under this scenario, investors short the commodity in the spot market and simultaneously buy the futures contract on the same. At contract expiration, they receive the commodity and cover the short position. Investors receive funds by shorting the commodities in the spot market and lending at the risk-free rate until the time of contract expiration, at which time they pay for the futures contract price.

From the above opportunities, it can be observed that investors buy whichever (either spot commodity or futures contract) is low and sell high, which can be generalized as "buy low and sell high."

There are three characteristics that influence arbitrage opportunities. They are lease rates, storage costs, and convenience yield.

Lease Rates

In the simple pricing technique, it was assumed that the opportunity cost is equal to the risk-free rate, which actually represents the return that the investor can receive without any risk by investing in treasuries or similar securities. However, if the commodity can yield some rental/lease income, then the investor must forgo that return by not holding the commodity. In other words, holding the commodity may help the investor by fetching some lease income. Therefore, the opportunity cost is reduced by the amount of the lease rate. Assuming a continuous lease rate of δ, the effective opportunity cost will become $r-\delta$.

Mathematically, the commodity forward price for time t with an active lease rate of δ is

$$F0, t = S0 * e^{(r - \delta)t}$$

Where $S0$ = commodity current spot price

$r - \delta$ = effective opportunity cost.

Storage Costs

In contrast to lease rates, the holder of the commodity will have to pay a fee for storing the commodity until the delivery of the contract. This will increase the opportunity cost by an amount equivalent to the storage cost.

Assuming that continuous storage cost is equal to γ, the effective opportunity cost will become $r + \gamma$.

Therefore, the commodity forward price for time t with an active storage cost of γ is

$$F0, t = S0 * e^{(r+\gamma)t}$$

Where S0 = commodity current spot price

$r + Y$ = effective opportunity cost.

Convenience Yield

Convenience yield represents the benefit that the holder of a commodity receives. The benefit can be in a form other than a lease. For example, a manufacturer may need raw materials on a continuous basis. If the manufacturer runs out of stock of the materials then the production process may slow down or even shut down temporarily. As a result, the manufacturer may lose part of his business income. Having the material purchased ahead of need and keeping it ready for manufacturing purposes increases the benefit. This benefit is called the convenience yield.

Convenience yield has the same effect as lease rate and represents the benefit the holder of a futures contract loses or the benefit the holder of a commodity receives.

Assuming a continuous convenience yield of α, the effective opportunity cost will become $r + \alpha$.

Therefore, the commodity forward price for time t with an active convenience yield of α is

$$F0, t = S0 * e^{(r-\alpha)t}$$

Where S0 = commodity current spot price

$r - \alpha$ = effective opportunity cost.

Impact of Lease Rate, Storage Cost, and Convenience Yield on Arbitrage Opportunity

Often there are situations where a combination of lease rate, storage cost, and convenience yield are applicable when pricing futures prices. For example, a manufacturing unit may be paying a storage cost while enjoying the benefit of convenience yield, or the jewel manufacturer may lease the old jewels while receiving the benefit of convenience yield before remanufacturing them.

Taking all three into consideration,

$$FO, t = SO * e^{(r-\delta+\gamma-\alpha)t}$$

It is necessary to set any nonapplicable terms to zero. Therefore, investors should consider the above equation while assessing the arbitrage opportunities.

Normal Backwardation Market

A market in which the futures price is below the expected future spot price is called a normal backwardation market. In the agriculture market, for example, farmers want to protect themselves from the fluctuations that maybe caused by weather. For this purpose, they sell the futures ahead of the harvest. Speculators, on the other hand, bear the risk and expect a risk premium. The risk aversion of farmers puts downward pressure on the futures prices, which fall below the current spot prices. This phenomenon is referred to as normal backwardation. Normal backwardation occurs if hedgers are net short in futures and speculators are net long in futures.

Contango Market

A market in which the futures price is above the expected future spot price is called normal contango. When hedgers are net long in futures, the futures price will be higher than the expected spot price to compensate speculators for the risk of selling short. For example, Kellogg's, a cereal company, wants to protect itself from pricing fluctuations of grain and buys long futures in grains. Speculators, on the other hand, bear the risk of pricing fluctuations and expect a risk premium. To compensate the speculators for bearing the risk, Kellogg's will pay more than the spot price for future deliveries. This will put upward pressure on prices. Speculators expect that the spot price at the time of delivery will be less than the price they receive for futures and cash in the profit. Normal contango occurs if hedgers are net long in futures and speculators are net short in futures.

There is a difference between normal contango and contango. As discussed above, normal contango refers to a price pattern where the futures price is above the expected future spot price, while contango refers to a situation where the futures price is greater than the spot price. There are many factors that make the market contango. One such factor is storage cost. Holding a commodity requires storage costs, which may make the opportunity cost higher than the risk-free rate. So the parties may pay a higher premium for futures, which will result in a price higher than the spot price. Similarly, backwardation refers to a price pattern where futures prices are below spot prices. For example, a stock that pays dividend falls, by an amount equivalent to the dividend, in price when the dividend is announced. So the futures buyers prefer to pay a lesser amount than the spot price. In the case of commodities, the lease rate replaces the role of dividend.

In other words, if $r - \delta + \gamma - \alpha > r$ then the market is said to be contango, and if $r - \delta + \gamma - \alpha < r$ then the market is said to be backwardation.

6.4 Risk Characteristics of Commodities

The basic risk factors that commodity futures are exposed to are basis risk, price risk, delivery risk, transportation risk, credit risk, and interest-rate risk.

Basis Risk: Basis is the difference between the current cash price of a commodity and the futures price of the same or a similar commodity. Basis is usually computed in relation to the next futures contract to expire and may reflect different time periods, product forms, grades, or locations. Basis risk exists when futures and spot prices do not change by the same amount over time. In other words, basis risk is the risk that remains after the hedging strategy has been implemented. For example, an airline company wants to hedge against a rise in jet fuel prices and will purchase NYMEX heating oil futures contracts. The contract may dictate various options for the grade of commodity, location, and chemical attributes. In other words, when spot and futures contracts are not perfectly correlated, then basis risk will appear. The magnitude of basis risk depends on the degree of correlation between spot and futures prices.

The effectiveness of a hedge is formulated as below:

$$h = 1 - \frac{\sigma^2(basis)}{\sigma^2(St)}$$

The closer h is to one, the more effective the hedge is. If the hedgers hedge the commodity prices using the same commodity, then the basis risk will be zero. However, the vast body of literature in futures contracts will be subject to various options of deliveries, which will make the commodities in a pair less correlated. In other words, the literature in the contract provides various alternative deliverable. The broad spectrum of alternative deliverables males the commodities less correlated. When spot prices increase faster than futures prices over the hedging horizon, basis increases and strengthening of basis is said to occur. When the futures price increases faster than the spot price, basis decreases and weakening of basis is said to occur.

Several sources of basis risk are the divergence of the futures and spot prices, changes in the cost of carry, and liquidity mismatch. In exchange-traded futures, margin calls are made based on the price movements of spot and futures. The cost of carry, which includes storage costs and borrowing costs, is influenced by interest rates. Fluctuations in interest rates will make margins and cost of carry fluctuate, which in turn will result in basis risk. If the hedger uses illiquid commodities in the hedging strategy, then greater price swings of illiquid assets will result in basis risk. Another source of basis risk is costs associated with the shipment of goods to the desired location. For example, if a hedger in Ohio purchases the futures that are contracted to deliver the goods from New York, then the hedger is required to bear the costs associated with transportation. In sum, the major factors Influencing the basis are the overall supply and demand for each commodity by variety or type, the supply and demand of other commodities that compete with each other, geographical disparities in supply and demand, transportation and transportation problems, transportation pricing structure, available storage space, quality factors, and market expectations.

Price Risk: The producer of the underlying commodities bears the risk of the commodity falling in value. Trading forwards and futures may reduce this risk.

Delivery Risk: Delivery risk emerges when either party disputes delivery of the commodity. In modern markets, this risk has been reduced drastically due to the involvement of clearinghouses and robust contracts.

Transportation Risk: Transportation risk may occur in the form of ordinary events, such as deterioration, spoilage, and accidents, or in the form of extraordinary events, such as acts of god, wars, riots, and strikes. Examples of ordinary risks are train-car overturns and loss of a ship at sea. Examples of extraordinary risks include hurricanes, border tensions, and so on. Some contracts include the cost of insurance and freight, in which case the seller is responsible for delivering the goods at the buyer's location. In this case, the futures sellers typically purchase forward freight agreements to hedge the associated transportation costs. On the other hand, in free-on-board contracts, the buyer is responsible for any ordinary or extraordinary events.

Credit Risk: Credit risk appears more in forward contracts and is minimized in futures contracts due to margin requirements. Futures are exposed to little credit risk in that if the party does not respond to the margin call, then the position may have to be unwound, which will result in some loss to the other party.

Interest Rate Risk: As the commodities are usually positively correlated with inflation and inflation is in turn related to interest rates, commodities are exposed to interest rate risk.

6.5 Hedging Techniques

Strip Hedge: Strip hedge employs a strategy that buys futures contacts matching the quantity and maturity for every month of the requirement. For example, if an airline company anticipates the need for X amount of oil every month, then the company will purchase twelve futures contracts that deliver X amount every month. At the end of expiration of each contract, the hedger unwinds the contract. This may result in higher costs, as the transaction costs and prices are higher for long-term contracts.

Stack-and-Roll Hedge: Short-term contracts are highly liquid and are less expensive than long-term contracts. Therefore, the airline company may employ a strategy that buys a one-month contract that matches the requirements of the next twelve months and rolls over every month. This strategy is called a stack-and-roll hedge.

6.6 Commodity Indices and Other Vehicles

Commodity indices are passive, long-only, unleveraged contracts that provide exposure to the commodity world. Unleveraged indices are assumed to be fully collateralized by US T-bills, which means that for every dollar invested in an unleveraged index, the investor indirectly invests a dollar in US T-bills and will receive interest. The interest earned on collateral is called *collateral yield*. The unleveraged commodity index is a true representation of commodity price changes without additional volatility. In addition to commodity price changes and collateral yield, commodity indices derive returns from the roll yield.

Roll yield is the return earned from the commodity futures term structure. While the futures prices and spot prices converge at maturity, disparity appears during the holding horizon. The roll yield is calculated as the difference between the futures price change and the spot price change.

Mathematically, roll yield = (F1 – F0) – (S1 – S0)

F1 = current price of futures contract

F0 = Previous price of futures contract

S1 = Current spot price

S0 = Previous spot price

Rearranging the above equation, roll yield = (F1 − S1) − (F0 − S0)

As the expiration time approaches, futures prices will converge toward spot prices. At maturity, F1 will be equal to S1.

Therefore, roll yield = −(F0−S0)

In a contango market, futures prices are higher than spot prices, and so the roll yield will be negative. In a backwardation market, the futures price is less than the spot price, and so the roll yield is positive.

A variety of commodity indices and vehicles are available in the market, and investors choose the desired indices based on investment goals. Some of them are discussed below.

6.6.9 The London Metal Exchange Index (LMEI)

The LME Index tracks the performance of the world's most traded nonferrous, base metal contracts. The metals include aluminum, copper, lead, nickel, tin, and zinc. The LME Index is a dollar-denominated index. The weighting scheme uses the five-year arithmetic average of each metal's source production data and volume data.

6.6.10 Bache Commodity Index (BCI)

The BCI provides institutional investors long-only, broad-based commodity exposure to nineteen commodities across the energy, metals, and agricultural sectors. The Bache Commodity Index utilizes a proprietary approach developed to combine the benefits of transparency, liquidity, and risk reduction, while providing additional sources of return beyond the commodity beta offered by traditional commodity indices. The energy group, which includes crude oil WTI, crude oil Brent, natural gas, heating oil, gas oil, and gasoline, contributes to 49 percent of the index. Energy contracts are traded every month. Metals constitute 21.5 percent, while agriculture constitutes 29.5 percent. Metals and agricultural commodities are not traded on a monthly basis.

6.6.11 Commodity Swaps and Swaptions

Similar to interest-rate swaps, a commodity swap involves a payment from one party based on the price of a commodity, such as gold, while the other set of payments can be either fixed or determined by some other floating price or rate. While payments could be made by delivering actual units of the underlying commodity, in practice cash is exchanged instead. In modern markets, commodity swaps are becoming increasingly common in the energy and agricultural industries, where demand and supply are both subject to considerable uncertainty. For example, airline companies often enter into contracts in which they agree to make a series of fixed payments and receive payments on those same dates as determined by an oil price index on a certain amount of oil. And the airline company will typically buy the actual oil from the spot market. The payment value of the index is based on the average value over a period of time, which could be weekly, monthly, quarterly, or the entire period between settlements. This feature removes the effects of an unusually volatile single day and ensures that the payment will more accurately represent the value of the index. The key advantage of commodity swaps over the futures contracts is that they are privately negotiated contracts and can be custom designed in order to meet the needs of hedgers.

6.6.12 Commodity-Linked Notes

The commodity-linked note is an intermediate-term bond whose value is a function of the value of the underlying commodity futures contracts or commodity options. In addition to par value at maturity, the commodity-linked note pays a periodical coupon. Just before the coupon payment, the value of the commodity-linked note can be calculated as follows. The bond is linked to a particular index, such as GSCI or DJ-UBSCI, and will typically set the strike price on the index and coupon payment. If the index exceeds the strike price, then the investor receives proportionate value and the coupon payment. If the index falls below the strike price, then the investor will receive only the coupon payment. Therefore, the commodity-linked note is a call option on the index. Investors typically receive reduced coupon payment on the bond compared to straight bonds, and the reduction in coupon represents the premium paid to the issuer.

Bond Value = [1 + max (0, (current index value − strike price for the note)/ strike price for the note)] * face value of note + coupon payment due

Commodity-linked notes offer several advantages to the investor over the regular futures contracts:

1. Investors do not need to roll the contracts at expiration. The task of rolling is taken care of by the issuer.
2. Certain institutional investors have restrictions on investing in commodities directly or through forwards/futures. Since a commodity-linked note is a bond, it provides access to commodities for such investors.
3. The investor does not need to worry about volatility and tracking error issues of underlying commodities.

6.6.13 Collateralized Commodity Obligations (CCOs)

CCOs are similar to CDOs in structure, backed by cash flows of a pool of instruments. The difference is that the pool represents commodity trigger swaps instead of credit default swaps or other credit-risky instruments. If the commodity prices increase over the trigger threshold, the CCO bond holder will be rewarded; on the other hand, if the commodity prices decline, the CCO bond holder will receive less than par value.

6.6.14 Spread Strategies

Various spread strategies can be employed using futures contracts. One such example is the calendar spread, which involves taking a long position in a near-term contract and a short position in a long-term contract, or vice versa. Fund managers make decisions based on the season and demand of the commodity.

For example, before entering into cold weather, the manager takes a short position in natural gas for October and a long position in a November contract. If the season experiences severe cold by November, the manager profits from the November long contract. Shorting the October contract reduces the funding requirement. However, the manager may experience loss if the weather becomes cold in October itself or a little warm In November. Developing such strategies requires both subject matter knowledge on weather and a large historical data set from where the patterns can be observed.

The example discussed just above is referred to as a *bear spread* and performs well in a contango market, where futures prices lie above spot prices. On the other hand, the opposite can also be implemented. For example, a manager takes a long position in March natural gas deliverable contracts and a short position in April contracts. If the weather becomes warm by April as anticipated, the manager takes profit from the April short positions as the demand declines for natural gas. This spread is referred to as a *bull spread* and performs well in backwardation markets.

A *processing spread* involves taking long positions in raw commodities and short positions in refined products. There are two types of processing spread: a crack spread and a crush spread. A crack spread, also known as a 5:3:2 spread, refers to a mechanism where five units of oil produce three units of gasoline and two units of heating oil. Hedgers employing a crack spread take a long position in one hundred oil contracts and a short position in sixty gasoline contracts and forty contracts in heating oil. The crush spread, also known as a 7:4:3 spread, refers to a mechanism where seven units of soybeans produce four units of soybean meal and three units of soybean oil. Hedgers typically take a long position in seventy soybean contracts and proportionate short positions in soybean meal and soybean oil. The difference between the price paid for a long position plus the processing cost and the price received from the short position is the profit from the processing spread.

6.6.15 Storage Strategy

Storage strategy involves purchasing physical commodities in the spot market and storing them in leased facilities for future delivery, while simultaneously selling the futures contracts on the same. The strategy locks in immediate profit at the time of creation and realizes the profit at the time of delivery. The competitive advantage that the manager possesses in acquiring, storing, and managing labor typically yields the profit for the manager.

6.6.16 Transportation Strategy

Transportation strategies involve purchasing the commodities in places where there is surplus and then employing leased transportation services to transport them to scarcity areas to sell them. The competitive advantage in managing transportation risk and potential headline risks yields the profits for the manager.

6.7 Agricultural Commodity Market

Long-run commodity demand is driven, in large part, by population and income dynamics. A country's demographic makeup by age and ethnicity may play a large role in determining food needs and preferences. However, demographic changes generally occur slowly and in accordance with well-known behavioral patterns. Similarly, per capita income growth usually trends upward or downward gradually and predictably with the national economy. As a result, short-term price movements are rarely driven by either of these phenomena. However, an important exception was the 1997 Asian financial crisis, which dramatically and quite suddenly curtailed commodity import demand in several major agricultural importing countries of East and Southeast Asia. The 1997 Asian crisis contributed significantly to the price declines in most international commodity markets of the late 1990s. Changes in currency exchange rates between trading nations can occur more suddenly and can have significant effects on international trade and prices. For an exporting country, a devaluation of its currency against other exporting countries has the same effect as a lowering of its export price against those competitor nations, thereby making its product more competitive. In contrast, for an importing country, a devaluation of its currency against the currency of exporting nations will make products from those exporters more expensive, thereby lowering its import demand. Currency appreciation will have the opposite effect. Currency exchange rate fluctuations and their economic implications are not unique to agricultural commodities, but affect all goods and services traded between nations.

By the nature of daily consumption, agricultural commodity prices typically respond rapidly to actual and anticipated changes in supply and demand conditions. However, there are certain characteristics of agricultural product markets that make agricultural product prices more volatile than other commodities. Three such noteworthy characteristics of the agricultural market include seasonality, demand, and price-inelastic demand and supply functions.

Seasonality: The cyclical nature of weather limits crop production to only a portion of the year. Even if there are some countries where agriculture is possible throughout the year, the same crop will not necessarily be repeated multiple times in a year. Therefore, most grains are limited to a single annual harvest. As a result, the cyclical nature of crop production plays an important role in agricultural commodity price behavior. Moreover, while in some countries farmers follow consistency year after year in crop selection, farmers in some countries look for expectations about future product prices and government support rates for crop productions. Also, expectations concerning international market conditions and the possibility for unexpected changes in the trade outlook are often relevant for most major field crops. As a result, the variable demand and competition for agricultural land influences the supply and demand of crop products, and the demand can ripple through the various agricultural markets, thus altering prices. Furthermore, it is possible that a producer's actual production maybe very different from the planned production due to unexpected variations in weather, pests, diseases, or other circumstances.

Demand: Demand for agricultural products primarily originates in two forms: primary and derived. *Primary demand* is associated with consumers who use the various food and industrial products that are produced from raw or unprocessed farm commodities, such as grains, oil seeds, and fiber. *Derived demand* refers to demand for inputs that are used to produce the final products. Thus, the demand for corn, wheat, and cotton is derived from the demand for their various end products. Similarly, the demand for soybeans is derived from the demand for soybean meal and soybean oil, the major products obtained from crushing soybeans. The demand also varies based on the quality and type of input fed to the crops because consumers look for special products, such as organic products. As a result, substantial price premiums and discounts may develop based on the commodities' end-use characteristics. This occurs frequently in the wheat market, where the different wheat varieties have very unique baking and milling characteristics. The demand also varies based on characteristics of the commodity, for example, rice based on grain length, corn based on color and oil or starch content, soybean based on protein or oil content, barley based on malting quality, and so on.

Price-Inelastic Demand and Supply: The demand and supply of agriculture products are relatively price-inelastic, which implies that even small changes in supply can result in large price movements. As a result, unexpected market news can produce potentially large swings in farm prices and incomes. The supply elasticity of an agricultural commodity reflects the speed with which new supply increases in response to a price rise or fall in a particular market. Since most grains are limited to a single annual harvest, new supply flows to market in response to a post-harvest price change must come from either domestic stocks or international sources. As a result, short-term supply response to a price rise can be very limited during periods of low stock holdings, but in the longer run, expanded acreage and more intensive cultivation practices can work to increase supplies. When the prices fall, producers might be inclined to withhold their commodity from the market. The cost of storage, the length of time before any expected price rebound, the anticipated strength of a price rebound, and a producer's current cash-flow situation combine to determine if storage is a viable alternative. If a return to higher prices is not expected in the near future, storage may not be viable, and continued marketing may add to downward price pressure. Similarly, demand elasticity reflects a consumer's ability or willingness to alter consumption when prices for the desired commodity rise or fall. Consumers consider both own-price and cross-price movements of complementary and substitute products in making their expenditure decisions. Willingness to substitute another commodity when prices rise depends on several factors, including the number and availability of substitutes, the importance of the commodity as measured by its share of consumers' budgetary expenditures, and the strength of consumers' tastes and preferences. Since the farm cost of basic grains generally amounts to a very small share of the retail cost of consumer food products, changes in grain prices generally have little impact on retail food prices, and therefore little impact on consumer behavior and corresponding farm-level demand.

Major Agricultural Commodity Futures Exchanges

Name	Abbreviation	Website
Minneapolis Grain Exchange	MGE	http://www.mgex.com
Chicago Board of Trade	CBOT	http://www.cbot.com
Kansas City Board of Trade	KCBOT	http://www.kcbot.com
New York Cotton Exchange	NYCE	http://www.nyce.com
Winnipeg Grain Exchange	WCE	http://www.wce.ca
Buenos Aires Cereals Exchange	BOLSA	http://www.bolsadecereales.com
Rosario Futures Exchange	ROFEX	http://www.rofex.com.ar
European Union Commodity Futures	Euronext.liffe	http://www.euronext.com

South African Futures Exchange	SAFEX	http://www.safex.co.za

Agricultural Data Providers

Estimates, Forecasts, and Projections: US Department of Agriculture (USDA)'s crop reporting schedule encompasses forecasts made during the growing season and estimates made after harvest. Forecasts and estimates represent two distinct concepts. *Estimates* generally refer to an accomplished fact, such as crop yields after the crop is harvested. In contrast, *forecasts* relate to an expected future occurrence, such as crop yields expected prior to actual harvest of the crop based on available information, such as current growing conditions, measurements of fertilizer usage, and so forth. *Projections* are an extension of forecasts, but made further into the future, where no objective supporting information is available. Instead, projections are based on extending historical supply and demand relationships, trade and demand patterns, and government policies into the future. Examples of projections include USDA's ten-year baseline projections, which project commodity supply-and-use balances starting in the year T+1 and extending for an additional nine years into the future.

Crop Area: National Agricultural Statistics Service (NASS) conducts three major acreage surveys in any given year (T). The prospective plantings survey in March provides early indications of what farmers intend to plant; the midyear acreage survey, conducted in early June, is used to estimate spring-planted acreages and acreages for harvest; and the end-of-year acreage and production survey is conducted after most of the field crops have been harvested.

Prospective Plantings: Field crop planted-acreage intentions are based primarily on a survey—conducted during the first two weeks of March—of the current crop planting intentions for about 55,000 randomly-selected farm operators from across the United States. These estimates are published in the *Prospective Plantings* report scheduled for release at the end of each March (in accordance with a preannounced schedule). The acreage estimates are intended to reflect grower planting intentions as of the survey period and give the first indication of potential plantings for the year. Actual plantings may vary from intentions in accordance with changes in weather or market conditions.

Acreage: Midyear estimates for planted acreage are made based on surveys conducted in early June, when field crop acreages have been established or planting intentions are firm. These estimates are published in the *Acreage* report scheduled for release at the end of each June.

Yield and Production Forecasts: The first forecasts of yield and production are published in the May Crop Production report for fall-planted winter wheat (with monthly updates through October); in July for barley, oats, rye, durum, and spring wheat; and in August for the remaining field crops—corn, cotton, hay, oilseeds, peanuts, rice, sorghum, sugarcane, and sugar beets—with monthly updates through November. Cotton yield estimates are updated again in the December Crop Production report. Objective yield surveys are conducted during the principal growing season for cotton, corn, rice, sorghum, soybeans, and wheat in each commodity's major producing states. A forecast of prospective yield or production on a given date assumes that weather conditions and damage from insects, diseases, or other causes will be about normal (the same as the average of previous years) during the remainder of the growing season. If any of these variables change, the final estimate may differ significantly from the earlier forecast.

Growing Conditions: In addition to the monthly Crop Production reports, NASS also publishes a weekly Crop Progress report during the principal growing season (April to November), including growing condition indices for the major crops as well as pasture and forage conditions. USDA, through its Joint Agricultural Weather Facility (JAWF), also publishes weekly information on US and international weather in its Weekly Weather and Crop Bulletin. These weekly reports on crop progress and conditions, as well as weather, provide a basis for evaluating crop yield prospects across the various global production zones for each year-end commodity. As a result, they are closely watched and reported on by other secondary market information sources.

Year-End Estimates: Year-end estimates of acreage, yield, and production for barley, durum, oats, rye, and wheat are published in the Small Grains Annual Summary, released at the end of September (T). For all remaining field crops, year-end estimates of acreage, yield, and production are published in the Crop Production Annual Summary report the following January (T+1).

Domestic Use Based on the Particular Commodity Being Monitored: Domestic use may be broken into various subcategories, such as feed use, seed use, and food and industrial use. Market information for this diversity of potential demand sources is less survey-based and less systematic than the information provided by USDA's many crop-production-related reports.

Export Demand: Since the market events of 1972, most market observers consider exports to be the great uncertainty underlying commodity supply, demand, and price forecasts. In 1972, the Soviet Union made unexpected purchases of large amounts of US grain. Prices for corn, wheat, and soybeans climbed to record levels in 1973, and then to still-higher levels in 1974. Congress responded by mandating export sales reporting by the USDA beginning in 1973. Today, there are three primary data sources that monitor the US trade situation and underlie USDA projections of US agricultural trade.

The weekly Export Sales report published by USDA's Foreign Agricultural Service (FAS) indicates the amounts of major US agricultural commodities that have been exported, as well as outstanding sales that have been contracted for but not delivered, during the current marketing year compared with the same period from the previous marketing year. The weekly Grains Inspected for Export report is issued by USDA's Agricultural Marketing Service and based on inspections undertaken by the Federal Grain Inspection Service of USDA's Grain Inspection, Packers, and Stockyards Administration. The Census Bureau (Department of Commerce) issues a monthly export report that indicates not only grain exports, but also product exports, including soybean meal and oil and wheat flour. At the end of each commodity's marketing year, the Census Bureau export data become the official USDA export estimate.

Market Price Information: USDA projects the season-average farm price (SAFP) for all major program crops contained in the *World Agricultural Supply and Demand Estimates* (WASDE) report except for cotton. The SAFP projection is usually presented as a range of high and low values that is tightened with each succeeding month until a single point estimate is reported near the end of each commodity's marketing year. Market observers and the various private market information services tend to use the midpoint of the USDA-projected SAFP range as a reference point from which all comparisons are made (such as "too high" or "too low"). In support of the SAFP estimates reported in the WASDE report, NASS releases a monthly Agricultural Prices report that contains monthly and marketing year average prices received (weighted by the monthly share of annual marketing) for most major crops at both the national and state level for major producing states. USDA's Agricultural Marketing Service (AMS) provides a portal to price and market information for a range of agricultural commodities. The Grain Market News Branch of AMS monitors and reports on: cash, barge, rail, and truck bids for grains and oilseeds at major terminal and export markets, including barge loading positions on the Mississippi, Ohio, and Illinois Rivers and at the Central Illinois (Decatur) corn and soybean processing location; nearby futures contract prices and cash-to-futures basis; and recent export sales by grain type with details on tonnage and delivery dates in the Daily Grain Review, Export Grain Bids, Daily National Grain Market Summary, and Weekly National Grain Market Summary reports.

Ending Stocks as a Summary of Market Conditions: USDA projects season-ending stocks for all major program crops contained in the monthly WASDE report. Ending stocks are calculated as the difference between total supplies (beginning stocks plus production plus imports) and total disappearance (all domestic uses plus exports). As such, season-ending stocks of an annually produced commodity summarize the effects of both supply and demand factors during the marketing year. In the early months of the marketing year, when most components of the supply-and-demand balance sheet are being forecast rather than estimated, expected ending stocks—expressed as a ratio over expected total use—are frequently used as an indicator of a commodity's expected price outcome by USDA and other market observers. For most seasonal commodities, annual prices tend to have a strong negative correlation with their ending stocks-to-use ratio. As a result, expectations for high stocks relative to use typically result in lower prices, while expectations for low stocks relative to use tend to raise prices. A certain amount of stocks at the end of the marketing year is necessary to provide a continuous flow of grain to processors and exporters before the new crop is harvested. These stocks are referred to as pipeline supplies. Although there is no hard-and-fast rule on what volume of stocks represents pipeline levels for the major grain and oilseed crops, whenever stocks approach historically low levels, market analysts speculate about what pipeline-stock levels might be. For wheat, pipeline stocks are thought to be in a range of 350 to 400 million bushels; for corn, 400 to 500 million bushels; and for soybeans, about 150 to 200 million bushels. Whenever USDA ending stock projections approach these levels, market prices become very sensitive to unexpected market news, and prices tend to be more volatile than during periods of abundant stocks.

6.8 Electricity Market

In most commodity markets, price movements are determined by supply, demand, and inventory levels. However, most electricity market prices cannot be modeled using traditional models. While electricity prices are mean reverting in the long run, they exhibit short-term volatilities due to strong seasonality, temporal jumps, and spikes. Electricity markets exhibit even hourly, daily, and seasonal uncertainty associated with fundamental market drivers and the physics of generation and delivery of electricity. As a result, electricity prices can deviate significantly from the forecast. The physical characteristics of the electricity market and the variability of the underlying drivers are the primary reasons for short-term volatility that is not observed in conventional commodity markets.

The following scenarios best describe the characteristics and drivers that influence short-term volatility:

- A sudden heat wave can strain the ability of even backup generator capacity to meet elevated demand in a timely manner.
- The generators are subject to unexpected outages and changing emission constraints, while transmission lines may experience congestion, creating electrical imbalances.
- Instantaneous demand and supply imbalances subject the system to unusual stress; this can only be captured by hourly volatility, not by day-to-day volatility.
- Ancillary services, emission allowances, and other products interact with energy prices and cannot be treated as isolated entities.
- Past conditions are unlikely to be repeated in any consistent manner useful in forecasting.
- In the past, the electricity market was strictly regulated and controlled by governments, and therefore, energy consumers were not exposed to any price fluctuations. However, due to the recent deregularization in the electricity market, the prices started depending only on market forces and needs. Now electrical energy has become a commodity that can be traded like any other commodity. In particular, it can now be traded in the form of delivery contracts on specialized exchanges.
- Nonstorability. The production of electrical energy has to cover demand instantaneously, as it cannot be stored efficiently. An exception is mountain reservoirs connected to hydroelectric plants and also man-made hydro pumped-storage facilities that usually are employed for shorter-term storage.

Thus, a more comprehensive forecast must capture the consequences of random and atypical fluctuations of fundamental market drivers and must be based on an accurate representation of the electrical system.

Extreme short-term price volatility in competitive electricity markets creates the need for risk management arrangements. Like any other commodities, the uncertainty in electrical prices can be hedged using derivatives. The most popular electricity derivatives are forward contracts, future contracts, and options. Limited storage means that forwards and futures cannot be priced using the standard arbitrage arguments involving cost-of-carry relationships. Forwards and futures prices are the result of supply and demand for hedging and speculation. Producers hedge by selling, and power marketers and the power-intensive industry hedge by buying (going long). Speculators, which often include producers and power marketers/consumers, enter both sides of the market depending on their expectations and risk-taking ability. These expectations about future spot prices are often formed by price forecasts from bottom-up models. In the former regulated regime, bottom-up models served multiple purposes, including prediction of the marginal cost of electricity production. The merits of such models typically include a detailed technical description of generation, transmission, and distribution systems as well as an extensive set of data on hydrological conditions, fuel prices, and consumer behavior. The main drawback of these models is that they cannot estimate or capture the risk premium or market price of risk determined by market forces.

6.9 Natural Gas Market

In the natural gas market, natural gas is traded as a commodity under contracts. These contracts are of two main types: physical and financial, traded in different markets. The main participants include producers, traders, suppliers, pipeline companies, and distribution utilities, depending on the industry's degree of vertical and horizontal unbundling. Natural gas prices are determined through the interaction of these two major types. The cash, or physical, market involves the purchase and sale of physical quantities of natural gas. The financial market involves the purchase and sale of financial instruments whose prices are linked to the price of natural gas in the physical market.

7. Managed Futures

Managed futures funds are part of the rapidly growing alternative investments. Although past performance is not indicative of future returns, investors have recognized managed futures as a means of achieving greater portfolio diversification. Managed futures are managed by professional managers. These professional money managers are also referred to as commodity trading advisors (CTAs) due to the historical association of futures trading with physical commodities. Though CTAs started trading futures contracts in the noncommodity sector, such as financial instruments, including stock indices, currencies, and global interest-rate instruments, they are still referred to as CTAs due to the popularity of the name.

7.1 Hedge Funds versus Managed Funds

While hedge funds invest in a vast number of products, both exchange-listed and over-the-counter (OTC) derivatives, managed futures are generally only invested in through exchange-listed futures contracts, regulated by the Commodity Futures Trading Commission (CFTC). While managed futures offer the same advantages offered by hedge funds, managed futures possess several other advantages that are discussed below.

Transparency: While transparency is not a major concern for some investors, most investors want to know how their money is being managed. For hedge fund managers, the tradeoff between transparency and performance is a big challenge. Hedge fund managers believe that their strength lies in the skill they possess and the proprietary nature of their strategies and are reluctant to reveal the fund details to investors. Transparency is an issue with any investment. Most investors want to know exactly what their money is doing at all times. Some investors believe that giving money to someone who claims to have returns of X without knowing what the manager is actually doing is generally a bad idea. Transparency is becoming more and more of an issue as the universe of investable products grows exponentially. The recent hedge fund "blow-ups" are a case in point. Some funds do not share the end net asset value with the investor even if the fund investments are revealed to the investor. There is absolutely no transparency. All the investors get is a quarterly statement informing them of gains or losses and maybe some commentary if the manager is not too busy.

A CTA, on the other hand, typically employs a specific strategy that is defined in the investor's disclosure document, which is similar to a prospectus. The CTA is required to state exactly what products the investor's money will be invested in, as well as exactly how the manager plans to invest. At the end of everyday, CTAs calculate net asset value (NAV) based on the closing price determined by the exchange. This allows investors to know exactly what their investment is worth.

Liquidity: Since hedge funds do not have any restrictions on type of investments, they heavily invest in illiquid assets if the profit opportunities arise. While illiquid assets yield the premiums, they also become sources of temporary or real losses, especially when markets perform badly. When all the hedge fund managers want to liquidate their funds at the same time, they will have to sell them at significant discount prices. Recently, many hedge funds have been forced to shut down because they were invested in highly illiquid derivatives linked to subprime mortgages.

Unfortunately the liquidity issue is not completely eliminated even in managed futures. While most managers only trade in highly liquid commodities, there are times when even the most liquid commodity can become illiquid very fast. In other words, even if the manager did not intend to invest in an illiquid commodity, the commodity can become illiquid after the investment has been made. Illiquidity can be caused by many factors, from politics to supply-and-demand imbalances to general investor fear and greed. A prudent manager will prevent investors from being too exposed to liquidity risks by implementing some sort of hedge, diversification, or proper position sizing of the account. Therefore, the investor should conduct proper research when setting investment goals for the CTA.

Lockup Period: A lockup period is an interval during which the investor is not allowed to withdraw funds from a particular fund. After the specified lockup period, investors are free to withdraw funds as defined in the disclosure document of each hedge fund. Almost all hedge funds have a lockup period ranging from as little as three months to longer than two years. Generally the more established the fund, the longer the lockup period. Lockup periods are established to give enough opportunity to the fund manager to draw the strategy and deploy the money. While managers prefer to establish lockup periods, investors may sometime feel it is an inconvenience. Managed futures, on the other hand, do not have lockup periods. There are a few that have lockups ranging anywhere from three months to a year, but this is not a stringent requirement in the industry.

7.2 Types of Managed Futures

Managed Futures typically achieve strong performance in both up and down markets, exhibiting low correlation to traditional asset classes, such as stocks, bonds. Managed Futures perform well in down markets because they employ short-selling and options strategies. There are basically two types of managed futures; managed accounts and future funds.

7.2.1 Managed Accounts

A separately managed account is an investment portfolio managed by a commodity trading advisor (CTA) that can potentially be tailored to meet specific investment objectives. While separately managed accounts are simple called *managed accounts*, they are sometimes called separate accounts, individually managed accounts, actively managed accounts, or privately managed accounts. Key features of managed accounts are listed below:

Management: Provide access to professional money management services.

Customization: Portfolio can be tailored to address each investor's specific needs. A separately managed account can be structured to automatically exclude investments that the investor may own in another account or investments he would prefer not to own.

Transparency: With a separately managed account, the investor will generally receive comprehensive communications and performance reporting. Account statements will give a complete picture of which individual securities the investor holds, as well as the number of shares owned. They will also usually provide the following:

- The current value of the positions
- The cost basis of each position
- Details of account activity
- Portfolio's asset allocation
- Portfolio's performance in comparison to a benchmark
- Market commentary from the portfolio manager

Liquidity: Although managers may hold cash, they are not required to hold cash to meet redemptions. However, managers are required to fulfill redemption requests when they arise.

Tax Efficiency: Because positions can be bought or sold at the client's instruction to harvest gains or losses, separately managed accounts allow the investor to address specific tax concerns. For example, investors can match capital gains and losses by selling select positions at a loss in order to generate tax write-offs at year-end.

Minimums: Significantly higher minimum investments than managed funds.

Fees: Investors generally pay one asset-based fee that includes ongoing advice from a CTA. a portfolio manager's fee, trading fees, and custody services for positions held in the account. Fees vary, but are generally higher than futures funds.

Managing Expectations: The CTA is obligated to fulfill a fiduciary duty, which means he or she has a legal or ethical duty to monitor the investor's assets according to the investor's own best interests. However, fulfilling these fiduciary obligations does not guarantee that the investor will meet his or her financial goals. When needed, investors can decide whether it may be appropriate to modify expectations to reflect a changing market, adjust risk considerations, or reallocate the assets in their portfolio.

7.2.2 Futures Funds

Futures funds are similar to managed accounts, but the funds are pooled from multiple investors. Therefore, the fund does not represent a single investor. Compared to managed accounts, futures funds provide less investor control, transparency, and liquidity. The advantages include: no margin calls, protection of the investor from liability beyond the amount invested, lesser expenses due to shared resources like trades, and auditing.

7.3 Benefits of Managed Futures

Managed futures funds have demonstrated the following attractive performance characteristics:

- Returns in line with equity markets.
- Low volatility or lower overall portfolio risk
- Low or negative correlations to equity markets

- Opportunity to profit in both rising and falling markets
- Limited drawdown due to a combination of flexibility and discipline
- Broad diversification opportunities

CTAs may be commonly associated with absolute return strategies, as returns generated can be independent of financial markets. Absolute return strategies enable CTAs to produce returns regardless of market direction. While traditional strategies implement long-only techniques to drive client return, absolute return strategies employ a broader toolkit of investment instruments. These instruments may include short selling, futures, options, derivatives, and use of leverage. It is this versatility of absolute return strategies that drives alpha generation, or risk-adjusted outperformance relative to a benchmark. Managed futures have historically outperformed competitive benchmarks while offering investors similar risk-adjusted performance and low risk exposure. The futures markets are highly volatile and risky, but adding a managed futures component to a diversified investment portfolio may actually help decrease volatility in the portfolio as a whole. This reduction of risk to a portfolio is possible because of the historically low or noncorrelation of managed futures with stocks and bonds. Because managed futures generally have not followed or mirrored the fluctuations of other asset types, they may complement a portfolio of traditional stock and bond investments.

Managed futures exhibits zero or negative correlation with both bonds and stocks providing diversification benefit. The diversification benefit offered by managed futures is higher than that is offered by other alternative investments. Managed futures are less correlated with other peers in the alternative world, and correlation between other managed futures is also very low. In sum, managed futures have noncorrelation to almost all investments. Both the skill of managers and flexibility to implement the strategy contributes to the low correlation. Futures markets enable strategies that can easily go long and short, or spread strategies that can go both long and short in the same product with different delivery months, or long and short in a product and its substitute. The core contract structure available in futures markets and the different delivery months and leverage usage provide enhanced strategy options when compared to the stock market or even to the hedge fund market.

Greater diversification achieved from the strategy is also an important contributing factor for low correlation. Managed futures funds employ computer-driven quantitative programs. While these programs tend to be primarily directional in nature, seeking to identify and take advantage of both upward and downward price trends across a wide range of markets, a number of managers have sought to achieve even greater diversification by introducing nondirectional, market neutral-type trading strategies. Additionally, managers are investing across a wider range of markets outside the commodity market, such as credit derivatives as well as emerging market stock indices, bonds, and currencies. Instruments such as swaps and exchange-traded funds have further enhanced the opportunity set.

Trend following systems utilize advanced quantitative processes and rules engines that detects price movements. The detected trend can exist from two to three days to several days. Trend following managers typically diversify the portfolio across several lengths of trends. Trade time frame is a considerable factor for the low correlation. Some managers establish positions that last for months, while others last for a few days or weeks. Integrating such a long-term frame with a short-term frame will produce a low correlation.

The establishment of global futures exchanges and the accompanying increase in actively traded contract offerings has allowed managers to diversify their portfolios by global geography as well as by product. Managed futures funds can participate in over 150 markets worldwide, including currencies, stock indices, interest rates, agricultural products, precious and nonferrous metals, and energy products. Managers have the opportunity for profit potential and risk reduction among a broad array of historically noncorrelated markets.

Because managers seek to take advantage of price trends in either direction, it is possible for managed futures to show gains in economic environments where other investments, such as stocks and bonds, are declining in value. Drawdowns are an inevitable part of most investments. However, because CTAs can take long or short positions and adhere to strict stop-loss limits, managed futures funds exhibit limited risk.

7.4 Risk Characteristics

The most pronounced risk characteristics of managed futures are leverage risk, manager-specific risk, and regulation risk. The other risk characteristics are discussed below.

Leverage Risk: Leverage is widely used in futures and option-based strategies. Leverage can work both for and against an investor, that is, the leverage can increase returns and also magnify losses. Margins also provide leverage, though implicitly, which enables the manager to gain higher exposure with little investment. When both explicit and implicit leverages are combined, it can create a risk mixture that must be carefully managed at all times. A fund manager gets a margin call when the account value falls below what is known as the maintenance margin. The maintenance margin can be considered a warning or cushion before an account goes debit. The margin call is the most feared aspect of the managed account and can cause unlimited liability to the investor. However, futures funds or commodity pool operator structures can limit the investor's liability and eliminate the potential for margin calls, making the futures fund a defined loss investment.

While past performance is not indicative of future results, the past volatility of margin calls is somewhat interesting, and investors are required to perform additional due diligence pertaining to margin call history. Margin levels are set by the exchanges and can change depending on market conditions. Managers are required to monitor the daily margin requirements and need to respond accordingly. If managers do not respond to margin calls within a specified time, then the FCMs liquidate the positions in the account to satisfy the margin calls. Liquidating the positions on an unfavorable market day may lead to losses to the manager and eventually to the investor.

Margin-to-Equity ratio is a useful tool to monitor and manage margin risk. A manager who uses low margin-to-equity ratio, for example 5 percent, is considered to be using a conservative level of leverage, while a manager who uses a higher margin-to-equity ratio, for example 70 percent, is considered to be risky. Margin-To-Equity ratio depends on the volatility of the underlying asset as well as the strategy. Assets with higher volatilities tend to have the highest margin-to-equity ratios. Similarly, short volatile strategies tend to have higher margin-to-equity ratios. However, margin-to-equity ratio does not give a complete view of the risk. It is just an indicator, and managers and investors should use this ratio as one of several risk measures.

Volatility Risk: Most managed futures funds are dependent on market trends to generate profits for investors. In the event of a reversal in market trends, managed futures funds can suffer heavy losses, which can be magnified by the use of leverage. Most managed futures funds are highly leveraged.

Liquidity Risk: Managed futures funds have limited liquidity and are subject to restrictions on transferability and resale. Most managed futures funds restrict liquidity to monthly intervals. Managed futures funds also typically require a redemption notice as much as two weeks in advance of the desired redemption date. Also, unlike mutual funds, there are no specific rules on managed futures fund pricing. Managed futures fund units may not be redeemable at the investor's option, because no secondary market currently exists for the sale of managed futures fund units, and none is expected to develop. In other words, the investor may not be able to get back the money he or she invested in the managed futures fund until the next redemption period.

Manager-Specific Risk: Manager-specific risk is tied to **the** diversification level the manager achieves. Manager-specific risk can occur if the CTA has a significant bad month, quarter, or time frame where he experiences significantly negative performance. Or the CTA might be facing issues with illiquidity, or the manager might have chosen the wrong market or strategy at the wrong time.

Model Risk: Most systematic managed futures funds are based on complex quantitative models that determine the trading decisions. There is little subjective intervention in daily trading activities of these managed futures. Quantitative models are limited in their ability to recognize rare and unpredictable events, such as extreme changes in the stock and bond markets, worldwide political crises, and natural disasters. In such scenarios, it is possible that the performance of such systematic models may suffer due to the lack of human intervention during such events.

7.5 Risk-Return Distribution

On a monthly basis, CTA/managed future strategies provide consistent returns of 0.96 percent, slightly higher than the average hedge fund index. The Sharpe ratio is in line with that of the average hedge fund index. CTA/Managed futures strategies are exposed to negative events in a reverse way and therefore exhibit positive skewness. As per the data available in Hedgefund.net for the period of 1998 to 2010, the skewness of CTA/managed futures on a monthly basis is 0.63. At the same time, the strategies exhibited slightly higher positive excess kurtosis of 1.10 on a monthly basis. The maximum drawdown was less than half of that of the average hedge fund index.

In general, the correlation of returns between CTA and other hedge funds and the S&P was low prior to the financial crisis. Since then, correlations have broadly increased, with a few exceptions. Discretionary CTA products had a large increase in correlations to equity markets during the financial crisis. On the other hand, the correlation of monthly returns between systematic CTAs, most other classifications of hedge funds, and the S&P have declined since the financial crisis. The correlation of returns for every submarket classification of

CTA, except FX, to other hedge funds and the S&P has increased in the more recent period, led by those managers focusing in the oil sector.

Year	HF Aggregated Index	CTA/Managed Futures Index
1991	28.76%	N/A
1992	16.92%	N/A
1993	29.93%	30.28%
1994	7.32%	8.48%
1995	28.10%	34.88%
1996	25.33%	23.36%
1997	23.25%	23.75%
1998	11.48%	21.05%
1999	36.22%	10.47%
2000	13.11%	16.18%
2001	9.04%	8.96%
2002	4.38%	19.38%
2003	21.30%	16.30%
2004	10.78%	6.51%
2005	10.94%	8.73%
2006	13.74%	9.58%
2007	12.62%	15.13%
2008	-14.37%	16.24%
2009	21.41%	2.56%
2010	10.48%	8.91%

Annual returns of CTA/managed futures index (Data source: Hedgefund.net)

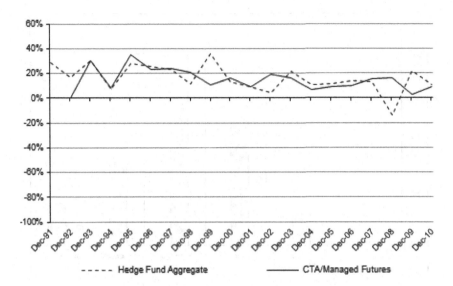

Annual returns of CTA/managed futures index (Data source: Hedgefund.net)

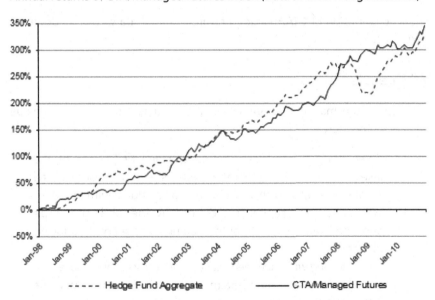

Cumulative returns of CTA/managed futures index (Data source: Hedgefund.net)

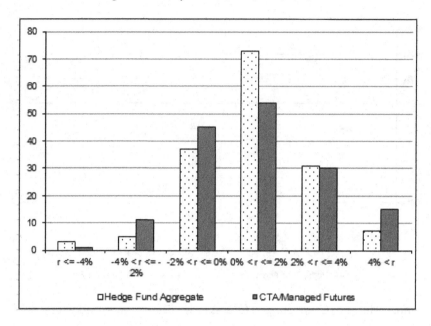

Return distribution of CTA/managed futures index (Data source: Hedgefund. net)

7.6 Due Diligence

At the minimum, managed futures investors should perform the following due diligence procedures:

- When investing a managed account or direct CTA account, the investor should ensure that the capital is placed in a segregated account held at a regulated FCM in good standing with the NFA.
- When allocating capital to a direct CTA, the funds should be deposited with the FCM, not the trading manager or introducing broker.
- When dealing with managed accounts, investors should make sure that they receive account statements directly from the FCM. While futures funds do not provide transparency, investors should ensure that they get at least some details pertaining to the investments.
- Investors should ensure results have been audited and see the NFA's audit report or NFA no-comment letter for further clarifications.
- Investors should review the fund's offering documents and summarize the fund's objectives, fee structure, and redemption procedures.

- Investors should confirm the CTA registration via the NFA website (www.nfa.futures.org).
- Investors should monitor the risks and returns and compare them against prior expectations and benchmarks.

8. Private Equities

As many things in the world do not have clear definition, private equity also does not have specific definition. By looking at the word *private*, we can say that it is something that is not available to the public. However, private equity firms do invest in some forms of public investments, such as convertible debt. As discussed in the first chapter, private equity firms are structured as general partner and limited partners. Limited partners are nothing but investors.

Private equities differ from hedge funds in the sense that most hedge funds deal with quoted instruments in public markets, such as stock exchanges, currency markets, and futures exchanges, and typically take paired positions, long on one side and short on the other side. Hedge funds also use derivatives. On the other hand, private equity firms deal with privately held companies with some exceptions, such as holding publicly quoted stocks that were taken public by the same equity firm.

The minimum qualification for investors, according to the SEC, is as follows.

- Should have net worth, or joint net worth with spouse, over $1 million.
- Or should have annual income over $200,000 in each of the two most recent years or joint income with spouse should exceed $300,000 for those years, with a reasonable expectation of the same income level in the current year.

Private equity funds are structured as limited partnerships, with the firm's principals acting as general partner and investors acting as limited partners. The general partner is responsible for making all investment decisions relating to the fund, with the limited partners responsible for transferring committed capital to the fund upon notice of the general partner. Limited partners are required to commit a minimum amount of capital. They do not deposit all the committed funds in the beginning. The general partner issues a notice, upon which the limited partners are required to transfer capital to the fund within an agreed-upon period of time. The term of the commitment period usually lasts for five to six years after the closing of the fund. General partners are granted an additional time period, which is reserved for managing and exiting investments made during the commitment period. Most funds' partnership agreements stipulate that the partnership may not invest more than 25 percent of the fund's equity in any single investment. The private equity firm generates revenue in three ways: carried interest, management fees, and coinvestment.

Carried Interest: Carried interest is a share of any profits generated by the private equity firm. Once all the partners have received an amount equal to their contributed capital, any remaining profits are split between the general partner and the limited partners. Typically, the general partner's carried interest is 20 percent of any profits. In some cases, limited partners enforce a hurdle rate. A hurdle rate is a minimum percentage of profits the fund should earn before distributing the profits to the general partner. The hurdle rate can be hard or soft. In a hard hurdle rate, the profits up to the hurdle rate are excluded from the calculation of the general partner's carried interest. In a soft hurdle rate, the entire profit is used to calculate the carried interest as long as the hurdle rate is met by the fund. Some fee structures enforce clawbacks, which make the general partner return some of his or her earlier distributions back to the fund if the fund does not perform well in later years.

Management Fees: Private equity firms charge a management fee to cover overhead and expenses associated with identifying, evaluating, and managing the investments. The management fee is intended to cover legal, accounting, and consulting fees associated with conducting due diligence on potential targets, as well as general overhead. Management fees typically range from 0.75% to 3 percent of committed capital, although 2 percent is most common.

Coinvestment: Executives and employees of the private equity firm may coinvest along with the partnership on any acquisition made by the fund, provided the terms of the investment are equal to those afforded to the partnership.

There are mainly four types of private equities: venture capitals, leveraged buyouts, mezzanine financing, and distressed-debt investing. Below we will discuss each type of private equity.

8.1 Venture Capitals

Venture capital as a financing institution was not a natural evolution. National leaders of the United States were thinking of various measures to help the recovery of the US financial system from the Great Depression and believed that new and small innovation-based science and technological firms seeking to upgrade and expand their businesses could provide a source of significant capital gains and that their growth could contribute to employment growth.

In order to support early-stage capital requirements, American Research & Development Corporation was incorporated in 1946. This was the first venture capital firm. The four primary goals for ARD were as follows:

1. To nurture new firms and assist existing firms in upgrading their technology or adding new product lines.
2. To encourage the commercialization of technological innovations.
3. To contribute to an economic revival in New England.
4. To assist in the diffusion of privately funded venture capital as an institution.

Following the ARD, approximately twenty venture capital firms were set up as closed-end funds over the ensuing twelve years.

To further spur the growth of innovation-based firms, in 1958 Congress created the Small Business Investment Company (SBIC) program. SBICs, licensed by the Small Business Administration, are privately owned and managed investment firms. They are participants in a vital partnership between government and the private sector economy. With their own capital and with funds borrowed at favorable rates through the federal government, SBICs provide venture capital to small independent businesses, both new and already established. All SBICs are profit-motivated businesses. A major incentive for SBICs to invest in small businesses is the chance to share in the success of the small business if it grows and prospers. The SBIC program has served as a launching station for several highly successful companies, such as Apple Computers, Intel, and FedEx. In 1958, venture capital investment took the organizational structure of general partner and limited partners, where limited partners contribute to the fund with no management responsibilities. In 1979, the Employee Retirement Income Security Act of 1974 (ERISA) was amended to permit pension funds to invest in venture capitals. Since then, ERISA has become a major source of capital for venture capital firms.

Due Diligence

The due diligence process is applicable to both venture capital firms as well as investors. The venture capital firm or general partner needs to evaluate various aspects before investing funds in companies, and the investor or limited partner needs to evaluate the general partner before committing funds into the pools. The following are the minimum areas where due diligence needs to be covered:

- Stage focus
- Geographic focus
- Industry focus
- Size of investment
- Return focus
- Investment-style focus
- Business management focus

8.2 Leveraged Buyouts

A leveraged buyout (LBO) is an acquisition of a company or a part of another company financed with a substantial portion of borrowed funds. Leveraged buyouts, as the name indicates, use extensive leverage and little equity. Leveraged buyout firms are a special form of private firms. In contrast to venture capital firms, leveraged buyout firms deal with existing or mature firms. The required equity portion of the LBO comes from a fund of committed capital that has been raised from a pool of qualified investors. The use of debt serves not only as a financing technique, but also as a tool to force changes in managerial behavior. Well-disciplined use of debt will force management to focus on certain initiatives, such as divesting noncore businesses, downsizing, cost cutting, or investing in technological upgrades that might otherwise be postponed or rejected outright.

LBO firms typically invest alongside management, encouraging top executives to commit a significant portion of their personal net worth to the deal. By requiring the target's management team to invest in the acquisition, the private equity firm guarantees that management's incentives will be aligned with their own.

If a deal is undertaken by the existing management together with some or all of the company's employees, then such a buyout is called a management buyout. When outside managers are brought in, the deal is called a buy-in management buyout. An LBO in which the new group continues to acquire companies in its sector so as to create industrial synergies is called leveraged buildup.

Due to the high degree of financial leverage, the financing search goes beyond traditional banking. The typical financing structure includes traditional or secured loans called senior debt, to be repaid first; subordinated or junior debt to be repaid after the senior debt; mezzanine financing, the repayment of which is subordinated to the repayment of the junior and senior debt; and last in line, shareholders' equity.

In order to eliminate diversifiable risk, specialized investment funds often invest in several LBOs. Due to the excessive use of debt, LBOs are considered to be risky, and investors will therefore require high returns. Indeed, required returns are often in the region of 25 percent per annum.

8.3 Mezzanine Financing

Mezzanine debt is used by companies in expansion projects, acquisitions, recapitalizations, and management and leveraged buyouts. Using mezzanine debt in conjunction with senior debt reduces the amount of equity required in the business, which in turn avoids dilution shareholders. As equity is the most expensive form of capital, it is most cost-effective to create a capital structure that secures the most funding, offers the lowest cost of capital, and maximizes return on equity. Mezzanine debt is subordinate in priority of payment to senior debt and senior in rank to common stock.

Mezzanine investing is typically a short-term investing. Mezzanine debt is more expensive than traditional financing. It shares the same covenant package as a bank deal, but the measurement characteristics are looser. For example, if the maximum leverage of EBITDA on a bank deal is three and a half times, a mezzanine deal would be four or five times. Sources of income take any of the following forms:

Cash Interest: A periodic payment of cash based on a percentage of the outstanding balance of the mezzanine financing. The interest rate can be either fixed throughout the term of the loan or can fluctuate along with LIBOR or other base rates.

Payment-in-Kind Interest: A periodic form of payment in which the interest payment is not paid in cash, but rather by accruing it to the principal amount of the security in the amount of the interest.

Ownership: Along with the typical interest payment associated with debt, mezzanine capital will often include an equity stake in the form of attached warrants or a conversion feature, similar to that of a convertible bond. The ownership component in mezzanine securities is almost always accompanied by either cash interest or PIK interest, and in many cases by both.

Participation Payout: Instead of equity, the lender may take an equity-like return in the form of a percentage of the company's performance, as measured by total sales or EBITDA as a measure of cash flow, or profits.

8.4 Distressed-Debt Investing

Distressed-debt investing involves purchase of the debt of troubled companies that may have already defaulted on their debt or may be on the brink of default. Distressed debt may be the debt of a company already under bankruptcy protection. Distressed debt includes subordinated debt, junk bonds, bank loans, and debt obligations. Distressed-debt investing is basically a value strategy of buying an asset for a price well below its intrinsic or fair value. Distressed-Debt investors look long and hard at distressed companies to see if their securities have been oversold, even accounting for the problems the companies face.

A distressed opportunity typically arises when a company, unable to meet all its debts, files for Chapter 11 or Chapter 7 bankruptcy. Chapter 7 involves liquidating the company's assets and paying down the proceeds to creditors. Chapter 11 gives the company legal protection to continue operating while working out a repayment plan, known as a plan for reorganization, with a committee of its major creditors. Creditors include banks that have issues loans, utilities and other vendors owed for their goods and services, and investors who own bonds. If in a bankruptcy a company does not have sufficient assets to repay all claims, the stockholders will be the last in line to receive any of the proceeds from the liquidation or reorganization. A distressed-securities investor focuses mostly on bank debt, trade claims, and bonds when looking for undervalued securities.

Many institutional investors, such as pension funds and endowments, are restricted from buying onto below investment-grade bonds even if the company is a viable one. Banks prefer to get rid of their bad loans in order to remove them from their books and to use the freed-up cash to make new investments. In addition, a bank typically does not have the resources or the focus to become actively involved in a reorganization process, which can last several years. Holders of trade claims are in the business of producing goods or providing services and have no expertise in assessing the likelihood of getting paid once a company has filed for Chapter 11.

All of the above situations put downward pressure on distressed debt and make it attractive to distressed-debt investors. Distressed-Securities fund managers best utilize their knowledge, expertise, legal experience, and patience that creditors of a company often do not have. Distressed-Securities investing is less correlated with the performance of the stock market, as performance is the result of the investor's research and financial analysis on the particular distressed asset, his or her knowledge and experience in the reorganization process, and overall familiarity with bankruptcy laws.

There are three types of distressed debt investment strategies: active investing seeking control, active investing not seeking control, and passive investing.

9. Real Estate Investing

Real estate investments generally involve one of the following three investment strategies: core, value added, or opportunistic.

Core: This is generally considered the most conservative strategy, characterized by lower risk and lower return potential. The fund will generally invest in higher-quality properties, with some of these properties requiring some form of enhancement or value-added element.

Value Added: This is a moderate-risk, medium-return strategy. Typically, this strategy involves managers buying properties, making some improvements, and selling at an opportune time for a gain. Value-added improvements can range from solving management or operational problems to physical improvements to solving capital constraints.

Opportunistic: Considered the most aggressive, this is a high-risk, high return-potential strategy. The properties often require a high degree of enhancement and generally include investments in development, raw land, and niche property sectors.

9.1 Real Estate Investment Trusts (REITs)

Through the centuries, wealth and power have been measured primarily in terms of the amount of land owned. Land distribution was concentrated among a small section of people throughout the world. The twentieth century witnessed industrialization and the rise of securitization and ownership of stocks and bonds. Slowly, real estate also evolved as an industry. But still real estate investments, such as shopping malls, corporate parks, and health-care facilities were concentrated among either wealthy individuals or corporations. In the United States, Congress passed the Real Estate Investment Trust Act of 1960. The legislation exempted special-purpose companies from corporate income tax if certain criteria were met. The financial incentives encouraged investors to pool their resources together to form companies with significant real estate assets, providing the same opportunities to the average American as were available to the elite. Shortly, the first REIT was formed. Real estate investment trusts provided an indirect way to get access to real estate in a way that is similar to stocks and bonds and became a convenient way for the average investor to profit without the hassle of direct property acquisition.

The original act required executives in charge of the business to hire third parties to provide management and property leasing services. These restrictions were lifted in the Tax Reform Act of 1986. In 1999, the REIT Modernization Act was passed, which allowed REITs to form taxable subsidiaries in order to provide specialized services to tenants that normally fall outside the purview of real estate investing. An REIT must meet a number of organizational, operational, distribution, and compliance requirements. Plenty of literature is available at http://www.reit.com.

- An REIT must be a corporation and must be formed in one of the fifty states or District of Columbia.
- It must be governed by directors or trustees, and its shares must be transferable.
- It must have at least one hundred different shareholders.
- Five or fewer individuals cannot own more than 50 percent of the value of the REIT's stock during the last half of its taxable year.
- Annually, at least 75 percent of the REIT's gross income must be from real estate-related income, such as rents from real property and interest on obligations secured by mortgages on real property.
- Additionally, 95 percent of the REIT's gross income must be from the above-listed sources, but can also include other passive forms of income, such as dividends and interest from nonreal estate sources (like bank deposit interest). As a result of these rules, no more than 5 percent of an REIT's income can be from nonqualifying sources, such as from service fees or a nonreal estate business.
- An REIT can own up to 100 percent of the stock of a "taxable REIT subsidiary" ("TRS"), a corporation with which an REIT makes a joint election that can earn such income.
- Quarterly, at least 75 percent of an REIT's assets must consist of real estate assets, such as real property or loans secured by real property.
- Although an REIT can own up to 100 percent of a TRS, an REIT cannot own, directly or indirectly, more than 10 percent of the voting securities of any corporation other than another REIT, TRS, or qualified REIT subsidiary ("QRS"), a wholly-owned subsidiary of the REIT whose assets and income are considered owned by the REIT for tax purposes. Nor can an REIT own stock in a corporation (other than an REIT, TRS, or QRS) the value of whose stock comprises more

than 5 percent of an REIT's assets. Finally, the value of the stock of all of an REIT's TRSs cannot comprise more than 25 percent of the value of the REIT's assets.

- In order to qualify as an REIT, generally, the REIT must distribute at least 90 percent of the sum of its taxable income. To the extent that the REIT retains income, it must pay tax on such income just like any other corporation.

- In order to qualify as an REIT, a company must make an REIT election. The REIT election is made by filing an income tax return on Form 1120-REIT. Because this form is not due until, at the earliest, March 15 following the end of the REIT's last tax year, the REIT does not make its election until after the end of its first year (or part-year) as an REIT.

- Nevertheless, if it desires to qualify as an REIT for that year, it must meet the various REIT tests during that year.

- Additionally, the REIT annually must mail letters to its shareholders of record requesting details of beneficial ownership of their shares.

- Significant monetary penalties will apply to an REIT that fails to mail these letters on a timely basis.

Advantages of REITs

No Corporate Tax: REITs do not pay taxes at the corporate level and let all income flow through to the investor. This structure is especially beneficial to tax-exempt investors, such as pension funds and endowments.

Easy Access to Real Estate Properties: With equity REITs, any investor can own a piece of a shopping mall or skyscraper. Real estate investment trusts purchase and manage real estate properties. When an investor purchase shares in an REIT, he becomes a partial owner of those properties, and from this perspective, he is also a partial owner of an operating business that manages properties for profit.

Investment Returns Through Dividends: Equity REITs are not taxed at the corporate level and are required by law to pay out 90 percent or more of their profits as dividends to investors. The best real estate investment trusts hire the best management teams. Their job is to manage the properties to maximize rental income and profits. With equity stocks, management decides whether to pay dividends or plow profits back into the company. With REITs, each investor can make his or her own decision about what to do with the dividends.

Low Volatility and Low Correlation: REIT share prices exhibit lower volatility than equity stocks and are less correlated with the performance of other asset classes. For this reason, they are useful for diversification of portfolios. As per historical evidence, when stock prices are down, REITs normally perform better, thus balancing the performance of the portfolio. As rental income is very predictable, analysts can be very accurate in their predictions for the performance of REITs. This reduces share price volatility.

Investment Returns Through Appreciation: Though equity stocks do not perform proportionately well in good markets, REITs have historically performed well due to the steady long-term appreciation.

Property Management Without the Headaches: REITs allow the average investor to own real estate that may not be reachable otherwise. The investor also enjoys the benefits of experienced property management without the headaches. A carefully selected management team handles marketing, rent collection, tenant management, and facilities maintenance. All the REIT's investor must do is collecting his or her dividends at the mailbox.

Reinvestment: REIT investors receive 90 percent or more of the profits of property management and ownership as dividends. If the investor chooses to reinvest, he or she simply purchases more shares of the REIT.

Liquidity: REIT shareholders are able to trade their shares on public exchanges and can purchase using margin accounts.

Disadvantages of REITs

Slow Growth: Because they can only reinvest up to 10 percent of their annual profits back into their core business lines each year, REITs tend to grow at a slower clip than the average stock on Wall Street. Over time, history has shown that the average publicly traded REIT tends to post annual earnings growth several percentage points below that of the S&P 500.

Cyclical Risk: Although the business tends to be a fairly stable one, its dividend payments are not guaranteed, and the real estate market is prone to cyclical downturns.

Individual Taxation: Due to the pass-through structure, investors are required to pay taxes on dividends based on their ordinary income tax rates. This may be problematic for investors in high tax brackets.

Systemic Risk: Since REITs are traded in public stock exchanges, they are exposed to systemic risk.

Types of REITs

REITs can be classified into various types based on structure, investment philosophy, and market focus. REITs based on structural classification are single-property REITs, finite-life REITs, dedicated REITs, umbrella partnership REITs, and down REITs. REITs based on investment philosophy are equity REITs, mortgage REITs, and hybrid REITs. Market-Focus REITs concentrate on investments according to location, size, and type of properties.

Single-Property REITs: These REITs invest in a single large property used for diverse purposes, such as shopping malls, residences, office space, entertainment spots, and so on.

Finite-Life REITs: These REITs operate for a specified period, which is typically eight to fifteen years. This provides ample time for managers to acquire, redevelop the properties, and enhance the profits to investors.

Dedicated REITs: These REITs typically invest in a single property type in a single development. These REITs differ from single-property REITs in that single-property REITs invest in a single property but diversified types, whereas dedicated REITs invest in a single type of single property. For example, a large health-care facility may be operated under an REIT structure.

Umbrella Partnership REIT: Under an umbrella partnership REIT, also known as an UPREIT, structure, the corporation does not own any real estate properties directly but instead operates investor properties. In a typical UPREIT structure, one or more individuals owning real estate contribute their holdings to an "umbrella partnership" in exchange for limited partnership units, sometimes called operating partnership units.

Down REIT: The down-REIT structure was created as an analog to UPREITs for those REITs that did not have a desire to form an umbrella partnership and also to provide additional structuring flexibility for existing REITs. UPREITs have used down REITs to provide additional structuring flexibility as well. In a typical down-REIT structure, a property owner becomes a partner in a limited partnership with the REIT, the umbrella partnership of an UPREIT, or a wholly-owned subsidiary of the REIT or UPREIT, as the case may be. The newly formed limited partnership owns and operates the property and possibly other income-producing property contributed by the other partner.

Equity REIT: As the name indicates, the management owns the underlying properties and is responsible for property renovations and development. Rental and lease payments and property appreciation contribute to the returns.

Mortgage REIT: A mortgage REIT purchases or invests in loans used to finance properties and earns interest. Though mortgage REITs can produce steady and significant returns, they carry significant added risks. Since they only hold debt instruments and not property, they cannot participate in the appreciation of the collateral properties. Their value is also quite sensitive to interest-rate fluctuations. As interest rate influences mortgage REITs, their prices tend to be more volatile than those of the equity type. Owned property values are more stable and predictable than the mortgages in the mortgage REIT.

Hybrid REIT: A hybrid REIT invests in both equity REITs and mortgage REITs in a proportion that is not explicit.

REIT Correlation with Other Asset Classes

REITs typically have low correlation with large-cap stocks and T-bills. REITs even exhibit negative correlation with ten-year T-bonds. Due to the similarities between REITs and small capitalization companies, they exhibit somewhat higher correlations with each other. The small correlation between large-caps and REITs can be explained by comparing the movements of the DJ-REIT index and DJIA index. At the end of 2007, the Dow Jones REIT Index was at 732.81, and by the end of 2008, it had dropped to 453.83, representing a 38 percent decline. During the same period, the Dow Jones Total Stock Market Index lost about 6000 points, from roughly 13,000 to 7000, registering an approximate 46 percent decline, more than the REIT losses. REITs have the highest correlation with high-yield bonds.

Inflation Hedge

Unlike most financial assets, REITs own real properties that generate rental income, most of which is paid to shareholders. Perhaps more important, REITs often have inflation step-up clauses in their leases, which means they have the ability to increase their net operating income (NOI) to keep pace with inflation. Some, such as apartment REITs, have short lease terms that provide similar flexibility. Banks, on the other hand, suffer from a flatter yield curve when the economy improves. Moreover, more investors adjust their portfolios to include real estate investments during high inflation, which in turn puts upward pressure on real estate prices. Over a short period of time during high inflation,

REITs exhibit negative correlation with inflation; but over the long period, the correlation will be positive. High inflation indicates higher interest rates and lower bond prices, which indicates poor performance of bonds. Thus, REITs and bonds are negatively correlated. However, due to the composition of mortgage loans in REITs, the correlation turns out to be positive with mortgage bonds.

While TIPS and commodities have long been traditional inflation hedges, real estate as a third option provides greater inflation protection. TIPS provide guaranteed protection against inflation by embedding the inflation rate into the income earned on a medium- to long-term US treasury bond. Every six months, the principal on the bond is adjusted based on the level of the consumer price index at that time. The investor receives an interest payment equal to the adjusted principal multiplied by one-half the stated interest rate for the bond. The trade-off for this assurance comes in the form of lower returns. Over the past thirty years, the CPI averaged 4.2 percent annually, which would have consumed half of the average 8.3 percent annual return from TIPS. On the other hand, by comparison, both commodities and REITs provide superior protection, but the volatility of commodities is higher compared to REITs. Thus, when choosing among the three options for inflation hedging, the investor considers the trade-off according to the style of the portfolio.

REIT Return Distribution

REIT monthly return distribution of the past two decades exhibits negative skew and excess kurtosis, which indicates that the REITs are exposed to outlier event risk. High correlation with small caps and exposure to mortgage loans will expose the REITS to event risk. Some REITs, which depend completely on property appreciation, may be speculative in nature, and general economic conditions may stall the growth of such properties. Real estate property typically goes through a boom–and-bust cycle. When demand for offices, apartments, and shopping malls is going up, developers rush in to build more of these properties. Due to various economic variables, it is sometime difficult to know when enough is enough; and within a few years, too much supply could cause rents and occupancy rates to go down. Overall, in the past decade, REITs performed well relative to other asset classes, with the second highest return and Sharpe ratio. The negative or low correlation with most asset classes provides a good source of portfolio diversification.

9.2 National Council of Real Estate Investment Fiduciaries

The National Council of Real Estate Investment Fiduciaries (NCREIF) is an association of institutional real estate professionals, such as investment managers, plan sponsors, academicians, consultants, appraisers, CPAs, and other service providers who have a significant involvement in institutional estate investments. They come together to address vital industry issues and to promote research. There are three types of memberships. A data contributing membership is for investment managers and plan sponsors who own or manage real estate in a fiduciary setting. An affiliated data contributing membership is for investment managers or other corporations who own or manage real estate in a fiduciary setting, but who do not currently qualify as data contributing members. And lastly, academic membership is for full-time real estate professors. NCREIF produces several quarterly indices that show real estate performance returns using data submitted to them by their data contributing members. More information about NCREIF is available at http://www.bis.org/publ/bppdf/bispap21zc.pdf.

NCREIF was established to serve the institutional real estate investment community as a nonpartisan collector, processor, validator, and disseminator of real estate performance information. NCREIF is a not-for-profit trade association that serves its membership, and the academic and investment community's need for improved commercial real estate data, performance measurement, investment analysis, information standards, education, and peer group interaction by:

- Collecting, processing, and reporting data in a secure environment;
- Producing performance measurement indices;
- Encouraging academic and member use of NCREIF data for objective research;
- Providing forums with strong educational content to address industry issues;
- Publishing informed industry-related articles and reports; and
- Contributing to the development of real estate information standards.

The NCREIF Property Index (NPI) provides returns for institutional-grade real estate held in a fiduciary environment in the United States. Properties are managed by investment fiduciaries on behalf of tax-exempt pension funds. As of the second quarter of 2003, the index contained 3967 properties with an aggregate market value of $127 billion. Office is the dominant property type, at 40 percent of the market value of the index; with apartment, retail, and industrial properties being about 20 percent each. Figure 2 shows the percentage of properties in each region of the country. The western region has the greatest proportion of properties (34%), followed by the East (29%), South (22%), and Midwest (15%).

The NCREIF index was the first available index to measure the performance of income-producing real estate and is still the primary index that institutional investors rely on for benchmarking the performance of real estate. It was created to understand how the performance of real estate compares with other asset classes, such as stocks and bonds, and also to provide a better understanding of the risk and return for commercial real estate.

The index is often used as a basis for developing diversification strategies, such as the percentage allocation to real estate to minimize risk for a target portfolio return. Also, subindices, such as for office, retail, industrial, and apartment properties, are used to determine how to diversify by property type. Similarly, subindices by regions of the country are used for geographic diversification. Investment managers also use the index as a benchmark to evaluate the performance of their portfolio against the index. Incentive fees paid by clients to investment managers might be based on outperforming the NCREIF index.

Calculation of Index

ERISA required pension funds to report the value of investments in retirement plans every quarter, and since most pension funds started adding real estate into their funds, fair market value accounting for real estate held by pension funds was incorporated into the Real Estate Information Standards (REIS) developed by NCREIF. The index measures the change in value of property between the beginning of each quarter and the beginning of the last quarter, that is, the change in value during a particular quarter. The return is calculated as the change in value plus any cash flow received during that quarter. Cash flow is net operating income (NOI) less any capital expenditures. The index is calculated on an unleveraged basis, that is, as if the property did not have any debt financing. Because the properties in the NPI are held in tax-exempt accounts, it is calculated on a before-tax basis. Returns are calculated for each individual property and then value weighted to produce the index.

Appraisal Issues

Since real estate in general, and properties in the index in particular, do not transact on a regular basis, the beginning and ending values used to calculate the NCREIF index are based on appraisals. There are certain issues in getting appraisal values accurately. Not all properties are actually revalued each quarter, as the managers don't always spend the time and money to do a complete revaluation of the property. They may just adjust the value for any additional capital expenditures and have a policy of only revaluing the property if they believe there has been a significant change in value. Information on transactions is often sparse and by nature historical—especially by the time the data is collected and verified. Market conditions often change more rapidly than can be reflected in data available to appraisers. This causes appraised values to be less than transaction prices in an up market and vice versa. As a result, the calculated NPI may exhibit low volatility and low correlations, causing inflated risk-adjusted performance and diversification effect, which in turn will lead to excessive real estate allocations in portfolios. This is called a smoothing effect. The smoothing effect can even be observed by comparing NPI with NAREIT.

Correcting for Appraisal Lag

Several approaches have been suggested in the literature to "correct" or adjust for the lag inherent in appraisal-based indices. The first is to "unsmooth" the index. This approach involves modeling appraisal behavior and then in effect "reverse engineering" the appraisal process in order to get an unsmoothed index. Appraisal behavior is modeled as a moving average of the value indicated by current and prior comparable sales (comps). We have

$$V^*_t = \alpha V_t + \alpha(1 - \alpha)V_{t-1} + \alpha(1 - \alpha)^2 V_{t-2} \ \dots \text{(moving average)}$$

where

V^*_t is the optimal appraised value in period t

V_t is the value from comps in period t

This reduces to $V^*_t = \alpha V_t + (1 - \alpha)V^*_{t-1}.$

We can now solve for the "true" value as follows:

$$V_t = V^*_t/\alpha - (1 - \alpha)/\alpha V^*_{t-1}$$

Empirical evidence suggests an α of 0.4 for the NCREIF Property Index (NPI) when estimating annual returns. Thus we can develop a simple unsmoothing model as follows:

$$V_t = V^*_t/0.4 - (1 - 0.4)/0.4 V^*_{t-1}$$

$$V = 2.5V^* - 1.5V^*$$
$${}_t {}_t {}_{t-1}$$

This adjusts for stale appraisals and lag in the appraisal process.

NPI from the Context of a Portfolio

The composite NPI is negatively correlated with treasury bonds and less correlated with investment-grade and high yield-grade bonds. NPI offers various advantages over REIT indices in regard to diversification. The composite NPI is less correlated with both large-cap and small-cap, whereas an REIT is highly correlated with small-cap stocks. NPI is positively correlated with inflation. NPI sector indices can also be used as inflation hedges. Adding NPI to a portfolio increases diversification and shifts the efficient frontier both up and left, thus enhancing the return and reducing the risk, whereas adding an REIT to a portfolio only provides parallel shift in efficient frontier.

9.3 Private Equity Real Estate (PERE) Investments

As discussed under the chapter "Private Equities", a private equity firm is a legal entity that acquires ownership interest in privately held companies. Investors of a private equity firm expect returns on their investment through liquidation, secondary, sale or public offer of portfolio companies. Private equity real estate (PERE) firms employ active management strategy consisting of both direct and secondary ownership of equity and debt interests. PERE firms diversify their investments across various, property types, locations, and property development phases such as new development, leasing, remodeling et cetera.

Though private equity investments are not usually available to the public, they are occasionally accessible to institutional investors and high-net-worth individuals through private equity funds, usually organized as limited partnerships. These partnerships establish investors as limited partners and pool investor capital to create private investment funds for the general partner(s) to manage. Many private equity fund strategies exist, including venture capital, leveraged buyout, and mezzanine financing.

A private equity fund's success depends on the ability of its portfolio companies to increase in value after a period of time and the fund's ability to dispose of its holdings. The fund's management often adds to this process by playing an active role in the portfolio companies, such as assisting the portfolio companies in achieving operating efficiencies, developing products or services, or reorganizing. Afterward, if a portfolio company increases in value, the private equity fund may seek to dispose of its investment, usually through the sale of the company to an acquirer or in a public offering of the portfolio company stock. The proceeds of these sales are generally distributed to the private equity fund's investors. Private real estate investments are typically made through private equity real estate funds. These funds usually have a seven- to ten-year life span, consisting of a two-to three-year investment period where properties are acquired, and then a holding period where active asset management is carried out and the properties are sold. These funds will generally have more flexibility than a real estate mutual fund in the types of investments they make. For instance, private real estate funds may include private direct real estate investments in multiple property types (such as multifamily housing, commercial, retail, or industrial), REITs (real estate investment trusts), debt instruments, or derivatives.

Capital Commitment

In a private equity or private real estate fund, the fund's managers can seek capital from a number of institutional or high-net-worth individual investors through "capital commitments," which can be a fairly large investment. A private equity or private real estate fund is generally a closed-end fund, which means that, after one or more fundraising stages (called "closings"), new investors are not accepted. A fund will not launch if it does not receive a minimum level of capital commitments.

Capital Calls

For the most part, private equity and private real estate funds are "needs-based" investments. This means that partners of the fund will commit to giving the fund manager installments of capital, up to a predetermined dollar amount, on an as-needed basis. As investment opportunities are identified, the fund's managers will send investors a formal notice to submit the money they have committed to the program. This formal notice is referred to as a "capital call" and is a contractual obligation that each partner must satisfy. A private equity or private real estate fund's offering documents typically provide a number of potential actions against investors who fail to meet capital calls. For example, a fund may require defaulting investors to forfeit their entire ownership interest in the fund and offer the other fund investors the ability to purchase the forfeited interest.

Capital Distributions

Over the long term, the investments in companies that the managers make in the portfolio may become a realized profit to the fund if those privately held companies are sold, merged, recapitalized, or brought to the public market at a higher value. If the fund makes such a profit, the private equity or private real estate fund will typically dispense those proceeds to its partners on a prorata basis through a capital distribution. This is how investors are paid for their involvement in the fund. Managers of private equity and private real estate funds may also choose to withhold capital distributions as a way of reducing the total amount of future funding required by their individual partners. In other words, if the program's investors have not fully funded the partnership up to their total committed amounts, the amount on the next capital call will be reduced in direct proportion to the withheld capital distribution.

Advantages of PERE Funds

- Diversification benefits
- Institutional investors can limit exposures by investing in multiple funds.
- Access to best-performing fund managers

Disadvantages of PERE Funds

- Lack of liquidity
- Loss of control
- Valuation issues

9.4 Commingled Real Estate Funds

Commingled real estate funds pool private capital and invest in real estate. They then issue ownership certificates that represent the proportional share of ownership in the underlying commercial properties. Mixed-together assets from various accounts provide investors with the benefits of economy of scale. Commingled funds are often called *pooled funds*.

Advantages of a Commingled Fund

- Efficient trading
- Cost reduction through economy of scale

- No need to own entire property. Ability to own a small portion of large complexes provides diversification benefit to investors.

Disadvantages of a Commingled Fund

- Lesser control on the property due to large number of owners
- Not available to small investors due to large capital requirements
- Lack of liquidity
- Valuation issues

9.5 Property Derivatives

Unlike the stock and bond market, there is no liquid market or facile means of hedging the attendant real estate risk. Case, Shiller & Weiss introduced the concept of real estate futures in 1992. The introduction of futures and options based on the S&P/Case-Shiller Home Price Indices at CME represents the fulfillment of that vision, forging the creation of a novel derivatives asset class. CME Housing futures and options are designed to provide a facile way for institutional and individual investors to gain exposure to real estate risk and effectively diversity their portfolios. Commercial and private asset holders are afforded an efficient hedging mechanism. In the process, this novel market may have the effect of reducing transaction costs for trading real estate. Cash settlement is based on the reported value of S&P/Case-Shiller Home Price Indices of home prices for the cities of Boston, Chicago, Denver, Las Vegas, Los Angeles, Miami, New York, San Diego, San Francisco, and Washington DC, and an index that represents a composite of the ten cities.

Commercial real estate property derivatives based on indices published by the National Council of Real Estate Fiduciaries (NCREIF) became available for trading in March 2007.

Property derivatives have some advantages over direct property investment, such as ease of execution, customization, and no property management. Property derivatives are associated with certain risks as well. Investment risks and returns may not be aligned with direct property investment. Derivatives have counterparty risk, lack of control over the referenced assets, and among other things there are index shortcomings.

9.6 Open-End Real Estate Mutual Funds

In open-end real estate, the fund manager continuously buys and sells shares from investors. New shares are created and issued on demand, and existing shares are retired if there is redemption pressure. Shares can be redeemed or terminated at any time.

Advantages of Open-End Funds

- There is no limit on the number of shares that can be issued— new shares can easily be created and issued. Therefore, a large number of investors can participate in a mutual fund scheme that is performing well.
- More liquid than underlying assets
- Regulated by regulatory authorities, such as the SEC
- Lower minimum amount

Disadvantages of Open-End Funds

Since the investor can redeem the shares, the fund manager will face redemption pressure. Selling well-performing shares to meet redemptions is not a good strategy. Therefore, most open-end funds keep a large balance of cash to meet any redemption pressure.

Since this cash is not invested in equities, and is kept either as cash or is invested in very liquid money market funds, it earns very low returns. Therefore, the overall return suffers.

Tax inefficient compared to exchange traded fund.

9.7 Closed-End Real Estate Mutual Funds

The shares of a closed-end real estate fund are issued only at the time of the initial fund offer. These shares are issued with a fixed duration. New shares are not issued on an ongoing basis, and existing shares are not retired before the term of the fund ends. At the time of the initial fund offer, an investor can buy the shares from the fund manager. The shares of such funds are listed on the stock exchanges just like ordinary shares, and can be bought and sold through a secondary market.

Advantages of Closed-End Funds

- No redemption pressure and so enhanced returns
- Highly liquid due to secondary market through exchanges
- Investors can take long and short positions.
- Can be purchased with margin
- Well regulated

Disadvantages of Closed-End Funds

Lack of broader participation. Since the number of shares of closed-end funds is constant, there is naturally a cap on the number of investors that can participate in such funds.

Difficult to gain access to a specific sector. This is true even for open-end funds.

9.8 Exchange-Traded Funds (ETFs)

ETFs are essentially index funds that track the performance of a specific stock or bond market index or other benchmark. There are quite a few different real estate funds available on the market. Investors can get exposure to global real estate, country-specific real estate, or REITs. The inverse ETFs are also available. There are even ETFs related to real estate, such as home builder ETFs and mortgage-backed funds. They are highly liquid and tax efficient. Investors can take long or short positions. The below is partial list of available real estate ETFs.

- DRN—Direxion Daily Real Estate Bull 3X Shares ETF
- DRV—Direxion Daily Real Estate Bear 3X Shares
- DRW—Wisdom Tree International Real Estate ETF
- FFR—First Trust FTSE EPRA/NAREIT Global Real Estate ETF
- FIO—iShares FTSE NAREIT Industrial/Office Cap Index ETF
- FRI—First Trust S&P REIT ETF
- FRL—Focus Morningstar Real Estate Index ETF
- FTY—iShares FTSE NAREIT Real Estate 50 ETF
- GRI—Cohen & Steers Global Realty Majors ETF
- ICF—iShares Cohen & Steers Realty Majors ETF
- IFAS—iShares FTSE EPRA/NAREIT Developed Asia Index ETF
- IFEU—iShares FTSE EPRA/NAREIT Developed Europe Index ETF

- IFGL—iShares FTSE EPRA/NAREIT Developed Real Estate ex-US Index ETF
- IFNA - iShares FTSE EPRA/NAREIT North America Index ETF
- IYR—iShares Dow Jones US Real Estate ETF
- KBWY—PowerShares KBW Premium Yield Equity REIT Portfolio
- PSR—PowerShares Active US Real Estate ETF
- REK—ProShares Short Real Estate ETF
- REM—iShares FTSE NAREIT Mortgage Plus Capped Index ETF
- REZ—iShares FTSE NAREIT Residential Plus Capped Index ETF
- RTL—iShares FTSE NAREIT Retail Capped Index ETF
- RWO—SPDR Dow Jones Global Real Estate ETF
- RWR—SPDR Dow Jones REIT ETF
- RWX—SPDR Dow Jones International Real Estate ETF
- SCHH—Schwab US REIT ETF
- SRS—UltraShort Real Estate ProShares ETF
- TAO—Claymore/AlphaShares China Real Estate ETF
- URE—Ultra Real Estate ProShares ETF
- VNQ—Vanguard REIT ETF
- VNQI—Vanguard Global ex-US Real Estate Index Fund
- WREI—Wilshire US REIT ETF